OXFORD ENGLISH MONOGRAPHS

General Editors

Boys in Khaki, Girls in Print

Women's Literary Responses to the Great War 1914–1918

JANE POTTER

CLARENDON PRESS • OXFORD

OXFORD
UNIVERSITY PRESS

Great Clarendon Street, Oxford OX2 6DP

Oxford University Press is a department of the University of Oxford.
It furthers the University's objective of excellence in research, scholarship,
and education by publishing worldwide in

Oxford New York

Auckland Cape Town Dar es Salaam Hong Kong Karachi
Kuala Lumpur Madrid Melbourne Mexico City Nairobi
New Delhi Shanghai Taipei Toronto

With offices in

Argentina Austria Brazil Chile Czech Republic France Greece
Guatemala Hungary Italy Japan Poland Portugal Singapore
South Korea Switzerland Thailand Turkey Ukraine Vietnam

Oxford is a registered trade mark of Oxford University Press
in the UK and in certain other countries

Published in the United States
by Oxford University Press Inc., New York

First published 2005

British Library Cataloguing in Publication Data

Data available

Library of Congress Cataloguing in Publication Data

Potter, Jane.
Boys in khaki, girls in print : women's literary responses to the Great
War, 1914–1918 / Jane Potter.
p. cm.
Includes bibliographical references and index.
1. English literature—20th century—History and criticism. 2. English literature—Women
authors—History and cirticism. 3. World War, 1914–1918—Great Britain—Literature and
the war. 4. Women and literature—Great Britain—History—20th century. 5. World War,
1914–1918—Personal narratives, British—publishing 6. Literature publishing—20th
century. 7. Women—Great Britain—Intellectual life—20th century. 8. World War,
1914–1918—Women—Great Britain. I.Title.

PR478.W65P68 2005 820.9'358—dc22 2005020147

Typeset by SPI Publisher Services, Pondicherry, India
Printed in Great Britain
on acid-free paper by
Biddles Ltd, King's Lynn, Norfolk

ISBN 0–19–927986–1 978–0–19–927986–9

1 3 5 7 9 10 8 6 4 2

For my father

HAROLD RUTHERFORD POTTER, JR.
1919–1994

Sing a song of Rule Britannia!
Sing in praise of Britain's boys:
Jolly Jack, the sailor with his breezy style,
Mister Tommy Atkins, of the rank and file.
They're lads we can depend on,
When danger comes our way,
For fathers all were fighters and what's bred in the bone
Is sure to come out, some day.

Refrain:
Boys in khaki, boys in blue,
Here's the best of jolly good luck to you!
You're all right, in love or war;
You'll get there again, just the same as you've done before.
Boys in khaki, boys in blue,
It's no idle boast or brag,
When we get you both together, there's sure to be dirty weather
For anyone who tramples on the flag!

Sing a song of Rule Britannia!
Now there's fighting work to do,
Ever staunch and ready, when the hour is nigh,
British boys know how to fight and how to die.
Lads, we know you'll do your duty,
Whatever fate may bring.
You have got the pluck and muscle, so make your battle cry
For Empire, for Home and King!

'Boys in Khaki, Boys in Blue' (1914)
lyrics by A. J. Mills
music by Bennett Scott

Acknowledgements

Vera Brittain's *Testament of Youth* got me 'hooked' on the Great War when I was 13. The television adaptation, which was screened in the United States on *Masterpiece Theatre* hosted by Alistair Cooke, led me to Brittain's memoir and her memoir to the poetry of Wilfred Owen. At the Long Beach Public Library I discovered his biography by a man called Stallworthy. It never occurred to me then to imagine that many years later Jon Stallworthy would not only supervise my doctorate but would become a trusted mentor and dear friend. He has read my work with meticulous care and his wise criticism has been invaluable. I shall always be enormously grateful to him.

I have had the opportunity to carry out research in many institutions, including the Bodleian Library; the Imperial War Museum; the British Library; the Publishing Archives at the University of Reading Library; the Huntington Library, San Marino, California; the Humanities Research Centre, University of Texas at Austin; the John Rylands Library, University of Manchester; the Manuscripts Collection at the University of St Andrews Library; and the War Poetry Collection at the Birmingham Reference Library. At each I was helped enormously by friendly and knowledgeable staff who went out of their way to assist this often bemused researcher. The staff at the British Red Cross Archive kindly provided the information about Kate Finzi's war record, and Sue Breakell at Tate Britain obligingly clarified Julian Allan's service in both world wars. I am particularly grateful to Dr Priscilla Coit Murphy whose research on my behalf in the J. M. Dent Archive at the University of North Carolina at Chapel Hill was instrumental in filling in details about the life of one of my more obscure subjects, Janet Laing.

I thank the following for their permission to reproduce published material: Bamforth and Co., Ltd., for the postcards 'How Can I Bear to Leave Thee?', 'Thoughts Unchanging', 'My Heart Is With You Always', and 'Jesu, Lover of My Soul'; the Bodleian Library for the illustrations from *The Girls' Reader, Khaki & Kisses*, *Richard Chatterton, V.C.*, *Good Old Anna,* and *Eighteen Months in the War Zone;* the Estate of Ruby M. Ayres and Peters Fraser & Dunlop for extracts from *Richard Chatterton, V.C.*; Paulo Lowndes Marques, Ana Vicente, and Antonio Leitão, the grandchildren of Marie Belloc Lowndes, for extracts from *Good Old Anna*; Dominick Jones for extracts from his mother Enid Bagnold's *A Diary without Dates*; and Dr Melissa Hardie and the Hypatia Trust Library for extracts from Violetta Thurstan's *Field Hospital and Flying Column*. Every effort has been made to trace the copyright holders of other material, but I should be glad to hear from those to whom I have not made proper acknowledgement.

A number of friends have cast their critical and rigorous eyes over this study, most importantly Dr Carol Acton, Dr Elaine Chalus, Dr Subarno Chattarji, Dr Margaret Connolly, Dr K. D. Reynolds, Dr Susan Skedd, and Dr Trudi Tate. I am extremely thankful for all of their comments and suggestions, which I know have made *Boys in Khaki, Girls in Print* a better book. Any infelicities are my own. I must thank my OUP editors, Andrew McNeillie and Tom Perridge, and my production editor, Jacqueline Baker, who have guided me through the publication process with patience and good humour. I am also grateful to my copy-editor, Charles Lauder, for his eagle-eyed attention to detail.

Others have, in their individual and various ways, advised, supported, encouraged, and cajoled me: the late Miss Julian Allan, Rosemary Batchelor, Jane Bellinger, Elizabeth Bonjean, Dr Grace Brockington, Lawson and Sheila Brown, Dr Michael Brown, Dr Alan Bryson, Sarita Cargas, Judith Curthoys, Dr Mark Curthoys, Dr Julie Curtis, Caroline Davis, Fleur Gooch, Sarah Jarvis, Denise Johnson, Harry and Mary Ann Kelsey, the late Dr Stuart McKerrow, Gwen Millan, Allan and Myra Milne, Atalanta Myerson, Pat Quinn, Dr Francis Ryan, Peter and Elizabeth Owen, Clare and Chris Priestley, Dr Roger Stearn, the late Mr Rayner Unwin, Cynthia and Stephen Wainwright, Janet and Martyn Woods, and Carol and Simon Wratten.

My family, of course, deserves my thanks for much encouragement over the years, in particular, my sister, Vickie.

Finally, but by no means least, I thank my husband, Dr Andrew Woods, without whose love and support this book would never have been completed.

My only regret is that my mom cannot share the completion of this book with my dad. But I like to think that he knows, and with her, is proud.

Jane Potter

Wolfson College, Oxford

Contents

List of Illustrations

Introduction

A battered pith helmet, a khaki pack, a canteen, and a shovel were kept in the garage of the house in Long Beach, California, where I grew up. They belonged to my step-great grandfather, James 'Dada Jim' Allan (1888–1950). An immigrant from Belfast, he joined the American Red Cross in 1915. When, two years later, the United States declared war he was inducted into federal service and served with the 101st Trench Mortar Battery as a Medical Sergeant (#2821). His demobilization papers record the 'battles, engagements, skirmishes, expeditions' in which Jim Allan was involved: Chemin des Dames; Bois Brule (Apremont); Jury Woods; the 2nd Battle of the Marne (18 July–4 August 1918); the St Mihiel Offensive (Les Eparges); and the Battle of the Meuse (Bois d'Haumont, Bois d'Ormont, Bois Belleau). On 10 May 1918, he was gassed at Bois Brule (Apremont), and was subsequently awarded the Purple Heart. I never met Jim Allan; I know him only by the military memorabilia of his time in France and by photographs.

Now, over 86 years on from the Armistice, few people have more than such indirect 'experience' of the First World War. The widespread fascination with that 'war to end all wars' is due also in no small part to the literature it generated. The poems of Wilfred Owen and Siegfried Sassoon or the memoirs of Vera Brittain, Edmund Blunden, and Robert Graves come immediately to mind. Their work has conditioned our twenty-first-century thinking about those years, often to the exclusion and devaluing—if not denigration—of other writers, particularly women writers. This study attempts to redress that imbalance.

Vera Brittain stands out in the preceding list as the lone female. Although specialist academics and Great War enthusiasts would also recognize the names Mary Borden, Enid Bagnold, and Helen Zenna Smith, Brittain has become for the general reader the token 'woman's voice' of 1914–18. Yet her characteristic tone—that of anguished pacifism—was articulated in the very different political and cultural climate of the 1920s and 1930s. Her memoir, *Testament of Youth*, which expresses the disillusionment of the interwar period, speaks to our late-twenty-first-century sensibilities, scarred by a Second World War, Vietnam, Bosnia, the 'war on terror', and other numerous national and international conflicts. We can see that the promises made to the Great War generation were not kept, but for the majority of the British population *at the time*, victory for the Allies did mean permanent peace and there was a certainty that soldiers would return to 'a land fit for heroes'. The 1916 trauma of the Somme may have marked a watershed in perception but it did not lower the resolve of the country as a whole. It may have severely shattered confidence, tested the nation's capacity to withstand enormous grief and suffering, and showed that war was not 'glorious', but even though some called for an end to hostilities, the prevailing cry was 'push through to the end'. This is the message of many literary texts published in the War years themselves. Indeed, Vera Brittain's own poetry and prose written *during* the War are very much like the literary responses of so many other women of her class and generation.

Boys in Khaki, Girls in Print seeks to illuminate the writing of now virtually unknown women writers and how they interpreted the Great War as it was happening. Recent critical studies have focused on the creation of women's identities, the relationship of motherhood to the state, and the development of female modernist texts.[1] Novels, stories, and memoirs by such famous writers as Virginia Woolf, Katherine Mansfield, and HD feature prominently. I will consider less elite literature and focus on texts that are not canonical and whose literary 'quality' may be debatable. It is not difficult, from an aesthetic point of view, to see why some of the novels have been forgotten. Yet they were part of 'an avalanche of

[1] These include Debra Rae Cohen's *Remapping the Home Front: Locating Citizenship in British Women's Great War Fiction* (Boston, 2002); Susan R. Grayzel's *Women's Identities at War: Gender, Motherhood, and Politics in Britain and France during the First World War* (Chapel Hill, 1999); Sharon Ouditt's *Fighting Forces, Writing Women: Identity and Ideology in the First World War* (London, 1994); Angela K. Smith's *The Second Battlefield: Women, Modernism and the First World War* (Manchester, 2000); Trudi Tate's *Modernism, History and the First World War* (Manchester, 1998); and Claire M. Tylee's *The Great War and Women's Consciousness: Images of Militarism and Womanhood in Women's Writings, 1914–1918* (Iowa City, 1990).

literature' that prompts certain questions.[2] To whom or to what were these books responding? What needs in the reading public were they attempting to address? Do they alter or confirm our sense of gender roles during the War? What function did they perform for their authors? With the exception of certain professional novelists, such as Ruby M. Ayres and Berta Ruck, most of these writers did not make a living from their pens, and many preface their books with disclaimers of any intention to publish, asserting that they were urged to do so by friends or interested publishers.

Arthur Marwick dubbed the Great War 'The Deluge', a description that might just as well be applied to its literary output.[3] The volume of books published between 1914 and 1918 is so vast that any study must of necessity be restricted to a representative number. Given that post-war texts have become our principal literary evidence of the Great War, and valorizing as they do the protest to the exclusion of other works, I will not be considering retrospective accounts from the late-1920s and early-1930s. Moreover, there are issues about the nature of the emotions recollected at such a distance and in a very different political climate that are larger than this study can address. Admittedly, as Samuel Hynes points out, all 'war narratives are by their nature retrospective',[4] including the ones with which I shall be dealing, but written within the atmosphere of a society at war, both the themes and the implications of the ideologies they express are distinct and different from those written much later.

In the years 1914–18, there *was* an ongoing current of protest from conscientious objection to feminist condemnations of militarism, yet most of what was published, particularly popular fiction and active service autobiography, was supportive of the war effort or, at the very least, accepted its necessity. This book is an outgrowth of a chapter published in 1997, which looked in detail for the first time at books normally dismissed as either unworthy of critical consideration or unpalatable from an ideological point of

[2] J. M. Winter, *The Great War and the British People* (London, 1985), 285.

[3] Arthur Marwick, *The Deluge: British Society and the First World War* (London, 1965).

[4] Samuel Hynes, *The Soldiers' Tale: Bearing Witness to Modern War* (London, 1998), 4.

view.[5] Six additional texts will be considered here and given close readings usually reserved for 'elite' works. The purpose is to show that these novels and memoirs can stand up to scrutiny and can tell us more than we may have anticipated about what these books were doing both on a public/readership level and on a personal/authorial level.

Sandra Gilbert and Susan Gubar have famously claimed that the War became a site of gender-inversion, and the thrill some women experienced led to the perception by male writers that females and other non-combatants were, in effect, feeding off the suffering of the men in the trenches.[6] Other critics, however, have taken issue with this idea. Mary Cadogan, for instance, asserts that

> Obviously many soldiers suffering the hell of the trenches *did* feel bitterness against non-combatants; there was often a great barrier between them and their wives or girlfriends who might not be able to empathize with their ghastly experiences. However, the blame that is heaped upon so many women in *Death of a Hero* seems totally unreasonable when the 'safe distance' which the author so much deplores was forced on them by social conventions that kept them away from the front line. In many instances, of course, girls got very near the trenches as ambulance drivers or nurses, but there is little evidence that the exposure to death or disablement that this involved produced the eroticism suggested by Richard Aldington.[7]

Similarly, Dorothy Goldman claims that 'women have not been listened to' because they were 'not part of the physical agony' of the trenches: 'we should consider whether the enormity of men's suffering justifies its being awarded the only place in our cultural awareness'.[8] Trudi Tate and Suzanne Raitt take this argument further, asserting that by studying women's writing we come to a fuller understanding of how the War affected *both* sexes: 'the war is not "about" gender; nor is it a metaphorical battle of the sexes. To transform the actual violence of the Great War into a trope of sex warfare is to deny the specificity of its trauma, both for women and

[5] Since then, scholars such as Susan Grayzel and George Robb have included the novels of Ruck and Ayres in their recent surveys.

[6] Sandra Gilbert and Susan Gubar, *No Man's Land: The Place of the Woman Writer in the Twentieth Century*, ii: *Sexchanges* (New Haven, 1989), 258–323.

[7] Mary Cadogan and Patricia Craig, *Women and Children First: The Fiction of Two World Wars* (London, 1978), 153.

[8] Dorothy Goldman (ed.), *Women and World War I: The Written Response* (Basingstoke, 1993), 2.

for men'.[9] This is not a comparative study, but women's writing should not be viewed in isolation. Hence, the female narratives are complemented, if only briefly, by men's novels and memoirs. Male popular writing differs very little in terms of language and ideology. The plot lines of their romance novels and the high-flown rhetoric of their memoirs can be as effusive and melodramatic as any composed by their supposedly 'over-emotional' women colleagues.

By and large, the women writers considered here are middle class, and it may appear that this study overlooks the experiences of working-class women. I am conscious of the class bias inherent in my chosen texts, but the 'introspective analysis of writing' required leisure time and the 'habit' of assessing one's life on the written page.[10] Samuel Hynes reminds us that 'the middle class is the great self-recording class, the class that kept diaries and journals and considers that the preservation of one's daily life is an appropriate and interesting activity for an individual'.[11] Documentation of the experiences of working-class women tended to come later in life, and usually at the urging of an interviewer or interested family members. Sharon Ouditt has tried to redress this imbalance by exploring how 'the experiences of the unglamorous go unrecorded'.[12] This important area of study, however, is beyond the scope of my book, but I will be drawing attention to biases, assumptions, and ingrained social values that govern these middle-class texts.

J. A. V. Chapple argues that, 'amongst all the documents that can speak out of dead mouths, works of creative literature have a special and unique status. At the same time, they were undoubtedly created in a particular period of history and can be only partially considered out of it'.[13] The First World War had been anticipated in some quarters for well over 40 years. When it came, old arguments, assumptions, and expectations were used to interpret it. Even when the realities of modern warfare became apparent, old attitudes prevailed, in varying degrees. They were, perhaps, hard to

[9] Suzanne Raitt and Trudi Tate (eds.), *Women's Fiction and the Great War* (Oxford, 1997), 15.

[10] Angela Woollacott, *On Her Their Lives Depend: Munitions Workers in the Great War* (Berkeley, 1994), 142.

[11] Hynes, 32.

[12] Ouditt, 738.

[13] J. A. V. Chapple, *Documentary and Imaginative Literature: 1880–1920* (London, 1970), 21.

relinquish in light of rapid and irrevocable change. Evoking past interpretations was a way of making sense of the enormous tragedy that became increasingly inexplicable and unfathomable. Placing contemporary events within the setting of a heroic past helps in the search for order and context, and provides 'a reassuring sense of continuity'.[14] These were the ideas of 'The Old Men', those who directed the War, but the term, used so derisively by Owen and Sassoon, was neither age- nor gender-specific. The relatively young—women as well as men—as much as elderly politicians and generals helped to perpetuate such ideas. That so many of the younger generation reiterated old values for so long, even in light of the suffering they had seen or experienced, is testimony to the potency and staying power of dominant and prevailing ideologies. Yet how did they receive them in the first place? This is the question Chapter 1 will attempt to answer by considering the popular literature and social commentary of the years 1899–1914, from the start of the Second Anglo-Boer War to the outbreak of the Great War. It will examine the ways in which Britain's imperial heritage was imparted to young women and girls through the periodical press. The years 1899–1914 were also marked by concerns over a supposed cultural degeneration, brought about by such deviant figures as aesthetes, suffragettes, and Germanophiles, not to mention the infiltration of British society by German spies. Such anxieties were played out not just in academic tracts and social commentary, but found their way into even the most seemingly innocuous stories, articles, and advertisements aimed at a female readership. The motifs that became common in the writing of 1914–18 were not new but easily adapted. The shock of 1914–18 was its scale, proximity, and duration, not war itself.

Interpreting this shock is what certain romance novels and active service memoirs accomplished. In this way, they responded both to the public need for reassurance and the political agenda that was 'the war effort'. Studies of war literature have generally overlooked the ways in which publishers figured in the creation and dissemination of novels and memoirs, so Chapter 2 will consider how the business of propaganda operated alongside the business of publishing. It will show how the concepts of country, conscience, and commerce were inextricably linked between 1914 and 1918, and

[14] Stuart Sillars, *Art and Survival in First World War Britain* (London, 1987), 8.

how the book trade responded to and helped to create public opinion. Literary culture became part of the war machine and Chapter 2 will also survey how media such as posters, postcards, and magazines helped to reinforce a climate of opinion that reached its fullest expression in the novels and memoirs that this book takes as its primary texts.

Popular writing reinforced the existing war effort, but created one of its own out of its particular methods of persuasion based on literary language, motifs, and fictional representations that drew on increasingly familiar and instantly recognizable images: wounds, khaki, women in uniform, public mourning, family grief. The romance novels scrutinized in Chapter 3 consistently claim that women should encourage their men in their duty to fight, but passive grief and suffering are never lauded—women must be emotionally if not sometimes physically tough. The narrative possibilities offered by the War were limitless and novelists rose to the challenge of creating 'amusing' and 'light' tales of entertainment while at the same time performing a patriotic function. Of course, not all novels written during the period 1914–18 dealt with the War, and reviewers in such periodicals as the *Times Literary Supplement* and *The Bookman* often expressed relief at its absence. However, the novelists that did weave the War into their storylines incorporated accepted notions of national duty, gender roles, and cultural difference. Print-run figures still available (the records of many firms were destroyed in the Blitz) show that demand remained high throughout the War, even for the most stridently patriotic stories.

The public appetite for realistic accounts also kept writers writing and printing presses rolling. Chapter 4 analyses the memoirs by women on active service that formed a large part of the diet of war literature. These are, for the most part, elegantly written, moving, and sometimes humorous. The incongruity between the graphic descriptions of wounds and the evocative portraits of the landscape and beauty of their surroundings is a key feature, as is the passionate, contradictory, and discordant language they employed. Women wanted to be active participants and there was a real need for their services as nurses, munitions workers, ambulance drivers, canteen organisers, etc. Visual imagery glamourized women's desire to be involved in the national effort: bloody Red Cross aprons, greasy munitions overalls, or chilblained feet do not feature in these visual representations, yet the memoirs are explicit about the less-than-romantic side of war. Aside from Bagnold, these women were not 'writers' or 'modernists' in the self-conscious sense. They did not see themselves as creating a new way of writing or looking at the world. Indeed, most would argue they are maintaining simple, everyday values that Britain was fighting to protect. Yet the War intruded and their texts exhibit some of the elements we associate with later writers.

The popular romance and the nursing memoir of the Great War do not challenge gender stereotypes. Far from suggesting a radical departure from accepted norms of feminine behaviour, the books I shall discuss provide (often shrill) justifications for adherence to such norms. The war effort depended on the shoring up of the values for which the conflict was supposedly started in the first place. This book is not intended to critique the pros and cons of the War, why it was fought, whether these were valid reasons, and whether the tactics used to complete the tasks were appropriate. These are for the military historians. What happened after the War, the economic depression and literary disillusionment are also topics for a different discussion. This study attempts to get to the heart of feeling *during* the War, as evidenced in the literary responses of women. Its aim is to examine the ways in which non-fiction and popular romance reflected, reinforced, and reiterated the values of the majority of the population of Britain. *Boys in Khaki, Girls in Print* seeks to provide a more rounded picture of the people of the time, who were flag-wavers, but who also thought about the implications of the War, even if they rejected an anti-war stance. These were people who were not simply war-mongering and ignorant, but a colourful generation who wanted to know about what was happening and who wanted to be distracted from these same events by books that both entertained and reassured them.

I

Before the Lamps Went Out: The Social and Literary Background of the Great War

The literary responses of British women to the First World War can and should be put into an ideological and historical framework: the ways in which they represented their experiences in their novels and memoirs were mediated and informed by their learned values, earlier reading habits, and the social atmosphere in which they were raised. Although it is not possible to establish whether particular women read specific magazines or novels, an examination of representative texts illuminates the kinds of concerns, language, and themes that dominated the writing of the decade or so before the Great War. The Second Anglo-Boer War (1899–1902), in particular, provides models for the literary representations of the later war. As opposed to earlier conflicts such as the Crimean War (1853–6) or the Indian Mutiny (1857–8), the Second Anglo-Boer War stands out not only as the most recent national—as well as imperial—war, but it was the only major conflict for half a century. Women's position in society, too, had dramatically altered since the 1850s so its literature speaks of their experience in ways that writing of earlier conflicts does not. Debates about woman's role in society, her duty to God, King, and Country that are such potent concerns in the popular writing generated in the Great War can, therefore, be traced back to much earlier ideological inculcation.

Britain in the late nineteenth century was a martial nation. Popular culture of the time 'legitimized war, romanticized battle and portrayed the warrior as a masculine ideal'.[1] Equally important

[1] Michael Paris, *Warrior Nation: Images of War in British Popular Culture, 1850–2000* (London, 2000), 13.

was the cult of the New Imperialism. With the idea of an 'historic destiny' at its centre, the concepts of 'Anglo Saxon manhood' and the Christian soldier incorporated the ideals of self-discipline, sportsmanship, patriotism, bravery, and physical toughness: 'A generation of university teachers, schoolmasters, clergymen, poets, journalists, and boys' fiction writers concentrated their minds and energies on popularising ... imperial duty'.[2] Although 'the language of Empire was molded first and foremost by its male exponents', women were also attracted to this imperial mission:

> It was an improving, self-reinforcing faith, designed to assert national vigour in an increasingly competitive world, but ultimately dependent upon the personal qualities of individuals.... [The] choice of familial, and especially maternal, metaphor offered important meanings to women who wished to share in the self-congratulatory adventure.[3]

The indoctrination of the young with the values of martial imperialism was also of paramount importance to the ruling class. Periodicals like *The Boy's Own Paper, Chums, Pluck,* and *Union Jack* aimed at young readers were filled with stories celebrating the adventure offered by the Empire. The prolific author, G. A. Henty, established most of the genre's clichés.[4] His boy heroes, who are 'not rounded characters but concentrations of national stereotypes', accompany famous soldiers on their campaigns to civilize 'unpromising natives'.[5] His characteristic use of 'with' in the titles of his novels reinforces the unlikely companionships they catalogue: *With Clive in India* (1884), *With Roberts to Pretoria* (1884), *With Buller in Natal* (1900), *With Kitchener in the Soudan* (1903). The 'parable' created by these books tells of 'the struggle between stereotypical hero and stereotypical villain [and] becomes emblematic of Britain's noble quest to civilise non-western societies.... there is no room for subtlety, introspection, or self-criticism'.[6] British civilization is always superior to any other culture. Working-class boys, who often received Henty's books as prizes for academic excellence or perfect

[2] Lawrence James, *The Rise and Fall of the British Empire* (London, 1994), 207–8.

[3] Julia Bush, *Edwardian Ladies and Imperial Power* (London, 2000), 2.

[4] Humphrey Carpenter and Mari Pritchard (eds.), *The Oxford Companion to Children's Literature* (Oxford, 1984), 7.

[5] Claudia Nelson, *Boys Will Be Girls: The Feminine Ethic and British Children's Fiction, 1857–1917* (London, 1991), 11.

[6] Ibid.

attendance at school, were drawn into the imperial 'adventures of their social superiors, learn[ed] about the deeds which shaped the empire, and absorb[ed] some of the imperial ideal.'[7] Imperialism's civilizing mission was thus not restricted in imperial literature to non-western cultures but extended to the domestic 'savages' of the working classes.

Nor were girls excluded from such a mission. Although their fictional representations were often one-dimensional,[8] and even less well-rounded than those of their male counterparts, Henty, among others, wrote pieces in which young women were given outlets for the kind of adventure enjoyed by their brothers. They occupy more than just the sidelines in such novels as *Out on the Pampas* (1871) and *A Soldier's Daughter* (1906). The latter was originally written for and serialized in *The Girl's Realm* magazine in 1903. A full-page advertisement in the April issue declares:

> THE LAST STORY
> (serial) Written by the late Mr.
> G.A. Henty
> Will begin in
> The GIRL'S REALM
> for May (Ready April 15th)
> With Charming Illustrations by Frances Ewan.

The added description 'charming illustrations' is crucial and interesting, for the 'charm' of the accompanying pictures undermines the masculinity of the text and thus saves the femininity of the reader. Henty employs the same 'breathless situations and exciting escapes' in a piece written earlier for the magazine. 'A Frontier Girl: A Tale of a Backwood Settlement' appeared in 1900, and its heroine, Mary Mitford, exhibits all the heroic qualities usually associated with boys as she saves her parents from an Indian ambush and takes part in the defence of the settlers' village. She possesses 'a certain alertness of expression and keenness of glance which would never have been seen in the face of a town-bred girl', and can judge a dangerous situation 'as accurately as an older settler would do'. She is also a crack shot, having 'learned to use her father's rifle with a skill equal to his own'. Much of her courage and coolness is the result of rugged upbringing: the adventure story highlights a

[7] James, *Rise and Fall of the British Empire*, 209.
[8] Carpenter and Pritchard, *Oxford Companion to Children's Literature*, 244–7.

frontier life that forces men and women into a more rigorous lifestyle.[9] The Henty heroine loses none of her marriageable prospects, for he tells us that ten years after her adventures, 'Mary, whose exploit had gained for her a wide reputation throughout the district for her courage and coolness, had long before married a young Englishman who came out with some capital with the intention of farming'. A perfect match. Her masculine behaviour does not compromise her essential femininity. Male and female characters in stories and novels reflected the ideological changes that occurred at the end of the nineteenth century:

> Ideas of the right and proper came to focus less and less on the exceptional, on the tract heroes who could achieve a saintliness beyond the reach of ordinary mortals. With increasing emphasis, glory fell instead on the normal. In the wholesomeness and freedom from morbid soul-searching John and Jane Bull were better than saints—they were British.[10]

Intelligent, plucky,[11] yet undeniably feminine heroines are the staple characters of other *Girl's Realm* stories. Fairly progressive, this 'magazine for the up-to-date girl' advocated female education, awareness of current events and issues, and a certain degree of independence. Alongside sections devoted to fashion ('Round About the Shops'), crafts ('Pretty Things Made Out of Queer Things'), and the lives of European royalty ('A Nestful of Princesses: The Four Little Daughters of the Tsar') are 'Sports for Girls' (which include basketball, tennis, and ice-skating), 'Clever Daughters of Clever Parents', and 'Careers for Girls', which highlighted such occupations as secretary, gymnastics instructor, and bookbinder. *The Girl's Realm*, in effect, professed a watered-down version of the 'New Woman', the cultural phenomenon that coincided with the women's movement at the end of the nineteenth century. The term was coined

[9] David Trotter, *The English Novel in History, 1895–1920* (London, 1993), 152. Sally Mitchell, however, argues that 'authors who tried to create adventure stories explicitly for girls were impeded by cultural "reality" ... a setting outside England is virtually essential' (Sally Mitchell, *The New Girl: Girls' Culture in England, 1880–1915* (New York, 1995), 115).

[10] Nelson, *Boys Will Be Girls*, 29.

[11] Paul Fussell equates this with being 'cheerfully brave' in his schema of '"raised", essentially feudal language' drawn from medieval romance, the adventure tales of Henty, and the poems of Robert Bridges and Alfred Lord Tennyson and which predominated in the late-nineteenth and early-twentieth centuries. Such '"high" diction' survived in fiction and non-fiction throughout 1914–18 (Paul Fussell, *The Great War and Modern Memory* (Oxford, 1975), 21–2).

in a pair of articles by Sarah Grand and 'Ouida' (Marie Louise de la Ramée) published in the *North American Review* in 1894. Other women writers associated with New Woman fiction and non-fiction included Mona Caird, Menie Murial Dowie, George Egerton (Mary Chevelita Dunne), and Olive Schreiner. The New Woman challenged the assumption that the goal of every woman is marriage and motherhood and she rejected the sexual double-standard that professed chastity—and sexual ignorance—for women but allowed licentious behaviour by men. Although some advocated sexual freedom for women, others, like Grand, maintained that social purity for both sexes was the only path.[12] Yet 'although *The Girl's Realm* encouraged its readers to discuss this new role of women in society, it was never radical enough to affront their parents'.[13]

The intersection of this cultural phenomenon with the Boer War of 1899–1902 meant that girls were written into an imperial event in ways different from any wars previously. Periodicals like *The Girl's Realm* not only encouraged them to be active, vigorous, and sensible young women, but stoic daughters of empire:

> A girl was complaining to me the other day, as girls are sometimes apt to do, of the uselessness of girls.... A girl never feels how useless she is as when her country is in danger. I think at last I managed to make her feel... that there was a part for everybody at all times, in war as in peace.... Be quite sure that the girls of the beleaguered cities of Ladysmith, Kimberley and Mafeking made the best of it; and girls who can be cheerful in the face of such terrors and such privations, are girls that deserved to be called heroines. We may be sure, therefore, that they made the best of it, not only in mere passive endurance, but in a thousand active ministrations that will make better and nobler women of them all.... Yes, the war will have made women of many girls.

Before the names 'Somme', 'Ypres', and 'Passchendaele' resonated in the public imagination, 'Ladysmith', 'Mafeking', and 'Kimberley' held sway. This excerpt from the February 1900 instalment of the *The Girl's Realm* feature, 'Chat with the Girl of the Period', shows just how potent they were. In an instant the editor could inspire the

[12] Sally Ledger and Roger Luckhurst (eds.), *The Fin de Siècle: A Reader in Cultural History c.1880–1900* (Oxford, 2000), 75–6. For an illuminating study of the international influence of New Woman ideology, see Ann Heilmann and Margaret Beetham (eds.), *New Woman Hybridities: Femininity, Feminism and International Consumer Culture, 1880–1930* (London and New York, 2004).

[13] Mary Cadogan and Patricia Craig, *Women and Children First: The Fiction of Two World Wars* (London, 1978), 55.

imagination and the patriotism of the magazine's readers. The sieges and reliefs of these towns were recorded and celebrated by the popular press of the day. Articles about the war in South Africa were everywhere and periodicals aimed at women and girls were no exception. Government and the tabloid newspapers had a symbiotic relationship during the Boer War.[14] Magazines of the period are also part of this equation. Just as the press helped to 'sell' the War, the War helped to sell papers. These periodicals did not question but appropriated the conflict for their own ends, to sell copy and to encourage readers in the imperial mission. Magazines helped to 'sell' the War in two distinct ways: first, ideologically, through their stories and 'I-was-there' accounts, and second, materially, by providing advertising space for manufacturers to tout their wares that, however tangentially, were linked to the War. Moreover, if the Boer War helped to sell magazines, so much the better for the proprietors. It is true that 'being inundated with evidence of Empire is not the same as supporting the economic or political ideal of British imperialism',[15] but women were part of the imperial mission and magazines went 'all out' to show them as actively engaged in supporting it.

The popular writing inspired by the Boer War shares a common element with that of the Great War: the assumed righteousness of Britain. Although the Second Anglo-Boer War and the Great War were fought for different political reasons, against different types of enemy, in different locations, and on different scales, they have more in common than is at first assumed. Instead of being 'the last of the gentleman's war', as it was perceived in the popular imagination, the Boer War of 1899–1902 was 'essentially a modern war'.[16] It challenged perceptions of Englishness, nationhood, and race, causing 'anxiety and introspection' to coexist alongside 'the bluster of imperial language'.[17] Many of its popular literary representations

[14] See Paula M. Krebs, *Gender, Race and the Writing of Empire: Public Discourse and the Boer War* (Cambridge, 1999).

[15] Ibid., 9.

[16] Carolyn Burdett, *Olive Schreiner and the Progress of Feminism: Evolution, Gender and Empire* (Basingstoke, 2001), 139.

[17] Steve Attridge, *Nationalism, Imperialism and Identity in Late Victorian Culture: Civil and Military Worlds* (Basingstoke, 2003), 3. For an historiographical review of the effects of the Boer War on South African culture and national memory, see Donal Lowry, *The South African War Reappraised* (Manchester, 2002).

could, with minimal revision to dates, locales, and combatants, be transposed to describe the events of 1914–18. The texts I shall highlight gloss over the causes of the War, its complexities and nuances, because what is important to authors/advertisers is that Britain wins and each Briton, male and female, must do their utmost to facilitate that victorious outcome. In these advertisements and stories the international politics of the particular war have little impact on the cultural ideology. It matters who is fighting and why but only up to a point, for popular entertainment aimed to reassure, especially in a world in which war brings such uncertainty. Popular entertainment made the politics of war seem simple and unambiguous. Neither imperialism nor the War fought in its name is critiqued or interrogated. Instead, we are given models of patriotic behaviour.

Between 1899 and 1902, periodicals such as *The Girl's Realm, The Girl's Own Paper* (*G.O.P.*), and *The Lady's Realm* devoted many pages to war themes in short stories, personality profiles, and first-hand journalistic accounts.[18] Their advertisements also illustrate how quick entrepreneurs were to jump on the bandwagon of public interest as the 'commodity culture tried its hand at propaganda'.[19] For example, the makers of 'Cerebos Table Salt' celebrate the fact that their advertisement, 'torn from the *Strand* magazine', was used by a soldier to write a 'letter from the Front'. They exploit the associations of the battle zone to make the analogy that their product 'is always "at the front" in Good-class Houses' (*The Lady's Magazine*, January 1901). In February 1900, Bovril announced its own 'War Picture', 'The Relief of Ladysmith' by John H. Bacon, 'a magnificent historic war gravure' that could be obtained with coupons available on every jar of Bovril. Bovril was particularly proud of its extensive use by the Royal Hospital Army Corps in South Africa. In the regular feature, 'Round About the Shops', *The Girl's Realm* describes how

> before each man was carried to the hospital train . . . , he was given a cup of hot Bovril, of which great kettles were kept in readiness just outside the Hospital tents and Red Cross trains! We can imagine how eagerly the poor fellows, who had been without food or drink, must have swallowed the refreshing draughts. (March 1901)

[18] See Appendix 1 for numbers of articles for each month and year.

[19] Thomas Richards, *The Commodity Culture of Victorian England: Advertising and Spectacle, 1851–1914* (1990), 155.

(Hospital tents, Red Cross trains, and the 'poor fellows'/soldiers would become ubiquitous images in the literature of 1914–18.) 'Van Houten's Brand' cocoa proclaimed that it was preferred by many wounded soldiers in hospitals in South Africa.

The consumerism of war did not end there. If one bought Vinolia soap, one could be proud that for every tablet purchased in November 1899, a half-penny would go towards the 'Transvaal War Fund'. One could also purchase the 'Cape to Cairo' inkstand featuring the profiles of Rhodes and Kitchener from Derry and Tom's for 10/6, or books out of the Invalid's Library, 'specially suited for wounded soldiers in hospitals' for three pence each or 1s 6d for the set of six (postage free). The ad proclaims that 'the Following are Now Ready':

1. Hymns for the Time of Weakness
2. A Short Story: Hetty's Pretty Face
3. A Short Story: The Blessing of the Rose Leaves
4. My Doves by Mrs Brightwen & Q&A
5. A Short Story: The Money Bags & Sayings of the Sages
6. A Short Story: A Prize in the Lottery & Comfortable Words

Notices praising the series are noted from *The Bookseller, The Quiver,* and *The Christian Leader.*

The Girl's Realm of March 1900 proclaimed:

> If you enjoy a THRILLING GAME with some skill in it, but not
> over
> difficult, you should
> ORDER AT ONCE
> EVERYBODY'S WAR GAME
> (copyright)
> Beautifully printed in Colours on Stiff Paper, with FLAGS,
> TEETOTUMS, and full directions.
> A THRILLING AND INSTRUCTIVE AMUSEMENT.
> Not only is this a capital Game in itself, but in addition, you get a
> splendid War Map with Sixteen Flags.
> A capital Game for Girls, or an excellent present for their Brothers.
> Sent for THREE PENNY STAMPS by
> W.R. Russell & Co., Limited,
> Paternoster Row, EC.

Such an ad reinforces the 'entertainment value of Empire'[20] as well as the imperial ideology that implicates 'everybody' in the War. War,

[20] Bush, *Edwardian Ladies*, 43.

here, is literally a game and girls, not just boys, are consumers of it. Girls can vicariously participate in the conflict and influence their brothers to do so also: 'an excellent present'. The phrase 'thrilling ... with some skill in it, but not over difficult' shows how the manufacturer gauged the sales pitch to echo the tone of this 'intelligent' girl's periodical. (It is acceptable to be 'bright' but not a 'bluestocking'!)

Clothing manufacturers, too, tried to boost sales by military associations. In February 1900, Hartley and Co. of Leeds featured a portrait of a famous general whose name they ascribed to one of their 'remarkable' products: 'Our "LORD ROBERTS" Cloth FOR LADIES'. Yet fashion was a problematic thing to discuss in time of war. The prevailing necessity for appropriate clothing for women, in particular for officers' widows—or ladies who could afford to be fashionable—is evident in the many advertisements for mourning wear. In its 'Expanded Fashion Edition' of 21 October 1899, the *Lady's Pictorial* featured 'Peter Robinson's Mourning Warehouse: Every Requisite for Mourning Attire, adapted to the latest fashion at moderate prices', as well as 'Mourning of Today at William Barker's (Islington)', and the 'Mourning Department of Jas. Shoolbred, Tottenham Court Road'. *The Lady's Realm* Double Number for Christmas 1900 showcased the following:

FOR FASHIONABLE
MOURNING
remember that
COURTAULD'S
CRAPE
Is Waterproof.
and therefore
IS NOT DAMAGED
BY A SHOWER.[21]

It cannot be claimed that Courtauld's intentionally meant for 'waterproof' or 'shower' to suggest the tears of grief, but the association is there nevertheless. As mourning became an increasingly familiar state, fashion editors adapted their features in order to retain interest in so seemingly trivial a thing as smart dressing in time of

[21] Courtauld's re-used this advertisement in its entirety fifteen years later in *The Lady*, 1915. See Kate Adie, *From Corsets to Camouflage: Women and War* (London, 2003), 115.

national and imperial crisis, for surely many readers must have challenged the preoccupation with '*fashionable* mourning'. *The Girl's Own Paper*'s regular feature, 'My Clothes Month by Month', is edited by 'A Lady Dressmaker'. On 27 January 1900, it is accompanied by an illustration of a smartly dressed woman depositing a coin in a box labelled, 'Soldiers' Widows and Orphans Fund'. Implicit in these advertisements are codes of social behaviour. Along with the sympathy, which she extends to those in mourning, 'A Lady Dressmaker' highlights how patriotic women should conduct themselves. Despite national grief caused by war, 'there are always children to amuse, and the young people whose brightness it is too soon to overshadow'. Mothers must be buoyant for the sake of their offspring. Ladies must also be sensitive to the concerns of others: 'if we wear no mourning ourselves, it seems to the leaders of the world of society, that it is in better taste that our garb should be quiet and retiring'. Above all, she emphasizes the familiar adage about maintaining a cheerful countenance: 'nothing is gained by meeting trouble halfway. Let us, therefore, try to look on the bright side of things, and turn our attention first to the always interesting subject of new spring millinery'. Like stories and other light entertainment, fashion is a form of amusement and distraction. This is 'retail therapy' at its early best. *The Girl's Realm*'s fashion editor strikes a similar if more serious note when she asserts that 'nothing but black will be possible for some months to come. Black serge coats and skirts, worn with blouses of black glacé silk, or very fine black flannel, are more suitable for day wear when in mourning'. As the Courtauld's advertisement proclaimed, mourning *can* be fashionable. Of course, the clothing industry had to find some way of confronting a potential loss in sales. It was therefore not simply catering to but inspiring public demand to sell its wares. The possibility that war might curtail the spending power of Britain's women was an unwelcome one, so there had to be some of way of ensuring that ladies remained concerned about their appearance, even in times of grief. How better to inspire than to appeal to their patriotic duty?

Even in the kitchen one could assert one's interest in and allegiance to the imperial mission in an appropriate way. Mrs de Salis in her monthly column for *The Lady's Realm,* entitled 'The Cuisine', notes that 'Our national anxiety prevents much entertaining, and all are willing to help the wounded and the widows and orphans of our heroes instead; therefore, I have given only some homely recipes for this month' (January 1900). These include Brain Cutlets *à la* Buller, Herring Roses *à la* Durban, and *Bonne Bouches à la* Rhodes. In subsequent months she suggests dishes like Africander Pudding (February 1900), *Anchois à la Natal*, and *Gelée à la Tugela* (May 1900).

The events in South Africa came to dominate other features. *The Girl's Realm* shows its more mawkish side in a series of photographs, arranged in the shape of a cross, and depicting a young girl of about five years old in different poses. In each, she wears a short white dress, with puttees and a colonial army hat. The first picture shows her holding a Union Jack and is captioned 'A Daughter of the Empire'. In the next, entitled 'Gentlemen, the Queen', she sits before a group of toy soldiers, imitating the monarch, whereas in another she carries a bayonet to illustrate the theme of 'A Bayonet Charge'. Finally, the bottom photograph shows her lying asleep, hand on weapon, and the Union Jack sticking up behind her with the caption 'The Day's Work is Done'. Girls can *pretend* to be soldiers, but unlike their brothers, their play will never become real. The child's play itself and the photographs that tell the story are indicative of the larger public fantasy of war, one which creative writers reinforced and developed not only in this war, but in the next, as we will see. Although the reality was far different from the imagined scenarios, there was an investment in the vision that depicted the familiar, the orderly, the successful, and the exciting.

The actual roles that women and girls undertook during the Boer War were for the most part not adventurous, confined as they were to the more mundane tasks of charity work on behalf of widows and orphans or knitting for soldiers. The nascent Welfare State, born partly out of the South African conflict, had, by 1914, taken on some of the obligations formally left to private initiative or charity. Women in the Great War were therefore more able to be involved in large numbers in some form of official war work, be it as nurses, ambulance drivers, or munitions workers. Between 1899 and 1902, however, magazines were there to help suggest ways of being of practical use for Queen and Country with features such as 'Socks for Our Soldiers in South Africa' (*The Girl's Realm*, February 1900) and 'Needlework of War-Time' (*The Girl's Own Paper*, 30 December 1899). In the 'Chronicle of the Schools' in *The Girl's Realm* of March 1900, the author points out:

There can scarcely be a girl in Great Britain to-day whose every thought is not turned to South Africa, whence all are watching with such heart-breaking anxiety for news of a loved father or brother, or some cousin or dear friend, who is fighting for Queen and country away out there on the veldt. But the English girl of to-day is not content with merely watching. She scorns to weep while her brother works; she, too, puts her shoulder to the wheel, and in the action shows as fine and unostentatious as does he. She finds out what there is to be done, and she does it, and well, too, because she does it so cheerfully and ungrudgingly. Indeed, the war had scarcely begun before the schoolgirl's fingers were busily fashioning shirts and socks and woollen tam o'shanters for the soldiers in South Africa, and her brain is actively formulating plans whereby she might materially assist the wives and chicks they had left behind.

To that end we are told the Leeds High School, through a series of concerts, raised £30 for a war fund whereas the Ladies' College at St Helier's, Jersey, was able to donate £63 to another.

Despite their suggestions for practical action, sentimentality abounds in these periodicals. In *The Girl's Realm* profile 'Some of Our Generals' Daughters' (January 1900), the author, Ignota, gushes:

at the present time much sincere sympathy cannot but be felt with the daughters of those of our gallant soldiers who have taken or who are taking part in the Transvaal campaign.... the outbreak of hostilities in any part of our great empire may, and indeed, generally does, change her existence from one where everything went pleasantly to one overclouded by the most wearing of all anxieties, often followed by bitter grief.

There is no questioning here of the politics that led to the 'outbreak of hostilities' and the language is characteristic of the emotional pitch of most of the magazine's articles. Words like 'sincere', 'sympathy', 'gallant', 'great', the use of the possessive 'our' in relation to soldiers or the empire appear often, and feelings are heightened by superlatives such as 'most'. Ignota suggests that the generals' daughters possess an extra degree of fortitude and commitment to empire because they are the offspring of military men. Such qualities are in their blood and are reinforced by example. The reader is also told about Lady Sarah Wilson,[22] a war correspondent in the Transvaal,

[22] Lady Sarah Isabella Augusta Churchill Wilson (1865–1923), Lady of Grace, St. John of Jerusalem and Red Cross, was the sixth daughter of the 7th Duke of Marlborough. She married in 1891 Lt.-Col. Gordon Chesney Wilson MVO (d. 1914) and they had one son. Taken prisoner by the Boers outside Mafeking on 4 December

and about Miss Frances Wolseley,[23] whom Ignota describes as 'devoted to the military profession and all that concerns it', but who is also 'like most modern girls' with her 'several hobbies' that include book-plate collecting and horse-riding. Wolseley and other women of her social set also appeared frequently in *The Lady's Pictorial*, which was devoted to fashion, society events, and gossip. From 1899 to 1902, the Boer War was mentioned in some capacity at least once in every weekly issue, mainly in the Editorial News. Not only are the lives and activities of such figures as Lord Roberts, Lady Buller, and Mrs Humphry Ward discussed, but 'American Ladies in the Transvaal' and 'Ladies Who are Aiding the War Fund and the Wounded' are profiled. Hints are also given for 'Practical Patriotism'. Certainly, the overriding impression of this periodical is that to be patriotic is to be *en vogue*.

Whereas Ignota and *The Lady's Pictorial* laud women for their interest in all things military, one writer, in the *G.O.P.*, cautions girls who seek military husbands. In 'Soldiers' Wives' (21 July 1900), the Revd E. Hardy, Chaplain to the Forces, claims that many girls are attracted by the uniform without realizing the dangers—'It sounds well to be a soldier's wife in war time, but the reality cannot be very pleasant'—or the important role army wives play—'Few people realise what it is to be the wife of a successful soldier'. He also talks about the 'designing fair ones', who, 'on the strength' of a married soldier's salary and the memory of the public generosity extended to the families of soldiers in the South African campaign, are induced 'to set their caps at soldiers on the approach of the next war. Wanted, a soldier going to be killed!' The Revd Hardy

1899, she was later exchanged for a Boer prisoner. She recounted her experiences in *South African Memories* (1909).

[23] Frances was the daughter of the commander-in-chief of the British Army, Garnet Joseph Wolseley, later Baron Wolseley of Cairo and Viscount Wolseley (1833–1913). She grew up travelling throughout Europe and Africa, and was a debutante in 1891. She preferred the country life, however, and when the family finally settled in Sussex in 1899, she pursued her passion for gardening. She founded the Glynde College for Lady Gardeners in 1902, which had the patronage of Gertrude Jekyll among others. She published *Gardening for Women* in 1908 and travelled extensively throughout Britain, Canada, and South Africa promoting women's role in countryside and horticultural issues. Her other books include *Women on the Land* (1916), *In a College Garden* (1916), and *Gardens, Their Form and Design* (1919). She became Viscountess Wolseley on the death of her father. She never married and spent her later years in Ardingly, Sussex (Jane Brown, 'Wolseley, Frances Garnet, Viscountess Wolseley (1872–1936)', *Oxford Dictionary of National Biography*, Oxford University Press, 2004).

anticipates Sassoon's poem, 'The Glory of Women', with his own damning assessment:

> Virgil sang of arms and the man; let us think a little of arms and the woman. Women can do almost anything they like with men, and there is little doubt that if they were joined together and set their faces against wars, these would never be waged. Instead of this they are attacked by scarlet fever, and favour the attentions of soldiers even more than they do those of parsons. They dote upon the military and are attracted by the pomp and circumstance of war. Since the Trojan campaign women have been either the direct or indirect cause of almost every great war, and it would seem that the Boer war is no exception.

Hardy thus rejects the assumption that women are natural peacemakers and betrays his own 'parson's' jealousy. In one fell swoop, the many catalysts of the South African War (and other conflicts) are reduced to one: females. The image of the war-mongering woman did not originate in the Great War.

Some women do merit his praise, however. Lady Roberts and Lady Wolseley (mother of the Miss Wolseley of Ignota's *Girl's Realm* profile) are particularly lauded, and Hardy admits that 'past heroes have shown that it is possible to be good soldiers though married'. Moreover, women can encourage men to 'behave as they ought':

> When the Guards were leaving London for the Boer war, a girl who had lately married one of them was heard to say to her husband, 'Keep your pecker up, Dick!' 'Taint me,' replied the guardsman, 'as needs keep my pecker up, but Kruger.' Sweethearts and wives have great influence in keeping up or keeping down the 'pecker' of soldiers.

The words used above would, in the words of Paul Fussell, 'constitute obvious *double entendres*'[24] in later years, but Hardy uses them with impunity. He uses them to reinforce his ultimate message that 'a young officer, before he unites himself to a girl, should ask himself, "What kind of a wife for a colonel or general will she be in case I reach that position? Will she fill the position with credit?"'

In order to show how exemplary women behave, *The Girl's Realm, The Lady's Realm,* and the *G.O.P.* give their newsworthy and factual articles a feminine edge. An appeal to womanly feeling and sensibility is always made as they attempt to bring the reader

[24] Fussell, *The Great War*, 23.

close to the scenes of action (but, of course, ones appropriate for the lady reader to 'see'). For instance, in 'How Our Wounded Soldiers are Nursed' (*The Girl's Realm,* March 1900), the author (again identified only by her first name), Sybil, says: 'I am sure that you all must be feeling great sympathy with the brave soldiers who are fighting our battles in South Africa, and to whom war brings so much suffering and distress.' Again, the politics of the War are largely ignored. The reference to 'our battles' simply and sharply implicates the reader in them. It is assumed ('I am sure . . . ') that she accepts the righteousness of the cause for which 'the brave soldiers' are fighting. The moral ambiguities of Britain's position are not even broached much less debated. As in Ignota's article, 'sympathy' is the byword, the breathless tone intrinsic. Come 1914, the idea that others are fighting on 'our' behalf will be even more potent.

The woman who, it was claimed, really understood her imperial duty and took the greatest interest in the conflict was Queen Victoria. Sarah A. Tooley's article for the June 1900 issue of *The Lady's Realm,* entitled 'The Queen and the Wounded',[25] profiles Victoria's concern for the men of her armies, particularly those at Netley hospital, which she visits frequently, striking 'the womanly note of sympathy and solace in all that she says or writes regarding the soldiers'. So great is the Queen's interest, Tooley tells us, that she is supplied with detailed accounts of the progress of the worst cases—'a history of that side of war which shows the price paid in human suffering'. In addition, 'choice flowers from the gardens at Osborne are constantly sent to the hospital, and fancy woollen goods and various little comforts from time to time find their way into the wards by the Queen's kind thought'. Tooley's comments are not just obsequious declarations. Victoria's correspondence and journals are filled with references to her 'brave troops' who inspire 'my admiration', 'my sympathy', and 'my deepest concern'. She writes of how 'my heart bleeds for these dreadful losses' and how 'I am horrified at

[25] Sarah A. Tooley was a familiar chronicler of nursing and of the monarchy. Besides her many contributions to magazines, she was a prolific author and her books included *The Personal Life of Queen Victoria I* (1896); *The Life of Queen Alexandra* (1902); *Royal Palaces and Their Memories* (1902); *The Royal Family by Pen and Camera* (1907); *The Life of Florence Nightingale* (1904); and *The History of Nursing in the British Empire* (1906). Her *Who's Who* entry declared that she 'discovered the birthplace and birth certificate of Mrs. Gaskell'. She died on Christmas Eve, 1946 (*Who Was Who*, vol. IV, 1941–1950, p. 1158).

the terrible list of casualties'. Her own version of a visit to Netley confirms Tooley's assertions:

Went up in a lift to the second floor, where all the wounded were assembled, almost all, with few exceptions, being able to stand in the corridors. They looked wonderfully well, considering how badly they had been wounded. Far the greatest number were from the Highland Brigade, which suffered so at Magersfontein. I handed flowers to those in bed. There were a good many Guardsmen, and also men from the Irish regiments. Then we went into the wards and corridors in which were the sick. It was sad to see so many with heart disease brought on by overmarching and hard work.[26]

The Queen reflected in her journal on New Year's Eve, 1899, on

the sad losses among my brave troops, which is a constant sorrow to me. In the midst of it all I have, however, to thank God for many mercies and for the splendid unity and loyalty of my Empire. I pray God to bless and preserve all my children, grandchildren, and kind relations and friends, and may there be brighter days in store for us![27]

Victoria, the symbol of the age, the figurehead of the Empire, is the ultimate patriotic mother, the ultimate exemplar of feminine behaviour in wartime.

How women lived in South Africa was also a subject of many articles. Neville Edwards depicted the 'Home and Social Life in the Transvaal' for *The Lady's Realm* (June 1900) and considered the future for *The Lady's Magazine* in 'The Transvaal after the War' (April 1901). Racial prejudices and stereotypes abound in these articles. For instance in the former feature, Edwards describes how women in England would not complain of their servants if they had to be 'confronted with the problem of having a native "boy" to do the household work'. While he might learn fast, he may also have a fondness for the whisky bottle and, if he is 'spoiled by contact with too much civilisation' he may just become vain:

He begins to realise the beauty of his snub nose and blubber lips. He develops into that truly appalling creature the "Kaffir masher"—the sort of native who, if he can write, tries to forge his master's name, or else he steals the money with which he buys the gorgeous ties, sashes, hat-bands,

[26] *The Letters of Queen Victoria: A Selection from Her Majesty's Correspondence and Journals between the Years 1886 and 1901*, vol. III, 1896–1901, ed. George Earle Buckle (London, 1932), 492.

[27] *The Letters of Queen Victoria*, 451.

and flash watch-chains in which he swaggers down the streets of Johannesburg on Sunday afternoons.

Although the Boer War differed from Britain's previous imperial conflicts, being fought as it was against white opponents, no effort was made to acknowledge the efforts of pro-British Africans. In fact, as Krebs points out, 'Baden-Powell consistently resisted attempts to publicize the efforts of the Africans who fought for the British, preferring to keep the conflict being seen as a "white man's war".'[28] Similarly, although the *G.O.P.* featured 'A Wedding in Native High Life in Zululand' (24 March 1900), it focused most of its attention on the experiences of British women in the colony in its articles, including 'An English Girl in South Africa' and 'Log of Voyage to the Cape, and Diary of Army Nursing in South Africa'.

We are not told the name of the 'English girl' who relates her impressions of life in the South Africa, but are given clear portraits of those with whom she comes in contact. A familiar emotionalism characterizes the exposé:

> At the present time the sympathy and interest of every Englishwoman is stirred to the uttermost by the knowledge of all the suffering and privation that are being endured by English people in South Africa. I know how anxiously at home people watch and wait for news, how eagerly the newspapers are read, and how sadly every heart beats when the news of a dearly-brought victory is followed by the tidings of individual loss and death. I know that no English girl could read with unmoved feelings the accounts of the great and noble deeds by our brave soldiers out here, deeds that will live in history long after the war is past.

The use of superlatives, dramatic language, and the rhetorical tripling of the adverbial phrases, 'how anxiously at home', 'how eagerly the newspapers are read', and 'how sadly every heart beats' gives the passage its high-pitched and melodramatic tone. What appears to be an article to further understanding between the two sides—'doubtless you have all read and heard about the Boer men of war...; but I feel sure that you will be interested in hearing about their lives in time of peace'—is actually a reinforcement of stereotypes that highlight the superiority of the English and the deficiencies of the Dutch. Their farms are 'curiously unattractive, internally as well as externally', situated as most are on a lonely

[28] Krebs, *Gender, Race, and the Writing of Empire*, 20.

and desolate veldt. The farmhouses are very plain, and contain no 'pretty pieces of embroidery, no dainty paintings, no cleverly-carved tables and chairs'. More damning is her assessment of the Boer communities, which, she claims, 'take an intensely morbid interest in all suffering'. They often can be found gathering in a sickroom, expressing 'just a little disappointment' if the patient recovers. Disagreeable traits will be found in the enemies of a later war, the Germans, who will also be characterized as callous barbarians.

Further reinforcement of unpleasant Boer stereotypes can be found in the 'Log of Voyage to the Cape, and Diary of Army Nursing in South Africa', which was serialized in ten parts by the *G.O.P.* from 24 February to 29 September 1900. The Boers are almost always described as dirty both in their person and in their living conditions; Dutch meals have a 'German sort of taste' and their coffee is 'execrable'. They are quite simply uncivilized. British Tommies, on the other hand, are dedicated and cheerful even in their suffering and defeat, and the wounded are 'keen on going back to have another slap at the Boers'. All that is English—a term used interchangeably with 'British'—is good, clean, and civilized, and throughout, the author, Maris, stresses that 'this is a righteous and necessary war. Even the most gentle-minded people say in the end, "I loathe the Boers."' She claims that South Africa is 'insufferable for English people to live in while the Dutch have the upper hand' and that if England asserts her will and civilizing power, 'the colony will flourish'. Tellingly, she likes the land far more than the people who inhabit it: 'One gets to admire this country more the longer one is in it, not things Dutch, but wild Nature, the vastness of everything, the lights and shadows on the wide veldt and rugged mountains.' In conversation with a Boer patient, who 'looks far more a Frenchman than an unkempt Boer', Maris is told about the 'intense faith of the Dutch in their own cause'. She seems incredulous at the fact that 'they have never believed themselves to be playing a losing game, and will not even now believe that they can lose their independence'. She is unequivocal in her belief—as her readers should also be—that 'the Dutch must be subjugated'.

Like her Great War sisters, Maris longs to get to the front. When she does, we are told that it is 'real nursing . . . , real war, and really interesting'. There is constant activity, hard work, and many casualties of battle and disease, but it is a very romanticized picture nevertheless. Tales of a more gruesome nature are recounted with a kind of relish. For instance, one of her 'delightful' Tommies

> told a very weird story this morning. He was dead tired after the battle, and lay down to sleep on his blanket, thought he was sleeping on saddles, but when he took up his blanket in the morning, he found two dead Boers underneath.

The suddenly discovered dead will be a feature of the writing about the Great War as bodies come to litter the battlefields, but Maris's tone in this retelling suggests that she is dismissive of the deaths of these 'evil' Boers. She makes even the unpleasant romantic:

> rather eerie, all alone, the only woman up in Sterkstroom. And no picturesque camp here by moonlight, as at Wynberg, but a dull schoolhouse full of the fevered and the dying, and some outlying huts and tents. The men have been lying in their blankets in stretchers on the ground; but now we have got beds for nearly all. Each hut is lit with a candle in a bottle or tin; so everything is primitive, you see, without the picturesque which is usually part of primitiveness.

Much of her account is characterized by this devotion to the picturesque, either as she tries to capture it in her writing or as she laments its absence. An open-air religious service, for instance, is called 'a study in khaki', and the colour becomes emblematic of the War itself. The scenery as well as the 'worshippers' are 'all khaki-coloured', and she finds it amusing 'to see suspicions of khaki puttees under the chaplain's surplice'. She turns war into something sublime, a subject for lyricism:

> No one who has ever been near to war, can think of it as anything but very dreadful, though I think the privation and wretchedness of much of the camp life in this sand, and the devastating sicknesses, are far worse than the actual warfare. Captain Montgomery's sudden death in the heyday of life . . . does not seem to me nearly so sad, for instance, as Captain R.'s death in our little ward. 'I want to live so much, Sister; you will help me fight for life,' he used to say in the night. He was so good, thinking always of the welfare of his men; and such an appreciative and grateful patient. It was dreadful to watch him slowly sinking, and to be with him dying; to do the last for him dead, and to follow him to the mortuary tent. And later in the day, to hear again the muffled drums and Dead March playing, and to see the long progression in khaki winding across the sand. I always think of that bit of Kipling—
>
> 'Hark to the big drums calling,
> Follow me, follow me home'.

One man is used to exemplify the many, and Kipling puts the seal on his sacrifice. The poet of empire supplants the Bible, as the factual descriptions of war are overlaid by this meditation on the supposed higher nature of the conflict.

The same strategy is used by Alice Cockran in her interview/article for *The Girl's Realm,* entitled 'Through the Siege of Ladysmith: A Chat with One Who Went Through It' (August 1900). Mrs Murray, the wife of a town councillor, describes the hardships, fears, and deaths she experienced before the rescue forces arrived. Cockran asserts that this female account 'of domestic sorrows will bring home to most of us the horrors of war far more than the rhetorical accounts of fields of dead and dying . . . than all the official horrors'. It is assumed that the reader will instantly feel a motherly tenderness when she considers 'a single one of these dead and think of all he represents, in the care of his childhood, the hopes of his manhood, the brutal severance from the ties that have made him part of other lives'. This singling-out of one casualty makes the appeal more direct and specific. In him, readers can imagine a son, brother, husband, or father of their own. It serves a function similar to that of picture-postcards and posters where the model becomes the image of everyman/woman.

Cockran does not just reserve this symbolism for the British dead, however. Although she too characterizes the Boers as bigoted, ruthless besiegers who 'made it a point to aim their fire at any passing group of persons', she also stresses how women on either side of the conflict are affected. Mrs Murray claims to have found letters from 'Dinah' to her sweetheart, a Boer soldier:

> Whatever may be our opinion concerning it, we cannot read them without being moved by their sincerity. Every girl who has a lover in the war will feel for Dinah's loyalty and fervour. . . . We need not be ashamed if we feel a throb of sorrow and sympathy for the true-hearted girl, whose letter, stained and creased was carried against her lover's heart to the last.

War brings grief to all women, irrespective of national allegiances.

The melodramatic note that distinguishes the previous passage is also sounded in the short stories featured in these magazines. 'Concerning One Volunteer' by Charles Kennett Burrow (*The Lady's Realm*, July 1901) describes how Guy Campion is reluctant to enlist:

> He had thought vaguely of volunteering for the front, but it had stopped at thinking. When he heard of other men, friends and neighbours in the country, sending in their names, he had had an impulse to do the same: once even he had put pen to paper with that very purpose; but, somehow, it all came to nothing.
>
> Guy Campion loved his ease—that was at the bottom of it. He admitted frankly that he loved soft living—indeed, he was inclined to make rather a virtue of it.... In spite of this dilettantism, he was popular both with men and women. Some day, they said, Campion will wake up and do something.

This description could so easily be transferred to the writings of 1914: the well-to-do, lazy, and comfort-loving type would become a favourite whipping-boy of novelists, memoirists, and commentators in the next war. Being 'soft' rather than 'hard', Guy Campion's manhood is called into question. It is difficult to imagine that the sexual connotations were not apparent to readers in 1901. The hope that he may one day 'wake up' enhances the belief that Guy exists in an artificial state; to awake is to re-enter the rational, real world of *men*.

True to the Revd Hardy's assertion that women can influence their men to 'behave as they ought', Bess Tennent wakes Guy from his dilettantism. She is his favourite cousin 'with whom he had imagined himself for some time to be a little in love' (Guy cannot even really muster the energy to be passionate about her, just as he cannot be passionate about the War). She is 'buried in newspapers' when he visits, for Bess takes a keen interest in the events unfolding in South Africa, and is appalled that Guy does not. She even has a large map pinned to the wall with flag-pins marking regimental positions that she alters from day to day 'as dispositions were changed or reinforcements arrived'. (Bess Tennent would certainly have enjoyed 'Everybody's War Game'.) The admiring Guy tells her that '"even most soldiers' wives wouldn't take the interest you do,"' but she claims he could not possibly understand either soldiers or their wives. It is her duty to be unkind to him so as to force him to do as he ought. When he makes the assertion, oddly pre-figuring Heming way's,[29] that '"duty towards one's country is such an abstraction,"' Bess's outburst anticipates that incessant cry of her Great War sisters: '"Oh, if I were only a man! Do you think I should be

[29] 'Abstract words such as glory, honor, courage, or hallow were obscene beside the names of rivers, the numbers of regiments and the dates' (Ernest Hemingway, *A Farewell to Arms* (1929), 191).

here if I were a man and could shoot? I wouldn't sit before maps, then!.... I should do a man's work. I couldn't bear to see others gladly doing what I could do better than they. To be shamed by boys—just think of it!"' Having internalized this masculine paradigm, she thinks Guy a coward for his failure to do likewise. Horrified by such a suggestion, he is shaken 'from his indolence and ineffectual ease', and the dilettante finds a new interest in life that is not only martial, but implicitly sexual: 'it was as though some sense, long sealed, had broken forth to life again; the spirit of action stirred in him, and with the change that should bring he saw old things newly... he moved in a changed atmosphere'.

His thoughts as he sets off on his horse are communicated in language strikingly similar to that which dominates similar tales between 1914 and 1918:

> The strange exhilaration that had come upon him was like a new pulse in his blood. The desire for action, which had been like to die out in him, was in full flood; he could have shouted for mere joy on the way to turning his manhood to account.

So preoccupied is Guy in this reverie of manliness, that he manages the aptly named Wild Robin carelessly and crashes into a low stone wall bringing the horse down on top of him. 'All that was left of Guy Campion was carried to his cousin's house. And as she bent over so much strength and beauty crushed to nothingness, she cried out: "Oh God, pity us poor women!.... But he meant to go—he meant to go!"' Bess feels no remorse for encouraging Guy's recklessness, but instead feels pity that she and his mother cannot take up his place as soldiers. Although he is redeemed in this rather ignominious death because he was on his way to enlist, Guy's fate suggests that he lost control because he succumbed to overemotional feminine excitement. This would not have happened to a more disciplined man.

Whereas Bess's war activity is confined to maps and newspapers, other women participated more directly in the events in South Africa. As the 'Log of Voyage to the Cape' shows, one of the primary ways in which females were active in the War was nursing. Florence Nightingale's work in the Crimean War created a romantic fascination with the profession despite her own protestations that it was not for the uninitiated, untrained, or delicate female. Magazines had a hand in keeping the popularized image alive by articles describing her early years ('The Girlhood of Florence Nightingale', *The Girl's Realm*, April 1899) and lauding her mercy and loving kindness (Eliza F. Pollard's feature in the *G.O.P.*, 1902). Idle middle-class women, especially, were encouraged to take first-aid classes, and the actively minded joined peacetime nursing yeomanries. The role of women was more limited in the Boer War than in the Great War, but nurses in South Africa attracted as much attention and interest. Both 'The Shield of Captain Credence' (*The Girl's Realm*, February 1900) and 'Hospital Jean: A War Story' (*G.O.P*, 10 March 1900) anticipate the language and sentiment discernable in romantic stories of 1914–18.

'The Shield of Captain Credence' opens as Curzon, a gunner, comes to the cavalry lines to borrow 'clean handkerchiefs and cigarettes' from his friend, Erskin. The two men grouse about the fact that real action has been temporarily halted by 'the last folly of the Chief's'. The narrator claims that this 'disrespectful sentence uttered referred to those placed in positions of trust and authority by the Imperial Government; but the Lieutenant of Artillery is a fine free critic of his Superior Officer'. Curzon goes on to explain his anger and the story belies its imperial prejudice with racial/racist stereotypes:

> 'They've got an idea that the niggers want an example of piety shown them, so all the troops, with massed bands, are going to march down to Ladysmith for a service on the Market Square. . . . ' Erskin looked as disgusted as Curzon. 'Fancy making soldiers a kind of penny peep-show for the niggers!' he said. 'What is the service coming to?'

There is little news of the enemy, according to Erskin, but a major called Barracleugh has come down with fever and is to be moved to Ladysmith. The point that has the two men chattering is that Barracleugh's sister will be at the hospital to look after him. Unlike other women, she has refused to leave the besieged town. We are told, ' "she's a plucky girl, and a true Briton!" ' What better accolade or credentials?

Fate has more in store for Erskin when he meets this paragon of women. He discovers that she is one of his childhood holiday playmates, Molly Bawn, Barracleugh's *half*-sister. Together they recall the games of role-playing they engaged in which centred around Bunyan's *Holy War*, a book they preferred to *Pilgrim's Progress*. Erskin says,

'I was always going to be a soldier you know, even then, and you were going—' He stopped in some confusion. In those days, when he was twelve and she ten, they arranged the universe for themselves, and were going to be married and live in a tent, and command a regiment in partnership, because Molly never would consent to be left out and told that, being a girl, she could not do exactly the same as Lionel Erskin—'Lal', as she called him. But looking at the grown-up self-possessed Molly at his side, he hardly liked to remind her of this.

Girls have always been fascinated by the adventures to which their brothers were entitled and from which, in real life, they were excluded. It is not surprising that many preferred the exciting world of deeds and daring to the closely circumscribed and domestic world which girls' fiction generally described and prescribed for them. Girls of the Edwardian generation

were closer to their brothers than any before or since. For a decade or two it was acceptable for girls to behave like boys when in their brothers' company; after 1920 single-sex schooling was nearly universal and adolescent gender roles were reimposed. The chivalry, manliness, and naive patriotism of the golden boys and girls thus become especially touching in the ironic glare of hindsight, and the brothers' loss in 1916.[30]

A forerunner of those young women who enthusiastically joined Voluntary Aid Detachments when they were founded some nine years later, Molly says with 'a little, quaint sigh': '"I couldn't be a soldier after all, you see! . . . So I trained as a nurse."'

The love that blossoms between Molly and Erskin is depicted in familiar love-story language common in romance novels of the period and after:

The weeks which followed were very happy for them both, though the sense of the war was upon them, and they snatched their intercourse from the very hands of uncertainty. At any moment there might be an action; at any moment the tragedy of battle might be upon them; and then, who knew what the end might be? They lived their lives ringed around by anxiety and the dread of death, and it drew them together as no other circumstances could have done.

Typically, war heightens romance and, once again, Fussell's assessment of *double entendres*, the 'curious prophylaxis of language', is pertinent here: 'One could say *intercourse*, or *erection*, or *ejaculation* without any risk of evoking a smile or a leer.'[31]

[30] Mitchell, *The New Girl*, 135. [31] Fussell, *The Great War*, 23.

Molly's own qualities, the stuff of British heroines, are described in similarly purple prose. She 'carried her shield of faith fearlessly and well... and moved about the danger-fraught town with willing hands and a brave heart that only shook with a pang of fear when she prayed with dumb lips that the sword of her hero might prosper'. Inevitably, Erskin is mortally wounded after leading a charge 'any man would be proud of'. It is therefore a given that any woman would also be proud. On his deathbed he tells Molly how that battle reminded him of their *Holy War* games. Play becomes real, and to comfort him, she repeats the words of Captain Credence almost as a prayer: '"Now take to yourselves your wonted courage, and show yourselves men even this once only; for in a few minutes, after the next engagement this time you shall see your Prince show himself in the field"'. With a murmur that 'it is very dark' and the exhortation for Molly to kiss him, Erskin dies, giving up 'the charge held so faithfully to the great Commander'.[32]

Prefiguring her Great War sisters, Molly experiences a kind of spiritual enlightenment and refuses to believe that Erskin's and his comrades' deaths are 'a terrible waste of life': '"I have faith that there is a beautiful interpretation even for the horrors and the apparent cruelty and barbarism of war!"' Despite her grief, and exclaiming that '"I serve England also!"', Molly refuses to be idle:

> 'Is it only the men who can do their duty in the face of death?' said Molly, quietly. 'I am proud to be associated with these'—her eyes wandered along the grim and ghastly line of beds. 'If the men do not grudge the personal pain—even the life—the women need not grudge giving their best, also, though it be their nearest and dearest, for their country.'

Such a rallying cry does not question the motives of the War, but ennobles the sacrifice. It is a crucial feature of romantic war literature, and it had tremendous staying power, as later chapters will illustrate.

A similar encomium of the fulfilment of duty is provided by G.E.M. in the story 'Hospital Jean'. Already a nurse at the outbreak

[32] The dying kiss would have had particular resonance for readers. Santanu Das in *The Sense of Touch in First World War Literature* (unpublished dissertation, Cambridge, 2002) discusses the many connotations of the dying kiss in his chapter on representations of male-to-male kissing in writing from the Great War. It was both religiously symbolic and historically resonant, evoking as it did the kiss of special significance in the national mythology: the dying words of Admiral Nelson, 'Kiss me, Hardy' (Das, *The Sense of Touch*, 97).

of war, Jean Kennedy gives up her position in an Edinburgh hospital when her brother, Jack, and George Campbell, the man she loved 'as few men have been loved', are ordered to South Africa with their regiment of the Gordon Highlanders: 'Jean couldn't bear the thought of the brave British soldiers lying wounded in the Transvaal while she remained at home.'

She goes out to South Africa along with three other nurses and is soon surrounded by artillery and horses, 'sharing in the dangers of her countrymen' for 'she had a soldier's heart within her'. Revelling in her part in the War, Jean's 'pride is stirred' as she watches 'her own countrymen . . . going into action' to the sound of bagpipes. Recalling Tennyson, 'she knew they would "do or die"'. As a member of a field ambulance, this patriotic nurse is able to come close to the scene of action, and she watches a battle from the top of a wagon. Short sentences mimic the bursts of actions: 'bayonets gleam amid the rocks'; 'The pipes burst forth'; 'The Gordons poured a volley and charged'; 'One big gun rang out'; 'On and on and on!' Despite 'murderous fire' which mows down lines of men, the enemy is 'hurled from the position' and the English flag is 'raised on the hill-top'. The Medical Corps then goes into action amongst the 'charred faces, mangled bodies, . . . lying everywhere'. Although two of the six nurses, 'horror-stricken with the spectacle', faint, 'Jean Kennedy worked as she never had worked before. The doctors marvelled at her strength.' The exemplary heroine always seems to overwork. This feverish rush to save lives is a key element, especially in nursing memoirs, and foregrounds the ways in which women behave unexpectedly in the service of the sick and the wounded. Healing soldiers is not just validated, it is celebrated.

It is not until the late afternoon that she finds her brother seriously, but not mortally, wounded. George Campbell is not so lucky. Jean finds him amongst four other dead soldiers: 'his head was buried in the grass, his coat was torn, there was a great gash in his neck'. The story ends with her pale and trembling, turning over the body: 'George Campbell lay before her!' Unlike 'The Shield of Captain Credence', this tale concludes without recording the heroine's emotions. The reader is left to infer, from the tone of the previous sentiments that, despite her grief, she will ultimately carry on without despair because her lover died for the Empire—even being the one to plant the Union Jack on Boer territory. He died an imperial hero.

Stories like this can be said to be acting as parables or textbooks for behaviour in the imperial cause—like a contemporary *Pilgrim's Progress*—how to put on a brave face; how to deal with sorrow as befits a true daughter of the Empire, with dignity; how to use patriotism to assuage any possible feelings that war is a useless waste. These stories also indicate to women how they should expect their men to behave, what characteristics are most admirable in the *sons* of the Empire. Yet the fact that so much effort seems to have gone into convincing the general population of the rightness of the War and of imperialism itself begs the question whether certain attitudes were actually more at risk than fully ingrained. They were, perhaps, not as widely shared as imperialists had hoped:

> even during the Boer War, commentators were already formulating analyses of the ideological function of the newspapers, the music halls, the schools, and the pulpits. An examination of such contemporary critiques reveals a complicated picture of how imperialism functioned culturally in turn-of-the-century Britain... Victorian imperialism was not a cultural monolith... empire was assumed and yet critiqued, was understood and yet always needed to be explained, was far away and yet appeared at the breakfast table every morning.[33]

The certainties expressed in fiction sit uneasily alongside the social commentary of these years. One outspoken critic of the celebration of imperial manhood and public fascination with the exploits of the War was Emily Hobhouse (1860–1926), who, among others, was outraged by the concentration camps that Kitchener set up to intern Boer families. *The Brunt of War and Where It Fell* (1902) offers 'an outline of the recent war, from the standpoint of the women and children', and describes the destruction of homes, relief work, life and death in the camps, and agitation in England for humane treatment of the 'enemy'. Maps and appendices listing rations, mortality rates, burnt farms, and native camp locations are intended to add further factual credibility to the personal experiences she recounts. Hobhouse defends herself against the accusation,

> so widely made in the Press and elsewhere that I have slandered the British troops. No one yet has substantiated this accusation from my words or writings. I have, on the contrary, done my utmost to uphold the honour of the army. It is true that as long as war exists the honour of a country is confided in its soldiers, who will never cease to shield it; but is not the

[33] Krebs, *Gender, Race, and the Writing of Empire*, 9.

converse also true, and is it not forgotten? viz. that the honour of the soldiers is confided to the country? If advantage is taken of the necessary obedience of soldiers to demand of them services outside the recognised rules of warfare, or in performance of which their moral duty must clash with their professional duty, the blame lies on the country and its Government but not upon the army.[34]

She trod on hallowed ground: implicit in her criticism of the government is a criticism of the cult of imperialism itself.[35] (Her cousin-by-marriage, Margaret Heyworth Hobhouse, would, as Chapter 2 demonstrates, also court public controversy with her 1917 pamphlet *'I Appeal Unto Caesar': The Case of the Conscientious Objector.*)

Although she was not a lone voice crying in the wilderness, Emily Hobhouse was outside the wide circle of social critics who tried to find more pervasive reasons for the failings of the British Army in South Africa. Underlying the defeats, they believed, was a degeneration of the race. This concern was not new and not confined to Britain. It had been brewing since the 1870s, with intermittent outbursts by writers like Max Nordau whose opus, *Degeneration*, first appeared in English in 1895.[36] The Boer War simply 'intensified the fantasies of racial decline'.[37] A royal commission charged with investigating how the War was handled catalogued a lack of army intelligence, mismanaged hospitals, and sickly working-class volunteers. The Inter-Departmental Committee on Physical Deterioration found that 60% of all recruits were physically unfit to serve in the army. This concern even found its way into *The Girls' Empire* magazine. In a ten-instalment feature of 1902, called 'How to be Strong—Special Features with the Sandow Grip Dumbell', the

[34] Emily Hobhouse, *The Brunt of War and Where It Fell* (London, 1902), xvi.

[35] Heloise Brown's illuminating study, *'The Truest Form of Patriotism': Pacifist Feminism in Britain, 1870–1902* (Manchester, 2003), provides a wider consideration of the activities of Emily Hobhouse and other women in the international peace movements of late-nineteenth and early-twentieth centuries.

[36] Max Simon Nordau (1849–1923), author and physician, was born at Budapest, the son of an Orthodox rabbi. He practised medicine from 1878 to 1880 at Budapest and then settled in Paris where he became a prolific writer and critic with his controversial attacks on European culture, art, and politics, including *The Conventional Lies of Our Civilization* (1883) and *Paradoxes* (1896) as well as *Degeneration*. He was a co-founder of the World Zionist Organization. He died in Paris on 22 January 1923 and his remains were reinterred at Tel Aviv in 1926.

[37] Ledger and Luckhurst, *The Fin de Siècle*, xvi.

author contends that girls and women 'will play a no less important part in the future progress of the British Empire' than their brothers. By 'working steadily at these exercises', the girl/reader will achieve a sound and healthy body: 'When you look at it from an Imperial point of view you see how very important it is. The nation is made up of the individual!' Personal laziness and social conditions rather than heredity were seized upon as the major factors in Britain seemingly losing ground to 'stronger, healthier beasts' like Germany, Russia, and the United States:

> The disturbing possibility that Britain might find itself amongst the also-rans promoted a bout of intense, national soul-searching among politicians, economists, social commentators, and journalists. Their diagnoses of national ills were usually accompanied by a quest for remedies that would revitalise the country, restore its self-confidence and reinforce its power abroad. Analysts of the right, and left, concluded that only radical nostrums had any hope of success.[38]

Baden-Powell, the 'hero of Mafeking', believed that 'a moral virus [was] already spreading amongst the young', and his Boy Scout movement was an effort to counteract this infection of 'wishy-washy slackers'. The working classes were to be made aware of the benefits of empire. Voluntary organizations like the Primrose League and the National Service League had been set up and funded by the middle classes, and 'patriotic race-thinking' was 'widely transmitted ... through the popular press, fiction, poetry, school texts and juvenile magazines'.[39] 'Race' became elided with national identity: Anglo-Saxon was equated with being British/English.[40] Social Darwinism inspired the foundation of voluntary organizations designed to promote public health, among them the Institute of Hygiene (1903), the Infants' Health Society, and the Eugenics Education Society (1908). The problem of physical and national degeneration 'was constantly linked with the question of child-bearing and rearing, and with the "ignorance" of working-class mothers'.[41] Advice and instruction on motherhood was disseminated by organizations such as the Women's League of Service for Motherhood and the Ladies Sanitary Association through leaflets,

[38] James, *Rise and Fall of the British Empire*, 320.
[39] Bush, *Edwardian Ladies*, 105.
[40] Ibid., 122.
[41] Anna Davin, 'Imperialism and Motherhood', *History Workshop: A Journal of Social Historians* 5 (Spring, 1978), 16.

lectures, baby clinics, and the often-unwelcome health visitors. The intrusion of these admittedly well-intentioned middle- and upper-class women into working-class homes was 'part of a general invasion . . . by authorities'.[42]

Similar indoctrination characterized organizations like the Girls' Friendly Society, founded in 1874 by a group of Anglican ladies intent on 'building up from the parish level a nation-wide organization which would ward off temptation by associating respectable young girls together, and by training them in religious principles and domestic duty.'[43] By 1913 the G.F.S. had over 39,000 working girl 'members' and over 190,000 upper-class lady 'associates': 'The model G.F.S. girl was expected to be devout, kindly, serious-minded, uncomplaining and (by modern standards) relatively uninterested in the opposite sex.'[44] It encouraged deference to one's social superiors and promoted the family as a 'preservative against class conflict'.[45] The Girl Guides, founded in 1913 by Baden-Powell's wife, Olave, was run along lines similar to those of the Boy Scouts. Captain Baker, an ex-Guardsman, was inspired in 1901 to found an organization for girls comparable to the Lads' Brigade. The story of his 'Drill Brigade for Girls' is told in *The Girl's Realm* of September 1908. Baker is lauded for his 'gentleness with unvarying firmness':

> One has only to see the healthy, happy faces of the children when they are at drill to realise how highly they value the privilege, and how greatly they benefit from the exercises. . . . Islington, Pentonville, and Clerkenwell contain many unhealthy areas, and the children from these districts are, as a rule, weakly and miserable, but not so those who are members of the Girls' Brigade. Watch a poor, wizened little wisp of a girl for a week or two after she has started drills. You will see her developing a grace you would not have suspected. The clubs and dumb-bells make her limbs firm, supple, and pliant; the breathing exercises bring her chest and shoulders into shape; the walking exercise teaches her how to carry herself. The natural result of all this is increased cheerfulness, for physical health inevitably imparts its benefits to the mind.

[42] Davin, 'Imperialism and Motherhood', 36–7.

[43] Brian Harrison, 'For Church, Queen and Family: The Girls' Friendly Society 1874–1920', *Past and Present*, No.61 (Nov. 1973), 109.

[44] Ibid., 116.

[45] Ibid., 127.

There is never too much 'body-building' or overexertion. The article is at pains to point out that these girls become *more* feminine from their training; there is no fear that they will become pseudo-men. Yet such emphasis on physical fitness surely must have contributed to women's conviction that they were more than mere ornaments of grace and beauty and were highly capable of playing active roles once war came in 1914.

The body of literature that documents the eugenic concerns of pre-Great War social commentators is vast.[46] Medical and quasi-medical discussions were carried out not just in 'specialist journals, but in magazines with a far broader readership, particularly the *Westminster Review* and the *Fortnightly Review*'.[47] Pamphlets and books with titles such as *The Physical Education of Brain and Body* (1900), *Education and Heredity; or, Eugenics: a Mental, Moral and Social Force* (1909), and *Parenthood and Race Culture, an Outline of Eugenics* (1909) were ubiquitous. A woman's emotional development was a key topic. In *Woman: Her Brain, Mental Capacity and Character* (1908), Bernard Hollander uses scientific terminology to describe the physical characteristics of the female, and extrapolates the effects of the body on the woman's psyche:

> Now, too little notice is taken of the fact that in women the sympathetic or ganglionic nervous system, which controls the vegetative and sensitive life, is more developed than in man, one reason being that it has to supply some additional organs not existing in man, the breasts, the womb, and the ovaries. It is due in part to this more elaborate sympathetic system that women feel more keenly the emotional side of mental life. Their affections are deeper, they are more subject to fear, more readily roused to joy and sorrow, and their grief is more intense. This increased susceptibility renders them easily moved to tears by trivial circumstances.[48]

[46] See J. Edward Chamberlain and Sander Gilman (eds.), *Degeneration: The Dark Side of Progress* (1985); Tracey Hill (ed.), *Decadence and Danger: Writing, History and the Fin de Siècle* (1997); Greta Jones, *Social Darwinism in English Thought* (1980); Frank Mort, *Dangerous Sexualities: Medico-Moral Politics in England since 1830* (1987); Daniel Pick, *Faces of Degeneration: Anatomy of a European Disorder, c.1848–1918* (1989); John Stokes, *Fin de Siècle/Fin du Globe: Fears and Fantasies of the Fin de Siècle* (1992).

[47] Kate Flint, *The Woman Reader: 1837–1914* (Oxford, 1993), 53.

[48] Bernard Hollander, MD, *Woman: Her Brain, Mental Capacity and Character* (London, 1908), 4. Other studies of this kind include, H. S. Drayton, 'Is the Brain of Women Inferior?' *Englishwoman*, 3 (1896), 493–6; Havelock Ellis, *Man and Woman: A Study of Human Secondary Sexual Characteristics* (1894); George J. Romanes, 'Mental Differences between Men and Women', *Nineteenth Century*, 21 (1887), 654–72.

It is the pelvic organs, he says, that are responsible for such complaints as headaches and neuralgia, and the feminine tendency to blush. Hollander does not discount the 'ancients'' explanation of hysteria, but asserts that the reason why modern women do not suffer as much from it is because their reason has been trained 'at the expense of their emotional nature', and they have experienced more outdoor life and physical activity. Women are not inferior to men or less intelligent, simply dissimilar: a woman's brain is 'smaller in circumference than [a man's] and five ounces lighter in weight'. Hollander is adamant, however, that women must occupy a different realm from men and never the twain shall meet. Reminiscent of the language of one war and in anticipation of the language of another, this medical man concludes, 'man loves power, woman loves admiration. A man respects, a woman adores. A man has pluck, a woman has fortitude. A man has push, a woman has patience.'[49]

Whereas Hollander's tract purports to be descriptive, Mary Scharlieb's is unashamedly prescriptive. Also an MD, Scharlieb sets out her ideas for *Womanhood and Race-Regeneration* in her 1912 pamphlet.[50] She says that in order for women to be fit for their important position—as mothers—it is necessary that they should, firstly, recognize their privileges and duties and, secondly, receive adequate training. As in Hollander's work, medical and scientific terminology is used to summarize the physical changes that occur in boys and in girls as they grow, with the intention of highlighting and justifying the emotional alterations. The main focus of Scharlieb's argument is education where, she claims, mistakes have been made in 'two almost opposite directions'. Some girls are taught little beyond languages, music, and other genteel accomplishments, whereas others are forced into rigorous studies like their brothers without 'any consideration for their own mental and physical peculiarities'. Women are sanctioned to be intelligent and well-educated for they are 'equally capable' and 'their brains are good and clear', but, she believes,

[49] His assertion about 'pluck' flies in the face of schoolgirl fiction that continually demonstrated the 'pluckiness' of its main characters.

[50] *Womanhood and Race-Regeneration* was part of a series called 'New Tracts for the Times' published by Cassell, which included Havelock Ellis's *The Problem of Race-Regeneration* (1911), Caleb Williams Saleeby's *The Methods of Race-Regeneration* (1911), and Frederick Brotherton Meyer's *Religion and Race-Regeneration* (1912).

the time is coming in which all these valuable distinctions and degrees will be prized, not as ends in themselves, but as the means whereby untold benefit is to be conferred on the race, and that, especially in the case of woman, this intellectual power is held in trust to pass on the great gift to the next generation, to her own children should she be so fortunate as to be a mother, to the children of others should that crown of womanhood pass her by.[51]

The language used to describe motherhood brings effusive romantic vocabulary to this initially scientific text. With each girl regarded as a potential wife and mother, 'half-trained, silly' women who are incapable of 'earnest work' are 'doing more harm to the race than those who are ignorant so far as actual knowledge goes.' The 'canker of superficiality', she says, 'eats deep into all ranks of society'. Women must accept their responsibility, because 'the nation will never rise higher than the women who bear and the women who educate its children'. Overriding her call for intellectual fitness is the need for a moral outlook. Scharlieb argues that eugenicists have neglected the spiritual side of life:

the regeneration of the race will never be accomplished until the women of the country, themselves deeply convinced of the importance of right belief and right practice, devote themselves to teaching their faith to their children, and to requiring it in a practical form from the members of their household.[52]

It was a worry, therefore, when women did not conform to this role. Although they may not have been pilloried in progressive magazines

[51] Mary Scharlieb, *Womanhood and Race-Regeneration* (London, 1912), 14. Mary Scharlieb (née Bird) first sought medical training after reading accounts of how Hindu and Muslim women suffered during childbirth, being prevented from seeking attention from Western male doctors. Living with her husband and their three children in Madras, she was admitted to Madras Medical College in 1874 and awarded the diploma in 1877. Back in England, she entered the London School of Medicine for Women, qualifying MB in 1882 and winning the gold medal for obstetrics. She went on to study midwifery at the Frauenklinik in Vienna. In 1883 she returned to India and helped to found the Royal Victoria Hospital for Caste and Gosha Women between 1884 and 1886. She returned to London in 1887 and the following year became the first woman to receive an MD degree from London University. In addition to being a lecturer at the London School of Medicine for Women, Scharlieb set up a private practice in Harley Street in 1889. It was in this period that she started to write for the press. She later published a number of books, including *The Mother's Guide to the Health and Care of Her Children* (1905) and *How to Enlighten Our Children* (1926). She was made CBE in 1917 and DBE in 1926 (Greta Jones, 'Scharlieb, Dame Mary Ann Dacomb (1845–1930)', *Oxford Dictionary of National Biography*, Oxford University Press, 2004).

[52] Scharlieb, *Womanhood and Race-Regeneration*, 63.

like *The Girl's Realm*, suffragettes caused great consternation among those most concerned about the collapse of society. Interestingly, however, although he condemned violence by suffragettes as 'coarse, stupid, and thoroughly inefficient', Max Nordau did not disapprove of women's suffrage. Using his characteristic terminology, he argued that

> to declare her intellectually incapable of exercising political rights is not an argument, but an impertinence.... We credit her already with the capability of ruling the small community of the family, and of shaping the future of the nation by the education she gives to her children; there is no reason for denying her the faculty of managing the public affairs which are now subject to the influence of voters who may be drunkards, prodigals, blockheads, or ignorant fools.[53]

Like eugenicists, anti-suffragists were prolific pamphleteers and writers of tracts. From, for instance, James McGrigor Allan's 1890 *Woman Suffrage Wrong in Principle and Practice* (1890) to Ernest Belfort Bax's 1913 *The Fraud of Feminism*, the debate was carried out with vociferous energy. The campaign committee of the National League for Opposing Woman Suffrage issued *The Anti-Suffrage Handbook of Facts, Statistics and Quotations for the Use of Speakers* in 1912, and the Women's National Anti-Suffrage League published its *Anti-Suffrage Review* between 1908 and 1918.[54] To many opponents of the female franchise, suffragists and suffragettes were de-sexed harridans. The romantic novelist, Marie Corelli, was one of those who denounced their claim for the vote. In an article published in 1902 in *The Lady's Realm*, she lamented 'The Decay of Home Life in England' and later saw the issue as a black-and-white question of '*Woman or Suffragette*?' in her pamphlet of 1907. Anticipating a cataclysm following the extension of the franchise to women, Corelli asks:

> Shall we sacrifice our Womanhood to Politics? Shall we make a holocaust of maidens, wives and mothers on the brazen altars of Party? Shall we throw

[53] Huntly Carter (ed.), *Women's Suffrage and Militancy* (London, 1911), 36.

[54] For more detailed discussions about the suffrage and anti-suffrage debates see Lucy Bland, *Banishing the Beast: English Feminism and Sexual Morality, 1885–1914* (1995); Jill Liddington and Jill Norris, *One Hand Tied behind Us: The Rise of the Women's Suffrage Movement* (1978); Jane Rendall (ed.), *Equal or Different: Women's Politics 1800–1914* (1987); Elaine Showalter, *Sexual Anarchy: Gender and Culture at the 'Fin de Siècle'* (1978); Martha Vicinus, *Independent Women: Work and Community for Single Women* (1985).

open the once sweet and sacred homes of England to the manoeuvres of the electioneering agent? Surely the best and bravest of us will answer NO!—ten thousand times no! Rather let us use every means in our power to prevent the consummation of what would be nothing less than a national disaster. For Great Britain is already too rapidly losing many of the novel ideals and institutions which once made her the unrivalled mistress of the world.[55]

Such dramatic language is indicative of the passions raised by the issue of women's suffrage and contrasts with the earlier examples of a tentative middle-ground espoused for women, not defeminized, but able to be intelligent and fit. Here Corelli returns to a reactionary and essentialist idea of womanhood. With the tone and cadences worthy of her status as a best-selling romantic novelist, her warning is meant to inspire profound fear. The convention of attributing the feminine pronoun to Great Britain is given even greater resonance in light of the maidens, wives, and mothers for whom Corelli predicts doom. Womanhood's tragedy is thus the country's tragedy.

'HOME', she sermonizes, is the foundation of the Empire, and when 'women desert their God-appointed centre, the core of the national being, then things are tottering to a fall'. With the suggestion of the Fall of Adam, due mainly to Eve, the threat to the stability of the nation transgresses both natural *and* divine law.

The suffragettes are characterized as short-sighted, obstinate, shrill, and discontented. They are also condemned for their frivolity, loose conduct, and coarse speech. Woman is destined to make voters, not be one of them, just as she is not supposed to be the musician but the muse. The existence of bad men, is according to Corelli, the fault of bad mothers—those who spoil, 'molly-coddle', and baby-worship their sons even on into manhood. Woman's responsibility is great and she must tread a precarious line between love and indulgence.

That a conservative, popular, and middle-class romantic novelist should oppose the franchise on grounds such as these is not, perhaps, surprising. It is no wonder she saw the suffragettes as coarse and unfeminine in their actions, particularly those who practised militancy. We would perhaps expect such a proponent of the 'sweet and sacred home' overseen by a Patmore Angel to be worried about the threat to middle-class values and stability should women

[55] Marie Corelli, '*Woman or Suffragette?*' (London, 1907), 3.

become involved in politics. What is more surprising is the opposition by working-class women, whom we would expect to have found, in the prospect of a vote, an emancipation from the impositions of the upper and ruling classes, and a chance for more control over their own lives. However, as Maud E. Simkins asserts in her book, *An Englishwoman's Home*, such a view is short-sighted and ridden with class bias.

Published in 1909, her title is surely meant to allude to a successful play running in the West End at the time. *An Englishman's Home* (by 'A Patriot', the pseudonym of Guy du Maurier) dramatized the invasion of a hypothetical (yet stereotypic German) army on the British mainland, beginning on the farm of an unsuspecting Englishman. Such an allusion suggests that the threat outlined by Simkins is as dangerous as the invasion from a foreign foe, and is also due, in part, to the ignorance of the average citizen.

Simkins's main argument is that working women do not need to add political responsibility to their worries; the franchise would be 'a placing of the last straw on camels already all but overweighted'. It is an imposition by the 'luxurious rich' whose 'blind egotism is at the root of their movement'. 'How *can* they know us?', she asks when there is such a gulf between the political activists and 'their humbler sisters'. The housework regarded as 'despicable and contemptible' by the rich is actually 'cherished and prized' by working women who are proud of being 'domestic creatures':

> We are the bed-rock, the great working-class, that works and endures in silence, that has not learnt to clothe in euphemisms that great fundamental fact of sex. . . . Down in the East End we have flesh and blood, stripped of all its trappings, no longer the curious composite that makes the so-called lady. And when we come to flesh and blood, honestly, bluntly, if you like, man is man, and woman is woman, still. And no one thinks to be ashamed of it.[56]

There is a suggestion in the phrases 'man is man, and woman is woman' that as well as being imitations of women, 'the so-called lady', the suffragettes are sexually deviant. Like Corelli, Simkins believes that if women take to politics they will lose all interest in the care of the home and the raising of children. Such an 'unnatural' turn of events would signal the downfall of English home-life. She

[56] Maud E. Simkins, *An Englishwoman's Home* (London, 1909), 16. Simpkins also published *Mixed Herbs: A Working Woman's Remonstrance against the Suffrage Agitation* (London, 1908).

utilizes the language of eugenicists when she asserts that the granting of the suffrage to women 'will be another downward step in the deterioration and degeneration of the English race'; it will 'speedily relapse into barbarism'; and 'all the old sanctities and decencies' will be abolished. The anti-suffrage struggle thus becomes aligned with other national efficiency campaigns designed to rejuvenate the country. This new kind of Mrs Jellyby is as every bit as malevolent as the anticipated German invader.

As the demonization of the pro-suffrage woman serves to focus the argument into a good-versus-evil dichotomy where there are no in-betweens, so too is the enemy clearly identified in soothsaying tales of invasion. The box-office success of *An Englishman's Home* in 1909 went hand-in-hand with (reputedly) a rise in enlistment in the regular Army, in the British Territorial Force, and in its medical wing, the Voluntary Aid Detachments founded that year. Although the invaders in this play are not specifically named as German, it was, by that time, generally accepted that Germany was Britain's most dangerous foe.

Ever since the Franco-Prussian War of 1870, a great conflict between the powers of Europe had been anticipated. George Chesney's *The Battle of Dorking* (1871) ushered in a new genre that fictionalized and fed on these fears. As I. F. Clarke points out, this was a 'purposive fiction [designed to] terrify the reader' with the disastrous consequences of a 'country's shortcomings'.[57] It created, as much as it responded to, a fear about Britain's unpreparedness for war: 'Between 1871 and 1914 it was unusual to find a single year without some tale of future warfare appearing in some European country'.[58] In the 1890s France and Russia were perceived to be the main threats, but by 1900, Germany became the most likely aggressor. The tone of Emil Reich's non-fiction book of 1907 is clear from the title: *Germany's Swelled Head* (Fig. 1). Reissued with a new introduction in 1914 in response to the outbreak of war, the book's original Preface compares the situation between Great Britain and

[57] I. F. Clarke, *Voices Prophesying War: Future Wars, 1763–3749* (London, 1992, 2nd ed.), 33. Clarke's *The Tale of the Future: From the beginning to the present day, a check-list* (1961), is a valuable resource for any study of future-war fiction, whereas his editions *The Tale of the Great War 1871–1914: Fiction of Future Warfare and of Battles Still-to-Come* (1995) and *The Great War with Germany: Fictions and Fantasies of the War-to-Come* (1997) provide selections of out-of-print texts.

[58] Clarke, *Voices Prophesying War*, 38.

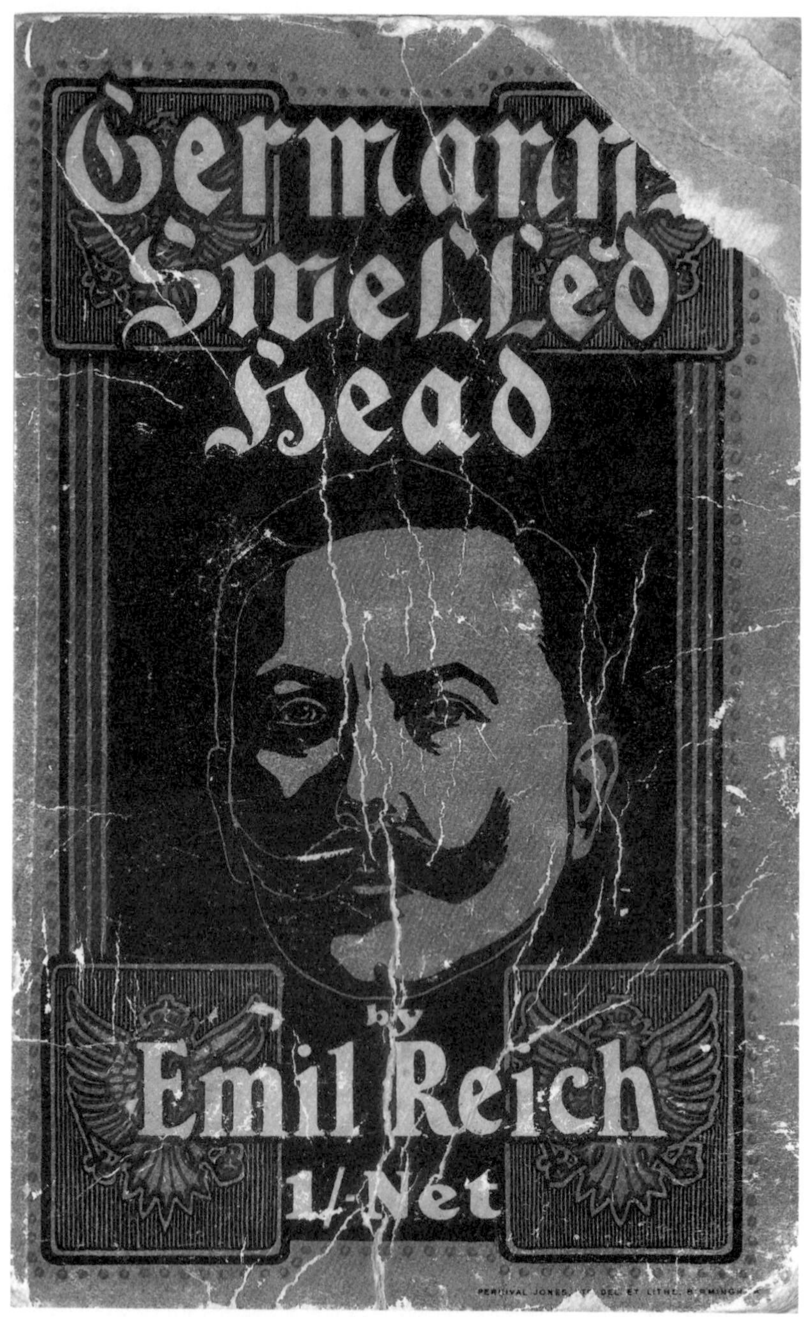

FIG. 1. *Germany's Swelled Head* (1907) by Emil Reich, cover

Germany to that between Rome and Carthage. The 'burden of the book', he outlines in Part I, is twofold:

The GERMANS are afflicted with the severest attack of swelled-headedness known to modern history.

The ENGLISH are practically ignorant of this dangerous state of mind in their greatest rivals.[59]

These are sentiments reiterated again and again by social critics at this time. The idea that the English are ignorant of another country's 'dangerous intent' serves both to admonish and to absolve. The English *should* be aware of Germany's malicious ideas, but their ignorance means they are innocent of any wrongdoing themselves. *They* are not the guilty, warmongering party. The Kaiser, on the other hand, is, and his cunning is severely underestimated in Britain. According to Reich, Wilhelm is seen either as impulsive or as a strutting buffoon. Readers are warned that he 'is nothing less than the very reverse of what most Englishmen imagine him to be'. An intelligent man of 'sober' judgement, his apparently rash and impulsive acts are nothing of the kind for he is well-versed in international politics and he is 'pursuing a definite, well-founded, and well-organised' plan. The German leader must be taken seriously, for although he is an 'upstart', he plans, according to Reich, to embroil England in a war. 'Kaiser Wilhelm has obligingly verified the prophecy', wrote the *Times Literary Supplement* reviewer on the publication of the second edition of *Germany's Swelled Head* in September 1914.

The book is only one of many claiming to raise the British awareness of the German menace. Fictional renderings of what an invasion would be like were 'appearing by the dozen every year—evidently a novelty that found a ready market'.[60] One could read about

[59] Emil Reich, *Germany's Swelled Head* (London, 1914), 1.

Emil Reich was born in Hungary and studied at the universities of Prague, Budapest and Vienna before emigrating to America with his family in 1884. He went to France in 1889 and finally settled in Britain in 1893. He was popular as a writer and a lecturer in Oxford, Cambridge, and London and contributed to the *Cambridge Modern History*. His publications included *Hungarian Literature* (1897), *The Failure of the 'Higher Criticism' of the Bible* (1905), *Handbook of Geography, Descriptive and Mathematical* (1908), and *Woman through the Ages* (1908) (W. B. Owen, 'Reich, Emil (1854–1910)', rev. H. C. G. Matthew, *Oxford Dictionary of National Biography*, Oxford University Press, 2004).

[60] Clarke, *The Great War with Germany*, 1. For more in-depth considerations of these texts see H. R. Moon, *The Invasion of the United Kingdom: Public Controversy and Official Planning, 1888–1918* (unpublished PhD dissertation, London

A New Trafalgar (1902) by A. C. Curtis; *The North Sea Bubble* (1906) by E. Oldmeadow; *The Death Trap* (1907) by R. W. Cole; or *The Swoop of the Vulture* (1909) by J. Blyth. William LeQueux's *The Invasion of 1910* (1906) caused a sensation when it was serialized in the *Daily Mail*.[61] That such scenarios did indeed penetrate the national consciousness can once again be gauged by popular magazines. 'Even the young readers of *Chums, Boy's Own*, and *Union Jack* were ready for the war the juvenile magazines told them would come sooner rather than later'.[62] The same is true for girls. Stereotyped images of Germans were already commonplace in 1902 when *The Girl's Realm* ran an article in October entitled, 'The Girls of the Fatherland' by Darley Dale. Illustrations show fat, mustachioed men wearing Bavarian hats, proud puffed-up soldiers, peasant girls, and stout ladies. In all things the German girl is 'a long way behind' her English sisters: 'not "up-to-date"'. She is tied to the home, being taught to be the ideal *hausfrau*, takes little exercise, and dresses 'without much taste'. Besides this, 'German girls have not good figures—they are too fat; it is their ambition to have what they call "an English figure", that is, to be slight and slender.' Dale admits that many are pretty when young, but they age quickly and the 'vein of coarseness in the German character' adds to their unattractiveness. The German girl reads novels of 'sentimental trash' (not like those reviewed in *The Girl's Realm*, of course!). The superiority of the English way of life is further upheld with the more charitable observation that

> German girls are just now in a transition stage; they are struggling to obtain the same position that English and American girls enjoy. They have a great admiration for English girls and English manners and customs, and whenever they come in contact with them, they pay them the most sincere of all compliments—imitation.

The warlike characteristics expounded in Reich's book come into play, albeit more lightheartedly and with a *happy* ending, in *The Girl's Realm* a decade later in 'Patriotism: A School Story' (April

University, 1977); Michael Moorcock (ed.), *Before Armageddon* (1975); Roger T. Stearn, 'Victorian and Edwardian Fiction of the Future', *Soldiers of the Queen* 69 (June 1992).

[61] See Roger T. Stearn, 'The Mysterious Mr LeQueux', *Soldiers of the Queen* 70 (September 1992).

[62] Clarke, *The Great War with Germany*, 22.

1912). A quarrel over the shape of Napoleon's nose threatens an 'international incident' between a German and a French schoolgirl. Observed by their fellow pupils at St Clare's School, the two bandy insults. Josephine, the German, says all the French are egotists, and Clorinde, the French girl, brands all Germans as '*stupide*'. She goes on to say, '"When I came to this school I was not informed that I should have to eat English bread and butter with an enemy of my country.... Between my beautiful country and the sauer-kraut-eating German there can be no friendship. This is what I, a French girl, do declare!"' Not to be outdone, Josephine agrees that the two are still enemies: '"Ja! France is a gontree full of vicked men.... Mine vaterland is ze only von great gontree in ze world. It is greater as England, and it vill von day England up eat."' Exasperated by their intolerance, Katie, the English head girl, walks away in disgust with other pupils. When no one is looking, Josephine and Clorinde exchange sweets, and agree to disagree while still being friends.

Rather more negative, however, is a full-page advertisement for Hall's Wine, which appears in the first volume of *Mrs Bull* in October 1910. Alongside an illustration of German officers raising their glasses is the phrase 'To the Day!' The four-column text that accompanies it is flanked by bayonet rifles and prefaced by 'The Anticipated German Invasion of 1913 Has Furnished the Text for this Advertisement.' Most of it is devoted to describing the threat and proffering advice on how to be prepared. As in Reich's book and other works of both fiction and non-fiction, Germany is methodically planning to conquer England, to rule her Empire by taking advantage of her physical and moral weaknesses. The advertisement asserts that the Army and Navy *are* ready, the Army especially, having learned its lessons in the South African War. It is the readiness of civilians that is now questioned. A *Weekly Dispatch* article is quoted, in which Robert Blatchford 'implores the people of Britain to wake up from their lethargy, and not to rest until every effort has been made to bring about [a] state of efficiency.'[63] The reader is exhorted by the advertiser not to be despondent, however, but to 'remember our splendid history, a continuous record of noble deeds and victories', and to keep fit. Such fitness, not only for war

[63] Robert Blatchford founded the socialist newspaper *The Clarion* in 1891 and was appointed 'Germany watcher' for the *Daily Mail* by Lord Northcliffe in 1909 (Clarke, *The Great War with Germany*, 14).

but for 'daily battles' in the office or factory or at home can be obtained by drinking Hall's Wine. With the endorsement of the medical and nursing world, the advertisement claims, Hall's Wine 'has no equal in the world of tonics and restoratives as a maker of new blood, as an instantaneous soother and strengthener of nerves'. It feeds the nerve centre and stimulates the brain, but best of all (it seems) '"*It makes a man!*"' That the makers of the product could have confidence that such a claim would appeal to the women readers of *Mrs Bull* indicates how important female consumerism—and their influence on the men in their lives—was, and how widespread and familiar were such fears.

The Girl's Realm, too, reflected the growing concerns about military threats. In an article entitled 'If Peace Reigned in the World: Can Our Christmas Dreams of Goodwill Ever Come True?' (December 1913), Stanhope W. Sprigg doubts whether Germany is the only site of aggression. He does suggest, however, that it is the main antagonist:

> The German Emperor, when not shaking his mailed fist and rattling his sabre on the pavement of some ancient fortress, strides up and down his Empire proclaiming that to him alone is due for at least the last quarter of a century, the peaceful days of the Great Powers of Europe.

The posturing of the Kaiser shows he is a hypocrite. Peace through sabre-rattling is not Sprigg's idea of goodwill or good intent. He praises Sir Edward Grey as the living embodiment of the golden mean of negotiation and arbitration (not surprisingly, as he is English), a foreign secretary whose treaties 'were torn up and trampled on before the ink on them had been decently dried.' Ordinary men and women are 'baffled', Sprigg says, and he questions whether world peace is really possible: 'Are we doomed for ever to hear the sound of those drums and those guns?' A photograph of dead and dying soldiers, presumably from the Boer War, is included. They are being tended to by some of their comrades on the battlefield, while others stand armed and ready at a parapet. The caption declares: 'WAR! It is splendid; and we admire the men who face death so bravely for their country's sake. But it is horrible; and when we think of it calmly, utterly foolish and wasteful.' Such a statement contradicts those made by others who refuse to see the waste, and chose to concentrate on the higher motives and patriotic ideals, as does Molly Bawn in 'The Shield of Captain Credence'. Despite such a comment, Sprigg does not advocate total and immediate disarmament or pacifism. A balance of power must be maintained, otherwise 'war might rear its ugly length across the rest of Europe and bathe half a continent in Blood.' It was a chilling prophecy of what would come eight months later, but not one to inspire the country to take the first step towards peace. In a particularly patriotic and nationalistic vein, Sprigg claims that altruism comes most naturally to England, 'the home and land of Freedom and of Christmas'. (He conveniently forgets that it was a German, Prince Albert, who brought the accepted notions of 'traditional' Christmas celebrations to England when he married Queen Victoria.) The imagery he employs to describe the effects of armed conflict—'blood-drenched plains'; 'ruined and ravished homes'; 'cruelty and suffering and barbarism'; 'thousands of mutilated men'; 'hordes of weeping women'—draws on recent memories of the Second Anglo-Boer War, but anticipates that of the Great War with 'plains' becoming 'Flanders Fields', and Belgian villages replacing the veldt as the theatre of war. The popular fiction and social commentary of the years preceding the Great War helped to create and to reinforce a climate of opinion that naturalized British superiority and imperialism. 'Such propaganda,' as Matthew Paris argues, 'alone cannot explain why Britain went to war in 1914, but it does go some way to explain why the nation slipped so easily into a major European conflict, and why that war was greeted so enthusiastically by so many young men.'[64] We might say the same of young women. Models for interpreting the new tragedy were already in place.

[64] Paris, *Warrior Nation*, 109.

2

'Is Your Best Boy Wearing Khaki?': Publishing and Propaganda

The fine line between so-called 'light-reading material' and propaganda discernible in the texts highlighted in Chapter 1, is even more clearly evident in the writing of 1914–18. Writers and publishers adapted quickly to the new atmosphere of a society at war. Influential press barons like Lord Northcliffe realized the commercial possibilities the conflict offered and his newspapers became convenient and powerful vehicles for propaganda. The visual image, too, played its part in influencing literary responses as well as the attitudes and actions of the public. Posters, postcards, book and magazine illustrations, and pageants became as powerful vehicles of propaganda as words on a page. The ideology and iconography that the more obvious forms of propaganda sustained and transmitted find their way into the various literary genres that later chapters will examine.

F. A. Mumby commented that the Great War 'shook the book trade, like everything else, to its foundations',[1] yet the demand for books, both fiction and non-fiction, for pamphlets and for periodicals was not diminished by the conflict. Although production was more difficult, the public need for reading material, both about the War and as diversion from it, was great. On the outbreak of war, however, publishers were uncertain about their commercial futures. Paper shortages and a loss of staff to the Forces were coupled with an anxiety over the reading public's readiness to exercise its spending power. The *Times Literary Supplement* for the years 1914–18 is

[1] F. A. Mumby, *Publishing and Bookselling* (London, 1930), 370.

an important source not only for its advertisements and reviews, which indicate what was being published, by whom, and in what manner marketed, but for its editorials, which provide valuable details about the state of the book trade at this time. On 13 August 1914, the *TLS* noted that 'the book trade, like the rest of the world, remains in a state of suspense. Publishers, however, are continuing their preparations for an autumn season in the hope that the reading public will presently be able to turn to literature again with a certain measure of relief.' By September it could report that 'war books, old and new, are being freely bought' (17 September 1914). *The Publishers' Circular* analysis of the year's literature was highlighted in December 1914:

> The war has left its mark on the book trade of 1914, but it has not proved so disastrous in that respect as some prophets foretold. The figures for 1914 show that, notwithstanding the great upheaval, the total number of books published during the twelve months amounted to no fewer than 11,537. It is true that this is 842 less than the total for 1913, but the heaviest drop occurred during the critical months of suspense in the first phase of the war, August and September. Afterwards the recovery was remarkable.[2]

On the whole it believed the situation was not too bad and showed every sign of, if not attaining pre-war levels, at least maintaining an even keel. Literature and poetry showed signs of increase, as did the numbers of pamphlets: 'A great national service is performed by

[2] A comparison of the figures for 1913 and 1914 for the months of August to December reveals the following:
August:
  703 in 1913
  427 in 1914
September (the month that inaugurates the chief season of the publishing year):
  1,203 in 1913
  853 in 1914
October:
  1,696 in 1913
  1,244 in 1914
November (recovery complete, numerically speaking):
  1,106 in 1913
  1,106 in 1914
December ('actual and substantial increase'):
  708 in 1913
  841 in 1914

writers who set forth in clear popular language the reasons why we have gone to war and the vital character of the struggle' (*TLS*, 15 October 1914).

A meeting of the English Association, held to discuss the production and reading of books during the War, was reported by the *TLS* in June 1916. Despite the doom-and-gloom attitude that prevailed months earlier, the situation was now viewed as healthy on the whole. Both John Buchan and J. G. Wilson felt that

> there never was time when more books of the best sort were being read in England, especially if we include that greater England which is now in France. Of course, there is a lot of rubbish read both at home and in the trenches. But there is nothing new about that; it has nothing to do with the war. What is new and has to do with the war is the demand for the best books, and especially for poetry.

This particular editorial, entitled 'Literature and the War', is especially interesting for the ways in which it so clearly delineates the reasons why there had been such an unexpected, yet extremely welcome, demand for books. There were four causes. Firstly, the trench war was monotonous and a soldier has more time for reading than he did in previous conflicts, 'under the old conditions'. Secondly, the modern army is demographically different, with officers and men drawn from 'classes far more interested in books' than their predecessors. Thirdly, the 'melancholy fact' that there are large numbers of wounded in hospitals, requiring diversion and amusement. Finally, the civilian population at home have had 'much more money to spend than before and fewer ways of spending it'. Fewer people are travelling and 'the new quietness of the evenings and the Sundays provided a harvest for the booksellers'. What were these readers—soldiers and civilians—buying? Soldiers, it seems, preferred fiction, but other books were 'surprisingly catholic': a Gothic grammar, an Anglo-Saxon dictionary, French and Russian novels, translations of the classics. 'But the most striking thing of all', said the *TLS*, 'is the general increase in the demand for poetry,' for Wordsworth, Shelley, and Rupert Brooke. At the beginning of the War, it comments, 'every one, bewildered by the sudden catastrophe, read nothing but war news and war books for such dim light as those could throw upon the problem. To-day people are turning with relief from the war news to fiction especially to the more popular novelists' (*TLS*, 5 August 1915).

Writers and publishers adapted quickly to the new atmosphere of a society at war. Almost immediately bookshops and newsstands were filled with pamphlets explaining and dissecting current events, novels that featured blushing heroines and their soldier-sweethearts, periodicals, especially those aimed at women and girls, containing practical articles on how to help the war effort, and a host of other media that promoted civilian support and patriotic thinking. This chapter highlights some of these in an effort to put them within a larger publishing context—that of country, conscience, and commerce—to illustrate the ways in which members of the book trade were complicit in the government's battle for hearts and minds, struggling all the while to keep their businesses afloat.

J. M. Dent established his business in 1888 and made his name producing fine-quality, yet inexpensive editions of classic works of literature. The 40-volume Temple Shakespeare, published between 1894 and 1896, was followed by other series such as the Temple Greek and Latin Classics. However, it is for the Everyman's Library that Dent is chiefly remembered. Established in 1906 and projected to include a thousand volumes, by 1914 the seven hundredth had been published. However, the outbreak of war brought work almost to a halt. War inflation forced the prices up and the gold leaf that was a characteristic feature of the books was replaced by imitation gold: 'war had literally taken the glitter from the Everyman's library, just as it had tarnished everything else'.[3] Dent recorded in 1917

> we cannot get the material to do our work with—either people or leather, and of course what we can get is very expensive, and so we find it very difficult to get along, but I am hoping still that the war will be over before we have to shut down. Everybody is doing his very best here, and we are going to put all our energies into the next year's work.[4]

The publisher suffered personally as well. Two of his youngest sons, Austin and Paxton, who both entered the firm in 1913, joined up soon after the outbreak. Reiterating familiar high-minded attitudes

[3] *Dictionary of Literary Biography: British Literary Publishing Houses, 1881–1965* (Detroit, 1991), 88.

[4] J. M. Dent, *The Memoirs of J. M. Dent: 1849–1926* (London, 1928), 211. The one thousandth volume of the Everyman series was not published until 1956.

about noble sacrifice, the publisher melodramatically describes his emotions in these early days:

> I cannot say that my heart leapt up as I thought of my country's stand for righteousness, though I was fully convinced of her cause—no, I was stunned and numbed and hopeless for many days, and recoiled in horror from the thought of a war so universal and with such weapons; but as the days went by and I saw the rush to the colours, and the exaltation of the nations, it came into my heart that after all it was a great thing to be called upon to defend the weak and uphold the nations in a great crusade against wrong. But alas! what did this mean to us? It meant asking our two young lads to take up arms to defend us—to take them away from their free and happy outlook, to the stern horrors of the bloodiest war the world has ever seen. . . . We could not cheat [Paxton and Austin] of their honour . . . proud and glad that we had two such find stalwarts to give to so noble a cause.[5]

Dent and his wife feel 'joy and exaltation' as, through their sons, they play their own 'part in the Great Sacrifice'. There are echoes of Jesse Pope here, and particularly when the publisher likens Paxton and Austin to Wordsworth's 'Happy Warrior': 'he that every man in arms should wish to be'. His sons, he tells us, have 'a clear sense of duty . . . to save the world from once more coming under the heel of tyrants'. Theirs is a 'living sacrifice' as they lay 'on the altar their joyous youth'.[6]

Dent does try to achieve some understanding of the horrific and unromantic nature of war in the trenches. Barbusse's *Under Fire*, 'which we know to be the absolute truth', presents him with a 'terrible picture' of the inhumanity and suffering: 'the whole story in its physical aspect is more terrible than Dante's Hell'.[7] It makes vivid for him 'the months of torture my dear lad Paxton lived through in the vile mud', but unlike Wilfred Owen, who was also greatly affected by Barbusse's novel, Dent can still believe that it is sweet and fitting to die for one's country—*dulce et decorum est pro patria mori*:

> as I brooded over it I said yes, there seems to be more regard for human life and human suffering and human pain, in spite of the fact that we are passing through the most awful war that has ever been seen upon the earth. And so I felt there was a product of perfect joy out of the infinite

[5] Dent, *The Memoirs*, 179.

[6] Ibid., 197. Wordsworth is Dent's favourite poet at this time; from his poetry, the publisher derives 'absolute subsistence' (211).

[7] Ibid., 184.

misery—I do believe the world is better.... I am content in thinking that my boys were in it... happy warriors.[8]

Perhaps it is not surprising that the publisher would turn to such beliefs for solace: both his sons were killed, one at Neuve Chapelle, the other at Gallipoli. How else could he bear the loss but to interpret it as a 'great sacrifice'? His daughters, too, did their duty. Muriel worked in a munitions factory and Olive was a V.A.D. nurse. (It appears that Dent's daughter Olive is *not* the same Olive Dent who wrote *A V.A.D in France*, one of the memoirs discussed in the next chapter. See Appendix 3 for biographical information.) Although he notes his pride in their patriotic service, he says very little else about them. It is male sacrifice that Dent privileges.

The death of the two Dent apprentice publishers added to the numbers lost to the book trade. 'Death was busy'[9] here as everywhere else. Capt. Tommy Nelson, a partner in the Nelson firm, was killed at the Battle of Arras on 9 April 1917; R. C. Jackson, who with Frank Sidgwick published Rupert Brooke's poems, was also killed; and so was John Heinemann, nephew and heir-apparent to William Heinemann. The Longman and Blackie houses 'each gave a son'[10]: eight weeks into the War, Frederick Longman was killed in action and the only son of Jack Blackie was killed on the Somme in 1916. Col. P. H. Dalbaic, a director of Allen & Unwin, also lost a son and himself served in France and Salonika in 1916 and 1917. Robert William Chapman, who succeeded Charles Cannan as head of the Clarendon Press, also served in Salonika with the Royal Garrison Artillery. Daniel de Mendi Macmillan, who had enlisted in 1914, was invalided out in 1915 and thirty-two of Cassell's employees were killed on active service. Despite the efforts of the Publishers Association, publishing was not classified as a trade of national importance whose employees could be exempted from military service; 'both in the initial enthusiasm for voluntary recruitment in 1914–15,' wrote John Feather, 'and in the later conscription to the forces, many good and essential men were lost.'[11] According to Arthur Waugh, managing director of Chapman & Hall, it seemed that 'work was the only anodyne' for the anxieties of war.[12]

[8] Ibid., 205. [9] Mumby, *Publishing and Bookselling*, 378. [10] Ibid.

[11] John Feather, *A History of British Publishing* (London, 1988), 196.

[12] Arthur Waugh, *A Hundred Years of Publishing: Being the Story of Chapman and Hall, Ltd* (London, 1930), 270.

If this was so then the effort with which the firm of Hodder & Stoughton took up its war work must have provided a great deal of solace. The firm's director, Ernest Hodder-Williams, and his editor and literary adviser, Sir William Robertson Nicholl, were extremely active in their support for the War. Both men believed 'their task was to preserve unity and boost morale on the home front: it was a prerequisite of victory. From the day the War was declared, they dedicated their minds and energy wholly to the common task with the high spirit of crusaders'[13] and they adapted their output to cater to and anticipate public interest. The *TLS* of September 1914 tells how the firm was 'organising a War Book Department for special books on the crisis'. It produced *Princess Mary's Gift Book* (1914), which sold 600,000 copies in two years, and *King Albert's Book* (1914) as fund-raisers. In May 1915 *The Bookman* (one of Hodder & Stoughton's periodical publications) announced that the firm 'arranged to pay to the Red Cross funds twenty-five percent' of the profit accrued during Booksellers' Week. The following year, the firm donated three pence in every shilling spent on their books during Red Cross Week. Yet Hodder & Stoughton also 'became increasingly identified with reading for entertainment. The demand for the novelist who could dispel the boredom of war was limitless.'[14] It published many of the most popular writers of the day, including John Buchan, Ian Hay, and Herman Cyril McNeile (Sapper). Unlike other firms, Hodder & Stoughton 'suffered remarkably few casualties' and its premises were undamaged by air raids, but its profits were 'deliberately reduced since large sections of the . . . list were devoted to the war charities.'[15]

If established firms, like Dent and Hodder & Stoughton were finding the demands of wartime publishing onerous, then it is remarkable that the firm of George Allen & Unwin survived the first year of the War, let alone its duration. Stanley Unwin was one of the few publishers who openly questioned the necessity of the War and did so in print by publishing radical and unpopular opinions. This entrepreneurial young man took over the bankrupt firm of George Allen on 'the very day of the declaration [of war]',

[13] John Attenborough, *A Living Memory: Hodder & Stoughton Publishers 1868–1975* (London, 1975), 76.
[14] Ibid., 78. [15] Ibid., 81.

4 August 1914. During his negotiations to purchase the firm, in July 1914, he thought '(before Sarajevo)... most people assumed that wars were a thing of the past; people were too civilised for anything so stupid'.[16] This assumption was soon proved wrong. On the practical level

> the outbreak of war had reduced the value of the assets we had bought by about a third on the very day we started. The turnover, which even during receivership, when nothing was being published, had always remained at over £1,000 a month, dropped to a few hundred.[17]

Two of his three directors were called up for military service, as were most male members of his staff. Old stock was rendered unsaleable, even as remainders, and sales of many of the standard publications were reduced by as much as 70%. At the time of his Directors' Report in 1916, the company was feeling more adverse effects like the 'enormous increase in the cost of production', especially with regards to paper, which was five times its normal price.[18]

As he weathered the workaday storms of the War, Unwin's personal response was no less difficult. He was, from the outset, 'a very genuine pacifist.'[19] The War, he believed, was preventable. Queen Victoria had been the 'grandmother of Europe' and disputes should 'all have been settled within the family.... There was no militarism that was not controllable.'[20] Unwin could not abide the rabid anti-German sentiment he saw developing around him, the 'hysterical mood' incited by the Northcliffe press.[21] He also disagreed with the

[16] Sir Stanley Unwin, *The Truth about a Publisher* (London, 1960), 130.

[17] Ibid., 131.

[18] The Trading Accounts document the worsening situation. In 1915 paper cost the firm £1,267.3d.; in 1916, the total was £1,474.3s.10d., and in 1917 the cost soared to £2,336.2s.6d. In the last nine months of 1918, Unwin wrote in his 1919 Directors' Report, that 'prices [were] so fabulous that more than double had been expended on paper than during the whole of the previous year'.

[19] Jane Potter, 'Interview with Rayner Unwin', *Publishing History* 41 (1997), 95. By 1917, the government would no longer grant Stanley Unwin an exemption from military service, and he decided that 'it was essential for me to do whatever I could conscientiously do'. In his book, *The Truth about a Publisher* (1960), Unwin records how he participated in air-raid rescues and a downed Zeppelin recovery, and assisted in many operations at Charing Cross Hospital.

[20] Potter, 'Interview with Rayner Unwin', 94.

[21] Unwin, *The Truth about a Publisher*, 157.

principle of censorship. The Defence of the Realm Act (DORA) was one of his earliest targets for protest: he believed its policies were ludicrous and its mindless rigidity severely restricted freedom of speech.[22]

As a pacifist, 'he made pacifist friends and ... their tough time brought them together'.[23] Unwin did not look for controversy, but 'controversy found him ... he was taking on that side of human expression which was a minority'.[24] He dared to publish, for instance, Bertrand Russell's *The Principles of Social Reconstruction*, the views of which more establishment figures like Lord Cromer, a member of the war government, though 'pernicious'.[25] However, as if to court even more controversy, Unwin put Cromer's opinion on the front cover of *The Principles*.

Equally controversial was *'I Appeal Unto Caesar': The Case of the Conscientious Objector'* (1917) by Mrs Henry Hobhouse.[26] She wrote, as

> the mother of sons in France, who are daily risking their lives, subjected to the horrors and discomforts of the trenches ... I feel less distress at their fate, fighting as they are their country's battles, with the approval of their fellows, than I do for that other son undergoing for his faith a disgraceful sentence in a felon's cell, truly 'rejected and despised' of men.[27]

[22] The Defence of the Realm Act, passed by the House of Commons on 8 August 1914, gave the government power to suppress published criticism, imprison individuals without trial, and commandeer economic resources for the war effort. After 1915, it was increasingly used to control civilian behaviour with restrictions on food and alcohol.

[23] Potter, 'Interview with Rayner Unwin', 95.

[24] Ibid.

[25] Like his publisher, Russell was vehemently opposed to the War: 'As a lover of truth, the national propaganda of all belligerent nations sickened me. As a lover of truth and civilisation, the return to barbarism appalled me. As a man of thwarted parental feeling, the massacre of the young wrung my heart' (Bertrand Russell, *Autobiography*, vol. II, 1967–9 (London, 1969), 18).

[26] Margaret Heyworth Hobhouse (*d.* 1921), née Potter, was the first wife of the politician Henry Hobhouse (1854–1937). The zeal for political and social reform was in her blood: the seventh daughter of Richard Potter, she was the sister of the famous social activists Beatrice Webb and Catherine Courtney. Stephen Henry Hobhouse later published *An English Prison from Within* in 1919.

[27] Mrs Henry Hobhouse, *'I Appeal Unto Caesar': The Case of the Conscientious Objector* (London, 1917), xiv.

The aim of her book was 'to remove the slur on the good name of our Government' by that minority of men 'who prefer driving the quill to wielding the sword'. The crux of her argument centres on the 'horrors of repeated imprisonment' for the conscientious objector, whose breach of the law 'is virtually one single offence, although technically it is a new offence on each occasion when he is released from prison. It is contrary to the practice of criminal law to punish a man repeatedly for the same offence'.[28] At the time of the book's publication in July 1917, between 800 and 1,000 men who refused any work under the Military Service Act were in prison. Her own son, Stephen, 'refused all forms of exemption or work under the Home Office scheme', whereby he might perform war-related, though noncombatant duties.[29] She discusses 'Facts about Conscientious Objectors in Prison' and 'Prison Conditions and Their Effects', and quotes a letter from a man in prison to sum up the injustice and inhumanity of the situation:

> 'Our choice has not been, and is not, between prison and the trenches... mad or sane—we are at least not cowards. It is not the fear of physical death in the trenches that has led to our remaining in prison, but rather a fear of spiritual death which we believe must follow our assent to any Conscriptive scheme, military or civil.'[30]

However, although it was endorsed by prominent men like Stanley Webb (Lord Parmoor), the Earl of Selbourne, Lord Hugh Cecil MP, and Lord Henry Bentinck MP, and contained an introduction by Gilbert Murray who called for readers to act sensibly rather than as angry fanatics, the book caused an uproar.[31] The *TLS* commented that her arguments 'will not convince many, but there will be a general determination to put down sternly every form of bullying and tyranny; and we shall be glad if her little volume receives the careful attention of the Home Secretary' (*TLS*, 30 August

[28] Ibid., 8.

[29] Ibid., 4.

[30] Ibid., 77.

[31] Unwin recalls in his autobiography that 'so great was the war-time prejudice on the subject that many booksellers refused to stock or even handle it. Over a thousand people came to our office to secure a copy. The book was referred to in Parliament and in the end thousands were sold, but it was an uphill fight with the book trade that I have never forgotten' (Unwin, *The Truth about a Publisher*, 154).

1917). Unwin's praise for Hobhouse's 'indefatigable' support and the Allen & Unwin seal on her 'little book' proclaims his own pacifism.[32]

Given Unwin's outspokenness on many of the policies associated with the War, particularly in terms of the books he published, it is perhaps surprising to discover that he was among the group of publishers who gave significant support to the government's propaganda work being undertaken at Wellington House.

The 'rush to the colours' that Dent witnessed in August 1914 was accompanied by a hunger for information about the events taking place, but Britain required an organization to counter German propaganda abroad and to encourage domestic support for the war effort. British propagandists had a 'field day' because 'they could assist in calling the nation to battle, in rendering the enemy hateful, in courting the sympathy and even the aid of important neutrals'.[33] Peter Buitenhuis's groundbreaking book *The Great War of Words* documents how the government carried out its mission. Charles Masterman was chosen as the head of operations at Wellington House, where the propaganda bureau was located. On 2 September 1914, a meeting of literary figures was held, the outcome being an Authors' Manifesto pledging support for the War. Among those who added their signatures to this document were Henry Newbolt, Arthur Conan Doyle, Mrs Humphry Ward, May Sinclair, and H. G. Wells. Printed with facsimile signatures in the *New York Times* on 18 September and reprinted in a full-page London *Times* Sunday supplement on 18 October, the manifesto claimed that Great Britain had to join the War or face dishonour. It was agreed at this meeting that the information disseminated by Wellington House be accurate

[32] Unwin also published *Militarism vs. Feminism* (1915), whose ideas about war, violence, and the subjugation of women are still being debated in the early twenty-first century. He could not, however, be termed a 'feminist'. He believed in the rights of the individual, but 'he was rather an autocrat at his own breakfast table', according to his son, Rayner. He would not have 'marched for Pankhurst, but wouldn't have disagreed with Pankhurst's right to march so long as he did not have to have her as an employee or as his wife.... But in so far as [feminism] was a reasoned, a well-reasoned view, he would support it in publication, but it doesn't mean he would necessarily have marched with it. You will see a lot of books of a feminist slant in father's list largely because his advisers were telling him these were serious people' (Potter, 'Interview with Rayner Unwin', 89).

[33] Trevor Wilson, *The Myriad Faces of War: Britain and the Great War, 1914–1918* (Cambridge, 1986), 747.

and expressed with measured argument—unlike, they claimed, German propaganda. Mass distribution was to be avoided; reputable public figures and distinguished scholars were more likely to be taken seriously, especially if it did not seem that such writers were working for an official agency. To this end, Wellington House pamphlets and books were produced by mainstream publishers.[34] Secrecy was further maintained by having the Stationery Office act as the official purchasing agent and A. S. Watt, the literary agent, carry out negotiations with the publishers on Wellington House's behalf. Distribution also took place through steamship companies, through labour organizations and peace societies, through the Central Committee for Patriotic Organisations, and even through the Religious Tract Society. Although they were intended for neutral countries and there was no organized effort to promote distribution at home, many Wellington House publications were no doubt read in Britain.

In his *Second Report on the Work Conducted for the Government at Wellington House*, Masterman asserted that

> We have endeavoured throughout to preserve methods of secrecy, to get our literature into the hands of those who will read it without any knowledge of any 'Government Bureau' behind it, and never to thrust it or force it upon those who resent its gifts, or who will merely treat it as waste paper. There are, of course, many objections to this secrecy.... All our literature, therefore, except definite Government publications, has been issued under personal names or distributed by well-known publishers.[35]

Each was paid five guineas for the use of their imprint and £5 towards to cost of advertising, the '5/5/-' arrangement, as it was called.

The Schedule of Wellington House Literature, now in the Imperial War Museum, confidential at the time, shows who these publishers were and what they produced.[36] Hodder & Stoughton published the most tracts for the bureau, over 120 pamphlets and books. These included Conan Doyle's *The German War* (1914) and *To Arms* (1914), *J'Accuse* (1915) by A German, and *The Western Front* (1917) by C. E. Montague with drawings by Muirhead Bone.

[34] Peter Buitenhuis, *The Great War of Words: Literature as Propaganda 1914–18 and After* (London, 1989).
[35] *Second Report on the Work Conducted for the Government at Wellington House*, with introductory remarks by C. F. G. Masterman, 1 February 1916, 6.
[36] See Appendix 2.

In this way Hodder-Williams and Nicholl were 'very close to the central direction of the war'.[37] T. Fisher Unwin, step-uncle of Stanley, follows Hodder & Stoughton, in the 'league table' of Wellington House publishers: his firm lent its imprint to 78 books and pamphlets. Darling & Son take third place with 45. Oxford University Press, including the Clarendon Press and Humphrey Milford imprints, contributed 13, including *Why We Are at War: Great Britain's Case by Members of the Oxford Modern History Faculty* (1914), which was translated into eight languages, including French, Italian, Swedish, and Portuguese. J. M. Dent produced only two: *The University of Louvain and Its Library* (1917) and *The Destruction of Merchant Ships under International Law* (1917). Stanley Unwin's firm was associated with 13 Wellington House documents, including *The Allies' Prospects of Victory* (1918); *Dangerous Optimism* (1918); *The Pan-German Programme* (1918); and *Three Aspects of the Russian Revolution* (1918).[38]

Women were the subjects of a number of Wellington House publications. Boyd Cable's *Doing Their Bit* (Hodder & Stoughton, 1916) chronicles female contributions to the war effort, as does *'Carry On': British Women's Work in War Time* (1917, no publisher or author indicated). Women themselves wrote about 'doing their own bit' in books such as *Munitions Lasses: Six Months as Principal Overlooker in Danger Buildings* (1917) by A[gnes] K[ate] Foxwell, *The Woman's Part: A Record of Munitions Work* (1918) by L. K. Yates, *The Story of British V.A.D. Work in the Great War* (1917) by Thekla Bowser, and *Women of the War* (1917) by Barbara McClaren. In the *Catholic Monthly Letter*, a serial Wellington House publication, Margaret Fletcher outlines the 'part played by Catholic women in national life', and *Our Flying Men* by Mrs Maurice Hewlett contains 'graphic stories of exploits and adventures of flying men on active service on various fronts'. Women authors, however, are not numerous in the list; there are only sixteen among the hundreds of men represented there.

[37] Attenborough, *A Living Memory*, 77.

[38] The other books were *German Socialists and Belgium* (1915) by Emile Royer; *War and Civilisation* (1917); *The Deeper Causes of War: Its Development and Resources* (1914) by William Sanday; *The Commonwealth of Australia* (1917); *New Zealand* (1917); *The Economic Weapon in the War against Germany* (1918); *The Military Outlook* (1918); *Germany Her Own Judge* (1918); *The Awakening of the German People* (1918); and *Canada: Past, Present and Future* (1918).

Of these sixteen, Mrs Humphry Ward was 'the most famous woman writer employed by the war-time Bureau of Propaganda'.[39] Her two books, *England's Effort* (1916) and *Towards the Goal* (1917), were published by Smith Elder and John Murray, respectively, and both under government auspices. Written as letters to 'an American friend', Theodore Roosevelt, Ward's books outline the cause for which England is fighting and laments the non-committal stance taken by the United States.

Texts were aimed at different audiences, and their physical appearances give clues as to whom they might have appealed. *The Meaning of the War for Germany and Great Britain: An Attempt at Synthesis* (1915), by William Sanday and published by the Clarendon Press, appears to have targeted an intellectual market, whereas *The Martyrdom of Nurse Cavell* (1915) by William Thompson Hill was directed at a more general readership, its subtitle, *The Life Story of the Victim of Germany's Most Barbarous Crime*, dramatically grabbing attention (Figs. 2 and 3). Sanday's book with its unostentatious cover and its black, sober lettering gives the impression of an official document. Hill's book conveys a different message. In the centre is a portrait of Edith Cavell in nurse's uniform. The title and subtitle are printed in brown, ornate, almost Gothic, lettering. However, the seeming neutrality of scholarship suggested by Sanday's book and the drama promised by the biography of Cavell are both of the same propaganda effort.

Sanday tries to counter the 'heightened antagonism' of wartime with a consideration of the conflict from both sides.[40] His three sections, 'The British Case', 'The German Case', and 'An Attempt at Synthesis', are prefaced by an introduction outlining the 'Christian By-Products of the War, to be seen in the contending nations': seriousness, national and social unity, capacity for sacrifice, a sense of brotherhood, internal and external, and heightened consciousness of national aims and international relations. He repeats the eugenic arguments of the pre-war period, and employs Biblical imagery when he talks about war's 'cleansing fires':

[39] Claire M. Tylee, *The Great War and Women's Consciousness* (Iowa City, 1990), 67.

[40] W. Sanday, *The Meaning of the War for Germany and Great Britain: An Attempt at Synthesis* (Oxford, 1915), 18.

The Revd William Sanday (1843–1920) was Lady Margaret Professor of Divinity and Canon of Christ Church, Oxford from 1895 to 1919. He also wrote *The Deeper Causes of War* (1914) and *When Should the War End?* (1917), both of which appear in the *Schedule of Wellington House Literature*.

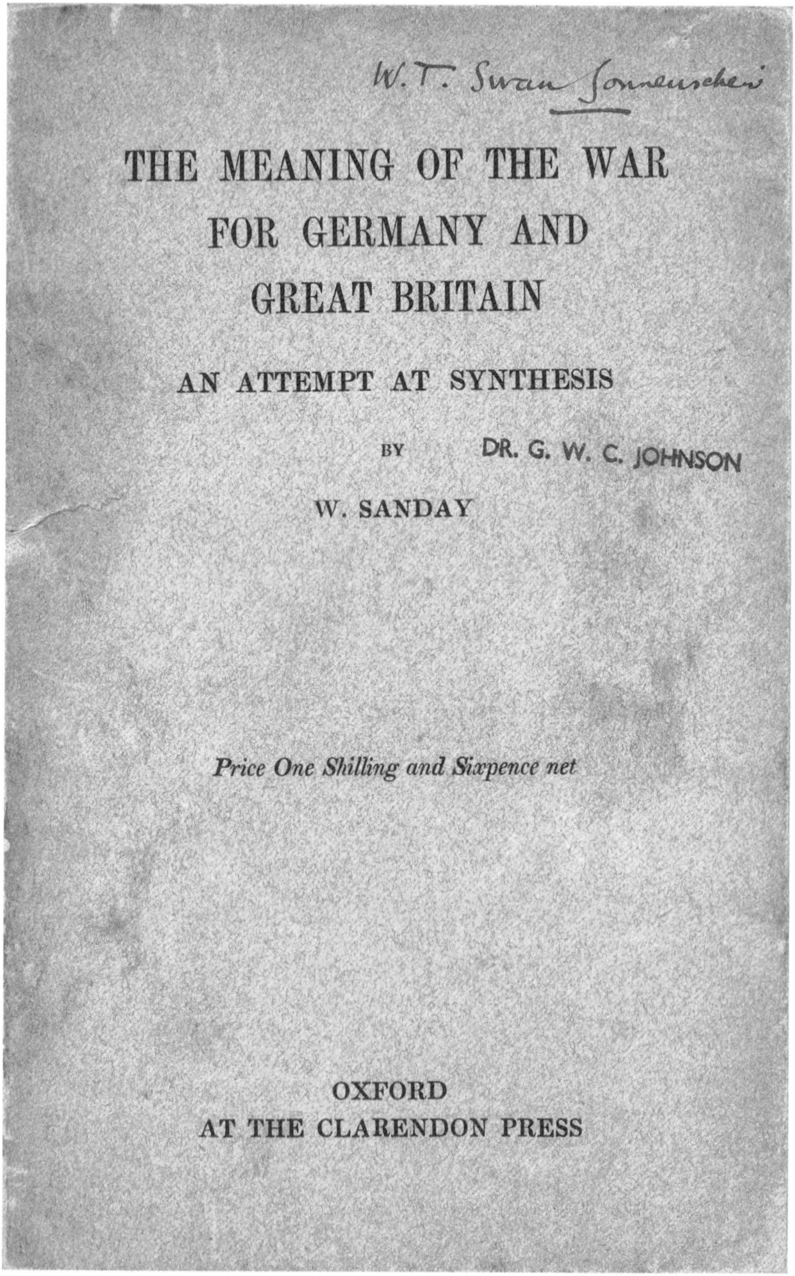
W. T. Swan Sonnenschein
THE MEANING OF THE WAR
FOR GERMANY AND
GREAT BRITAIN
AN ATTEMPT AT SYNTHESIS
BY
DR. G. W. C. JOHNSON
W. SANDAY
Price One Shilling and Sixpence net
OXFORD
AT THE CLARENDON PRESS

FIG. 2. *The Meaning of the War for Germany and Great Britain: An Attempt at Synthesis* (1915) by William Sanday, cover

FIG. 3. *The Martyrdom of Nurse Cavell: The Victim of Germany's Most Barbarous Crime* (1915) by William Thompson Hill, cover

All Europe was in need of some such sobering and solemnising influence. The great cities, more especially, were becoming more and more luxurious and pleasure-loving. It seemed as if the higher aims of the spirit were being drowned in gross and growing materialism.... Our enemies were saying that we were a decadent people. We did not believe it, but we also did not feel sure that there might not be some truth in it. We had had a long time of peace, so far as any great demand upon the nation as a whole was concerned, and such a time is apt to weaken the moral fibre; we did not know how far it might have done so.[41]

Although Sanday claims to have stated his arguments so that a German reader would not be offended or insulted, and certainly he is less bellicose than other propagandists, we are left in no doubt that his aim is to convince his audience of Britain's innocence and Germany's culpability. He is careful to distinguish righteous indignation from what he calls 'the ugly "jingo" temper, which came in the 'eighties and 'nineties'. Again invoking well-worn pre-1914 arguments, he locates the war in South Africa as a turning point in national outlook and sentiment by asserting that Britain 'was chastened by the wholesome discipline of the Boer War and by defeats of various kinds in athletics and other fields which the Briton had been in the habit of regarding as his own'.[42] Conflating war with sport, Sanday also celebrates the 'finer type of British manhood', the young men of the universities, who showed what they were made of in the newly raised armies. He affirms 'with great and confident emphasis' that Britain went to war against Germany without malice or animosity:

I was never so proud—I never thought to be so proud—of my own nation as I was in the first week of the war. Everything about it seemed to me noble. Its statesmen were noble; its Parliament was noble; its fighting services were noble; its Press was noble; its people were noble.... The war was a stern necessity—not to be avoided, but to be waged calmly and without hate.[43]

The word 'noble', here repeated to emphatic effect by Sanday, is used frequently by other writers between 1899 and 1919.[44] After

[41] Sanday, *The Meaning of the War for Germany and Great Britain*, 11.

[42] Ibid., 85.

[43] Ibid., 50.

[44] Over 35 books with 'noble' in their title were published between these years, most of which concerned women, including *Our Noble Queen* (1899); *Noble Work by Noble Women* (1900); *Noble Women of Our Time* (1901); *Noble Deeds of the*

her execution in 1915, Edith Cavell, in particular, is often accorded the epithet, 'noble', not least conspicuously in Ernest Protheroe's biography, *A Noble Woman* (1915).

Although Sanday does not really achieve his aim of an unbiased assessment in *The Meaning of the War for Germany and Great Britain*, he does urge his readers to have charity and forgiveness. William Thompson Hill, on the other hand, makes no pretensions to a 'balanced and dispassionate' argument in his book about the noble nurse Cavell. Chronicling her life from earliest, and seemingly idyllic, childhood to her 'barbarous' execution by the Germans in 1915, *The Martyrdom of Nurse Cavell* is written in dramatic and sensational language. At times, Hill seems to be overwhelmed by rage. For instance, in the first chapter entitled 'Childhood', his romantic descriptions of Cavell's birthplace, a village parsonage abutting a cemetery (reminiscent of the Brontës's Haworth parsonage), are interrupted by

> Some day, when the war is over, another grave may be dug in this quiet spot. If the poor mutilated frame of Edith Cavell is ever permitted to be brought back home, her countrymen will come to look upon the place where she lies. In this October of 1915 she sleeps in a land ravaged by war, and those who killed her will not stoop even to the tardy pity of giving back her body.[45]

There is no evidence that Cavell's body was 'mutilated' but myths grew up around the facts of her execution, many of which became increasingly sexualized and prurient. Her body became a site for propaganda for, interestingly, Cavell seems to have been used more as an example to inspire men than women. Certainly she was the ultimate nurse and ministering angel, that apex of feminine self-sacrifice, but in Hill's book, she encourages male chivalry and duty. They could not save this damsel in distress, but they can make retribution: 'there are wounded British soldiers who have pressed the doctors to send them back quickly to the firing line. "We will go back willingly," they say, "to avenge this great woman's death."'[46]

World's Heroines (1903); *A Book of Noble Women* (1907); and *The Golden Book of Youth, Noble Deeds by Boys and Girls* (1910). In 1913, Frederick James Gould published *Noble Pages from German History*.

[45] William Thompson Hill, *The Martyrdom of Nurse Cavell* (London, 1915), 3.

[46] Ibid. 16. In her fascinating book, *Female Intelligence: Women and Espionage in the First World War* (2003), Tammy Proctor contrasts the public image of the virtuous Cavell with that of her evil 'foil' Mata Hari.

Hill's melodramatic description of the execution is worthy of the 'Lives of the Saints': blindfolded and led in front of the firing squad, Cavell's 'physical strength was not a match for her heroic spirit. She fell in a swoon. The officer in charge of the soldiers stepped forward and shot her as she lay unconscious'.

The myth of Edith Cavell was disseminated in many other books, for like the sinking of the *Lusitania* and the invasion ('rape') of Belgium—detailed by the *Bryce Report on Alleged German Atrocities* (1915)—it could be used to great propagandistic effect. This was especially crucial after the illusion of swift victory was dispelled, and action was needed to bolster public morale.

Pamphlets were not the only means by which the Wellington House bureau hoped to influence public opinion at home and overseas. It produced and disseminated thousands of photographs, maps, cartoons, lantern slides, and eventually, films. Calendars and writing pads were also on offer. The 'British Victory Calendar' is printed in black and red and includes illustrations 'commemorating notable British achievements, 1914–1917'. By contrast, the 'German Crimes Calendar' records that country's 'outstanding Crimes against civilisation, 1914–1917'. One could also acquire stationery like 'The British Empire at War' bearing an 'illustrated cover with a portrait of Field-Marshal Sir Douglas Haig, and photo illustrations on each page of letter-paper'. The Wellington House *Schedule* also lists numerous postcards, such as 'British War Pictures: A Series of Postcards' from 1917 that includes images of 'Tracking a German Submarine', 'An English Girl in 1914 & 1917', and 'HMS Iron Duke'.

Visual media helped to codify the behaviour and actions of the wartime public, and postcards, especially, often overlooked in studies of Great War propaganda, 'were the social currency of the Great War. They were the language through which the soldier at the front and his people at home communicated'.[47] For women, this meant that all kinds of everyday heroines were depicted, from the mother and sweetheart to the nurse and munitions worker. Mediated by

[47] John Laffin, *World War I in Postcards* (Gloucester, 1988), 2. Laffin notes how 'publishers were quick to see the opportunities of the war and there is reason to believe that some already had their designers at work on 4 August 1914, on the day Britain declared war. Postcards were on sale within three days of the declaration and were widely available before the first troops of the BEF crossed the Channel to France and Belgium'.

class and part of a culturally available pattern of expectation and role-playing:

> postcards had to reflect the tastes, interests and sentiments of the various sections of the community to which they were primarily addressed. For this reason, publishers kept a close watch on the symptoms of changing tastes. Their cards provided a barometer of how people's interests varied, comparable to the modern public opinion poll, inasmuch as popular approval or disapproval was revealed in sales.[48]

A picture-postcard that features an elderly mother shows not just that every patriotically minded woman should send her son to war, but also how mothers permeated the consciousness of their male offspring. Captioned 'Mother o' Mine', this particular card invokes Kipling's poem, adapting its sentiments of a mother's undying love to the Great War (Fig. 4). With fighting raging in the background, a young cavalry officer on horseback prepares to go into battle. Above him floats the image of his elderly mother. Her cap denotes she is a widow and will have to face old age alone should her son be killed. His concerned expression as he thinks of her reinforces this possibility. But she selflessly pushes him onwards, says, 'GO!', as presumably she did when he enlisted, because she believes in his role as defender of the country. She may mourn her loss, but she would not wallow in grief, being proud of her contribution to the nation.

Young women, too, had their exemplars of behaviour presented in picture-postcards. Romantic and melodramatic, they show women embracing, saying goodbye to, or thinking of their beloveds. Often they are captioned by portions of song or verse. 'How Can I Bear to Leave Thee?' depicts what would have been a familiar image of lovers' farewell (Fig. 5). Having encouraged their men to go, they remain true, loyal, and deeply in love with their soldier, illustrated by the postcard entitled, 'Thoughts Unchanging' in which a young woman, dressed characteristically in pink, extends her arms to the image of her soldier that floats above her (Fig. 6). The soldier-lover, it seems, is dead, reinforced by the aureole that surrounds his image and the (rather phallic) sword that strikes through the picture between the two figures. The ideas and images communicated

[48] Richard Carline, *Pictures in the Post: The Story of the Picture Postcard in the History of Popular Art* (Bedford, 1959), 9.

FIG. 4. 'Mother O' Mine', postcard, circa 1915

FIG. 5. 'How Can I Bear to Leave Thee?', postcard, circa 1915, Bamforth & Co., Ltd.

here are typical of much bereaved women's writing of the War—and its aftermath—prose and poetry, that expresses longing for a supernatural communication with the dead beloved.

When they are not being embraced, or looking longingly at their men or imagined versions of them, everyday heroines stare into space, as in the postcard 'My Heart Is With You Always', where above the young woman floats the image of a line of soldiers in khaki, bayonets poised, advancing towards the smoke of battle (Fig. 7). The Union Jack brooch she wears proclaims her patriotism in this reverie of romantic warfare.

A more active, yet supremely feminine image of a patriotic woman is depicted in 'Jesu, Lover of My Soul' (Fig. 8). Accompanied by a stanza of the hymn, it shows a woman nursing a dying soldier on the battlefield, a true ministering angel. The light that shines from the left corner touching the man indicates that he is being called to his heavenly rest. Like other postcards and posters, it is a highly sanitized picture of death on the battlefield—there is no blood, no visible wound—and it bears no resemblance to the act of nursing near the front. The memoirs of women on active service, discussed in Chapter 4, paint a very different picture.

Postcards gave rise to and continued to reinforce the stereotype that women were stridently pro-war while remaining oblivious to the suffering of soldiers. Such daughters of Britain provide the model for Sassoon's females in 'The Glory of Women'. No doubt his anger at what was certainly reprehensible behaviour on the part of civilians can be appreciated, but it is important to acknowledge his bias, his own internalization of the roles he, as a man, was taught to play, and especially the fact that he condemned the 'Old Men', the generals, politicians, and war-mongering clerics, far more than he did the allegedly ignorant and bloodthirsty women.

Whether it is ghostly film footage or Kitchener staring out from behind his pointed finger claiming 'I want YOU', the impact of the visual was enormous. Images such as these became ammunition in the battle to win and maintain public support. The now (in)famous poster, 'Women of Britain Say, "GO!"', is an archetypal image of female persuasion. As the postcards illustrate, much effort was put into the appeal to women of all ages. Posters, too, were aimed at the young sweetheart ('Is your best boy wearing khaki?') and at little girls ('What did YOU do in the War, Daddy?'). These were effective, because, as Peter Stanley points out, posters 'do not seek a dialogue:

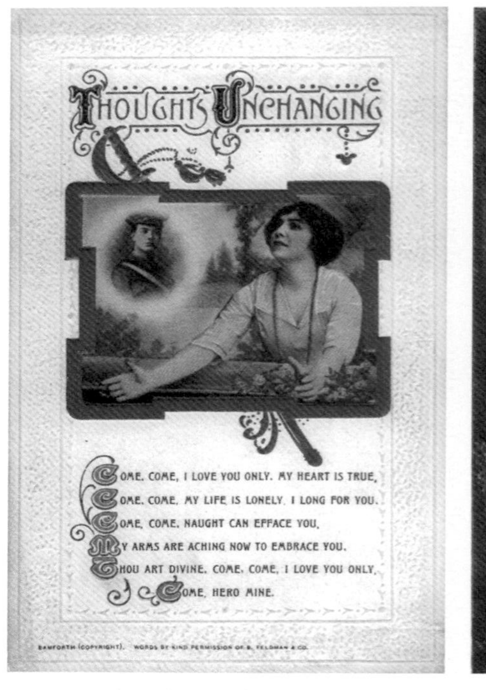

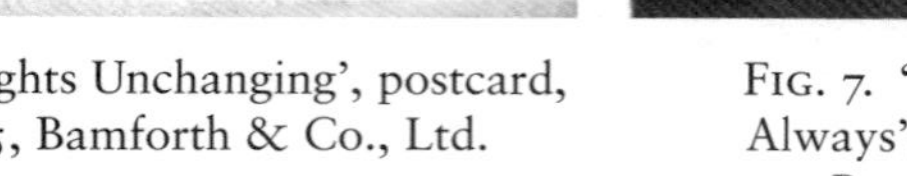

Fig. 6. 'Thoughts Unchanging', postcard, circa 1915, Bamforth & Co., Ltd.

Fig. 7. 'My Heart is With You Always', postcard, circa 1915, Bamforth & Co., Ltd.

Fig. 8. 'Jesu, Lover of My Soul', postcard, circa 1915, Bamforth & Co., Ltd.

they imposed, imparted, and impelled, but did not inquire'.[49] The output was massive with as many as 2.5 million copies of 110 different posters in the first year of the War alone.[50]

Recruitment posters that appealed to women to take up active service presented images of noble-looking VADs,[51] WRAFs (Women's Royal Air Force), and WRNSs (Women Royal Naval Service). All these use the lure of the uniform alongside patriotic exhortations and the opportunity for action to inspire women to do 'their' duty. In recruiting posters that appealed to men, however, women are depicted either as victims of the evil, rapacious Hun or as glamour girls who cry 'If only I were a man!'

Although class is not explicit in these visual representations, it is certainly implicit, despite wartime attempts to stress a kind of class-blindness. As Sharon Ouditt reminds us, British tradition relied 'heavily on voluntary contributions and a deeply-structured sense of place and position. Women's war experience, on the whole, did little to fracture this tradition.'[52] The exemplary female portrayed in the munitions poster, 'These women are doing their bit—Learn to make munitions', is almost certainly of the working-class.[53] It shows a young woman, eager and already in action by putting on her coat, not waiting for any instruction from her sisters in the VAD or the WRNS. She does not even turn around to acknowledge the wave of her soldier, whose figure appears in the background. No

[49] Peter Stanley, *What did YOU do in the War, Daddy?* (Melbourne, 1983), 7.

[50] Wilson, *The Myriad Faces of War*, 734.

[51] Although the acronym denoted the collective organization designed to provide medical assistance to the British Territorial Force and although men were also members, serving especially as orderlies, the term 'VAD' came increasingly to represent in the public imagination a young female nurse. Since the work was voluntary and low paid, most hailed from the middle and upper classes. In her book *England's Effort* (1916) Mrs Humphry Ward praised

> the army of maidens . . . who as V.A.D.s (members of the Voluntary Aid Detachments), trained by the Red Cross, have come trooping from England's most luxurious or comfortable homes and are doing invaluable work in hundreds of hospitals; to begin with, the most menial scrubbing and dishwashing, and by now, the more ambitious and honourable—but not more indispensable—tasks of nursing itself (Mrs Humphry Ward, *England's Effort: Six Letters to an American Friend* [London, 1916], 184).

[52] Sharon Ouditt, 'Tommy's Sisters: The Representation of Working Women's Experience', in Hugh Cecil and Peter H. Liddle (eds.), *Facing Armageddon 1914–18: The War Experienced* (London, 1996), 740.

[53] It is interesting to note, however, that Bessie Marchant made the heroine of her novel *A Girl Munition Worker* one of the genteel class. This will be discussed further in Chapter 3.

gazing longingly out of the window for her—this girl not only says, 'GO!', but seems to add, 'Let me get on with *my* job!'

Just as they had been during the Boer War, women's and girls' magazines published between 1914 and 1918 were sites of patriotic inculcation and fervour. As Chapter 1 illustrated, before the outbreak in August 1914, they touched on a variety of social issues, but war with Germany soon became a popular theme. Alfred Harmsworth, Lord Northcliffe, was undoubtedly the most famous periodical publisher of his day, and he admonished his staff, 'Don't forget the women.' His Amalgamated Press produced numerous penny papers aimed at working-class women and extolled the virtues of the plucky (usually East End) heroine.[54] The covers of his magazines are meant to entice the reader with their fine pen-and-ink, action-packed illustrations, along the lines of the nineteenth-century penny dreadfuls. The headlines are sensational. Titles are in large print with tag lines finished by exclamation points, such as 'ALL STORIES BRIGHT AND HEALTHY!' Accompanying the cover illustration is usually a synopsis of the week's serial instalment. A typical example reads

> CAN LOVE BE BOUGHT? But he could not buy HER love, no matter how much he spent on her—No! Even if he threw all his wealth at her feet in a glittering heap!
>
> (SEE THE GRAND STORY, 'He Thought Her False!')[55]

These are romance tales of poor girls made good. They achieve the love of a wealthy, but true man because of their honest, down-to-earth charm. Such heroines are the mainstay of *The Girls' Reader.* Fantasy love affairs are meant to provide the ordinary, overworked reader with an escape from real life drudgery. The characters can also be said to illustrate the particular qualities working-class girls should emulate: frankness, fidelity, and good humour mixed with a feminine, yet plucky personality. Although they are not the refined, intellectual females of *The Girl's Realm,* they are nonetheless thoroughly feminine and, most importantly, British.

These qualities were easily transformed for use in wartime. The magazine's pre-war subtitle, 'The Home Paper for All,' became, in

[54] Among Northcliffe's periodicals for women were *The Girl's Own Paper, The Girls' Empire, The Girls' Friend, Horner's Pansy Library, Home Chat*, and *Cosy Corner* with its tag-line, 'Just the Very Paper for Every Nice Girl'.

[55] *The Girls' Reader*, 11 July 1914.

September 1914, 'The Paper for British Homes' and its title appeared on the front page flanked by the furled Union Jack and the French *tricolore*. Beside each was the image of a British girl and a French maid wearing a Phrygian cap. Heroines of *The Girls' Reader* also became more overtly patriotic. 'Kitty the Coffee-Stall Girl' with 'her infectious gaiety, her bigness of heart, her ever-ready sympathy and dazzling wit', who featured in stories in 1913, metamorphosed into 'Emma Brown, the Girl Who Beat the Kaiser' (Fig. 9).

Emma is a plucky, warm-hearted house-maid. Yet it is her thrilling adventures, defying the Kaiser and his army at the Front that provide the escapist element. However unrealistic, and indeed absurd, its daring deeds, the serial plays upon prejudices and echoes the patriotic propaganda prevalent at the time about Germany. There is, of course, romance, but like earlier war stories, such as 'The Shield of Captain Credence', it takes a back seat for 'England's sake'.

The serial begins with the 24 October 1914 issue. The cover shows Emma dressed in a domestic servant's uniform and standing in a resolute manner gazing into the distance—like many representations of women in recruitment posters. She clutches in one hand a sword and in the other a huge Union Jack that waves out behind her. At her feet is her grimacing bull-dog, inevitably named 'John Bull', and in the background is the tower of St Bride's and the dome of St Paul's. The caption reads, 'Emma Brown says: "Come the three corners of the world in arms, and we shall shock them!"—And she's right!' Touted as 'The Girl Who Beat the Kaiser', Emma sets off to play an active role in the War.

With her fiancé, Ernie Dobbs, at the front, Emma is enraged by the stories she reads of German atrocities (probably in a Northcliffe newspaper!), and she longs to 'tell that ole Kaiser something!' She gladly and 'insolently' leaves her job—refusing her severance pay—and gives her employer, Mrs Yexley, a piece of her patriotic mind: 'I'd like to work at a place where they're true Britons—where they do stick up for their country!'[56] Emma is a 'fiery, quick-tempered little thing, but with a heart of gold' and 'what she lacked in size, she made up for in spirit'. She wants to 'be doing something myself', and like so many women of her time and before, she exclaims, 'If only I'd been a man!' No horror stories about the 'Uhlans', or,

[56] 'Emma Brown', *The Girls' Reader*, No.143, Vol. III (24 October 1914), 2.

EMMA BROWN: THE GIRL WHO BEAT THE KAISER!

FIG. 9. 'Emma Brown', *The Girls' Reader*, cover illustration (Per. 2537 d. 24) (24 October 1914), Bodleian Library, University of Oxford

as she calls them, the 'Yewlands', can scare her. With faithful John Bull to accompany her, Emma rounds up her own army of old men and young boys in France and proceeds with this ragged band systematically to win numerous battles against the Germans, stunning the British Army, and winning its grateful thanks. The description of her first encounter with the Germans displays all the resoluteness and cool-headed bravery that characterizes the girl's subsequent exploits. As the German guns get closer, Emma and her men 'seemed to be in the midst of it', but she holds them back until the appointed moment for hand-to-hand conflict: 'It was what she was waiting for'. Her cry of 'Charge!' sounds out 'clarion-like' and 'with one yelp they were up, those 200 veterans and striplings'. They 'were hurling themselves on the enemy with all the fury and impetus they were capable of'. As for Emma, their leader, her

> hair had come undone, and was falling about her shoulders. She had her military coat over her dress, and she waved her sword above her head, urging her men on, heedless of her own great risk. She was, indeed, a modern Joan of Arc.[57]

She is the image not only of Joan of Arc, but of Ophelia with her loose and flowing hair—there is something of madness in her exploits—and of Boadicea in her sword-wielding power. She manages, as well, to make every man fall in love with her—she is the sexiest soldier around!

Emma is later involved in more land battles and in a dogfight against the Germans with the French Flying Corps lieutenant, Andre Fevere, a rival suitor to Ernie ('"It ain't proper for there to be any quarrelling among the 'ontong cordial, is it?"'[58]), and thus the source of romantic intrigue. The two are shot down over enemy territory and taken prisoner. Emma meets the 'arch-enemy of the country she loved better than life' without fear. The Kaiser is portrayed as a large imposing figure who 'could not rest anywhere'. Speaking in perfect English to emphasize his British connections, he stresses that the final victory will be his and that of his glorious army. He declares that 'God is fighting on my side.... It is a great pity you belong to England—England the pirate—the treacherous serpent!'[59] The Kaiser is here depicted, typically, as a madman, a

[57] 'Emma Brown', *The Girls' Reader*, No. 144, Vol. III (31 October 1914), 5.
[58] Ibid., Vol. III (26 December 1914), 8.
[59] Ibid., Vol. III (14 November 1914), 2.

blasphemer, and a fiend. Emma's anger is roused and her response is one right out of the Northcliffe press:

'You're talking about my country—about Britain! Britain, wot's the land of the free—the country that stands for everything that's good and true and noble—the country that's got 'onour enough to respect the promises it makes.

'I—I ain't eddicated. I don't profess to be; but I know what I am talking about now. I know that we're in the right, and you're wrong. And I know'—she flung up her head—'that Old England is going to win. BRITAIN ALWAYS WINS!. . . . I've got a bull-dog. It ain't a snappy, snarling sort o' beast, but when it's roused—it's roused. And when it grips it don't let go. And that's England. Britain's roused now—and the British bull-dog won't let go until Germany's been brought to her knees!. . . . I've heard you've got a toast—"Here's to the Day!" Well, I want to drink it to-night for me. Drink to the Day when the old Union Jack will be flying over Berlin. Three cheers for dear old England! Down with Germany where the sausages come from!'[60]

The Kaiser listens to her diatribe and then dismisses her as a raving lunatic who belongs in an asylum.

Emma and Andre make a daring escape and the Cockney heroine is free for more exploits, including recapturing a French town for the Allies. The allied commanders exclaim: '"If only she had been a man she would have made a splendid general."'

Throughout, Emma's working-class credentials are stressed, especially by Emma herself, who is very proud of them: '"Who am I . . . A Skivvy. That's what I've been all my life. A domestic servant's as good as anybody else—ay, and perhaps a bit better. Anyway, they can't do without us."' With this, Emma falls in line with other heroines presented in the Amalgamated Press stories like 'The Queen of the Laundry' or 'The Heart of a Servant'. There is nothing highbrow about her; she must work hard for her living, her lover is an ordinary bloke, and she is the backbone of British society.

She disbands her army and goes to Ernie, wounded and due to be sent home to England where she will nurse him. Emma falls back into her conventional role at Ernie's side, still fervently patriotic, but knowing her place, and no longer desiring to do man's work. Ernie's goodness and heroism (he is awarded the V.C.)—not her own exploits—make her '"the happiest girl in the world!"'

[60] 'Emma Brown', *The Girls' Reader*, No. 145, Vol. III (14 November 1914), 2–3.

The wild scrapes in which Emma Brown places herself are entertaining and exciting, but they are far-fetched and certainly the magazine did not encourage its readers to do the same. Instead, Emma's final sentiments reinforce the traditional place of women in wartime. They can be patriotic, but their place is not leading an army. They must carry on courageously at home and, if necessary, nurse their wounded lovers. As with other heroines, Emma is conquered by love without losing all of her strength of character. She simply must channel it into the woman's part—as her readers must do also.

A more philosophic and active line was taken by *The Girl's Realm*. As in the Boer War, it was directed at a middle-class audience and prided itself on its forward-looking attitude to women and young girls. The arty covers do not change—the outer look of the magazine remains consistent—but slowly the War begins to dominate its pages. In the September 1914 issue, one can clearly see the haste with which the editors had to adapt to the mood of the moment. Obviously planned far in advance of the outbreak of hostilities, the September issue is tagged with a strip of blue paper announcing the special supplement contained within: 'THE WAR—What Women May Do To Help—Full Directions Inside'. Inserted between the middle pages, this supplement is made of cheap, brown paper, lower in quality than the usual pages: paper-rationing was already beginning. 'How Girls May Help in Practical Ways' announces that nurses are wanted by the Red Cross, but garments, too, are needed for the wounded. The article provides instructions for sewing from 'odds and ends of flannel' a chest and back protector and for knitting bedroom slippers, body belts, and nightshirts. It comments that 'Every girl or woman with time to spare should at once start work.'

The *Girl's Realm* publishers, Cassell, also thought it important to explain to their readers their practical position with regards to operating costs and its duty to its employees. They explain that, despite the rising cost of paper and the decrease in advertising, they meant 'to go on'. Cassell proclaims that it is the company's patriotic duty not to down-size its staff to improve profit. Furthermore, the reader, by continuing to buy *The Girl's Realm*, will help Cassell in this patriotic 'resolve [that] not one worker must go.' (Presumably, Cassell is referring to those not fit for or exempt from military service.) Another instance of how country, conscience, and commerce were inextricably linked and a clever marketing tool: the reader's purchasing power is also her patriotic duty.

A pleasing appearance can also assert one's patriotism. Mrs Mary Whitley, in her regular fashions column, notes in October 1914 that 'so many grave and terrible things have happened...that I feel almost as though some apology were needed for attempting to write at all on so avowedly frivolous a subject as dress'. Yet, she asserts, women of Great Britain 'owe a certain duty' to dress 'as tastefully as they can' and, in doing so, they are helping to keep British trade afloat. As with other *Girl's Realm* articles on dress and taste, this clearly reinforces the sense that the audience is middle and upper-middle class. These girls are not just looking for diversion or escapist entertainment, but more intellectual or informative entertainment of a kind that reinforces their status and their privilege.

While readers of the magazine are given instructions on how to knit for soldiers or to sew their own frocks, they are also encouraged to fend for themselves—something the audience of *The Girls' Reader* was supposedly already used to doing. In 'War and Women—The Influence of the World Conflict on Women's Status and Work', the editor stresses that the War will bring more disproportion among the sexes: women may *not* find husbands. With this comes economic as well as emotional implications for women: 'We cannot afford to keep an idle womanhood.... Every woman as well as every man, has in times like these, to show "the reason of her existence".... The War has made us all face reality, and, not the least of all the women of world'.

To support the war effort and to do war work, then, is to 'face reality'. Yet, at the same time, much emphasis was placed on having an *escape from* reality, and literature, whether periodical or book, aimed to provide this. However, as I have argued, there was a fine line between what was 'escapist' and what was 'propaganda'. This was also true of the theatre, as L. J. Collins in his *Theatre at War, 1914–18* (1998) asserts:

> the generally held opinion that the theatre in 1914–18 was simply an antidote to war is not true. Theatre was much more than a diversionary and escapist tactic employed to provide temporary relief; indeed, the theatrical profession, in order to justify its existence, had to produce a theatre that was seen to be purposeful and relevant.... the theatre was employed as a recruiting and propaganda agent, and raiser of funds for war.[61]

[61] L. J. Collins, *Theatre at War, 1914–18* (London, 1998), 3.

The idea of theatre as a remedy for the burdens of war was, not surprisingly, touted during the conflict. In his book *At Home in the War* (1918), G. S. Street contends that 'anything that helps to keep the nerves and spirits normal is a national service'.[62] He argues that theatrical entertainment is a refuge for servicemen on leave, and that actors who, despite air raids, carried on with their performances should be deemed 'heroes'. As many romance novelists and memoirists would assert, Street believes also that the war has brought a graver outlook in the once-frivolous society:

> while it has given them an added abandonment to their brief gaieties, has created and deepened the gravity of thought and outlook underneath, and this is shown even in playgoing, here and there.... Some plays of serious import have had a vogue they could not have had a few years ago, and I believe the war, with its stir of feeling, is the cause. I have no doubt at all that this graver outlook will continue and show itself in the theatres as elsewhere.[63]

Julie Holledge describes the link between actresses and the suffrage movement, and illustrates how, on the outbreak of War, both suffragettes and performers became 'patriotic women', setting aside their campaign for the vote to canvass for enlistment and support for the war effort.[64] The rhetoric of the suffrage pageants was well suited to be adapted to the needs of wartime. Propaganda plays full of militaristic references were written and performed. By the end of October 1914, actresses, mainly from the Actress Franchise League, were working as entertainers for the troops. By 1917, there were twenty-five acting companies in France performing over 1,400 shows per month. Their average programme consisted of scenes from Shakespeare, Barrie, Sheridan, and Shaw.[65]

Numerous pageants were also written and performed between 1914 and 1919, among them *Britannia's Revue*, *Britannia Goes to War*, *Britannia's Pageant of Peace*, and *Britain's Defenders*.[66] Their

[62] G. S. Street, *At Home in the War* (London, 1918), 106.

[63] Ibid., 111.

[64] Julie Holledge, *Innocent Flowers: Women in the Edwardian Theatre* (London, 1981), 97.

[65] Ibid., 98.

[66] None of these are listed by Collins, but are archived in the Birmingham Reference Library's 'War Poetry Collection'.

very titles indicate the propagandistic slant as personifications of national stereotypes and ideals parade on stage. *Britannia's Revue* (*c.*1914) by Gladys Davidson, for instance, has four sets of characters: 'Britannia's "Hearts of Oak"', including John Bull, Jack Tar, Tommy Atkins, Red Cross Nurse, and An English Rose; 'Britannia's "Little Acorns"' or nursery rhyme characters; 'Britannia's Colonies', among them Canada, India, and South Africa; and 'Britannia's Allies' consisting of France, Russia, Belgium, Japan, and Serbia. The individual characters of History, Hope, and Peace also make appearances. Patriotic songs and verse-speeches by each character add to the rousing intention of the pageant that ends with a tableau of all the members on stage. As Collins points out, the tableau was an effective 'method of stirring nationalistic pride... because it was both visually and, combined with the singing, emotionally evocative'.[67]

Other dramatic pieces were equally ubiquitous. Sketches and scenes often appear in volumes of poetry or in magazines. *Britannia Goes to War* by May Bell appears in her volume (classified as verse) entitled, *What of the Night? And Other Sketches* (1919). Similarly, 'Discipline', a short three-scene play with speaking roles for two women and two men, appears in the *Women's Volunteer Reserve Magazine* (July 1916). It depicts the meeting of Miss Earle, 'a young lady, fashionably dressed' and Emma Jones, 'a coster girl, dressed in the approved fashion of that species.'[68] Like *The Girls' Reader*'s Emma, Miss Jones speaks in a cockney accent and describes how she has come to want to join the Women's Volunteer Reserve (W.V.R.):

MISS JONES a lidy in kharki was passing along the street... when Hi was a-calling out my wares—(*shouts at top of voice*)—'Co-o-o-ckles hand mu-u-u-ssels.'... And the lidy comes up to me and she says, says she, 'That's a beuutiful vice yer've got, yer ought to be a Sergeant in the W.V.R., that's what yer ought to be,' says she.... Then she told me all about the work of the W.V.R. is doing of, and 'ow the women of hall classes kin jine and do their bit for the blessed old country.[69]

[67] Collins, *Theatre at War*, 189.

[68] 'Discipline', *Women's Volunteer Reserve Magazine*, vol. 1, no. 7 (July 1916), 135.

[69] Ibid., 135.

Class stereotypes are reinforced while, paradoxically at the same time, conflict or disparity is repudiated: 'women of hall classes kin jine'.

The only thing that worries Emma is the drilling and discipline, but 'the lidy' assures her that if soldiers ''ad no discipline, they couldn't lick this yere ol' 'orror called a Kaiser'. Miss Earle, typical of her middle-class status, begins war work as a hospital assistant but leaves to join the W.V.R. because she 'had come to be a *nurse*, and not to be a charwoman'.[70] In the second scene, the Sergeant-Major and the Lieutenant sing the praises of the two 'Ptes. Jones and Earle'. None are 'keener in the Corps' and they have each learned how to be disciplined volunteers:

> SERGEANT-MAJOR If anything were needed to show what a real blessing the W.V.R. is going to prove to the country, there it is, in those two girls. Nine months ago we took them, one full of zeal . . . but never having been trained to be of use to anyone. . . . *Now*, not only is she one of the smartest in the Corps, but she has passed her First-Aid and Home Nursing exams., is proficient in Camp Cooking and Signalling, and has brought in six recruits. As for Jones, she is a real treasure. Her patriotism knows no bounds, and it would be a bad day for the Kaiser if he fell into *her* hands.[71]

Both privileged and working women can find a useful part to play, and in the process, such a sketch suggests, become better individuals. The patriotic nature of 'Discipline' is reinforced further by the final scene, the direction for which indicates a pageant-like tableau: 'The Corps is discovered on the Stage, National Anthem is played, and Curtain falls with Company standing to attention and Officers at the salute.'[72]

However, there was another side to this influx of patriotic drama. Edy Craig and her Pioneer Players designed a new repertoire that eschewed the rhetoric of the pageants to produce works like Gwen John's *The Luck of War* (first performed on 13 May 1917, at the Kingsway Theatre in London).[73] The play concerns the plight of Ann who believes her husband, George, has been killed in the War. With three children to support on a widow's pension, she re-marries. George, however, was only missing and returns to the marital

[70] Ibid., 136. [71] Ibid., 137. [72] Ibid., 138.

[73] Holledge, *Innocent Flowers*, 137.

home one night, leaving Ann to explain herself. Holledge notes how the play, 'while never belittling the horrors of the trenches, successfully draws attention to the problems faced by working-class women'.[74] Craig was concerned with moving away from socio-realism, from the melodrama of the nineteenth century, and was interested in providing a stage for more experimental works by European writers, but 'her choice of plays was still influenced by the war—which increasingly affected civilian life'.[75]

Despite the efforts of many women and men to write contrary to nationalistic and wartime ideals, the majority of authors, critics, and dramatists—aided by publishers and the book trade—reinforced beliefs in the righteousness of the cause. When a government inquiry in 1917 questioned the money being spent at Wellington House, H. T. Sheringham, Masterman's colleague, defended the payment scheme, asserting that publishers' cooperation 'reflect[ed] a great credit on their feelings for the work and their patriotism' and that they did 'not make anything out' of what they distributed on behalf of the government.[76] This may seem a disingenuous remark, but the fact remains that publishers did *not* make vast amounts of money from Wellington House. Stanley Unwin's participation in the scheme was not a primary factor in his firm's survival in the difficult commercial climate of war. Nor did his cooperation with the government agency come with any mandate to 'tow the party line' in other publications. Wellington House had 'no authority either to give or to refuse permission for the publication of any book'.[77] The dust jacket of *Three Aspects of the Russian Revolution,* which publicizes, among other tracts, *I Appeal Unto Caesar,* attests to this. That Hodder & Stoughton made far more money from the sales of Ruby M. Ayres's *Richard Chatterton, V.C.* (discussed in the next chapter) than it did from any of its 134 government-sponsored tracts indicates that the reading public was absorbing propaganda from sources that had no 'official' government backing. The texts highlighted in this chapter—postcards,

[74] Holledge, *Innocent Flowers*, 138.

[75] Ibid., 140.

[76] Propaganda Inquiry, Report of the Proceedings of meeting held at Wellington House, 15 November 1917, Statement by H. T. Sheringham, PRO INF 4/11.

[77] T. O. Willson to Stanley Unwin, 22 December 1917, Allen & Unwin Archive, University of Reading.

periodical stories, plays—did much to foster the kind of patriotic right-thinking so essential to the war effort and they offered encouragement in the face of anxiety, uncertainty, and loss. The attitude expounded in newspapers as well as public advertisements that the War was a national necessity was shored up by novelists who, as the next chapter will demonstrate, eagerly responded to the demands of a reading public.

3

'Putting Things in Their Right Places': The War in Romance Novels

> 'George, it's dreadful now—to be a woman!'
>
> She spoke in a low appealing voice, pressing up against him, as though she begged the soul in him that had been momentarily unconscious of her, to come back to her.
>
> He laughed, and the vision before his eyes broke up.
>
> 'Darling, it's adorable now—to be a woman! How I shall think of you, when I'm out there!—away from all the grime and the horror—sitting by this lake, and looking—as you do now.'
>
> . . .
>
> 'Will you ever have time—to think of me—George?'
>
> She bent towards him.
>
> He laughed.
>
> 'Well, not when I'm going over the parapet to attack the Boches. Honestly, one thinks of nothing then but how one can get one's men across. But you won't come off badly, my little Nell—for thoughts—night or day. And you mustn't think of us too sentimentally. It's quite true that men write wonderful letters—and wonderful verse too—men of all ranks—things you'd never dream they could write. I've got a little pocket-book full that I've collected.... But bless you, nobody *talks* about their feelings at the front. We're a pretty slangy lot in the trenches, and when we're in billets, we read novels and rag each other—and *sleep*—my word, we do sleep!'[1]

The exchange between newlyweds Nelly and George Sarratt in Mrs Humphry Ward's 1918 novel '*Missing*' not only encapsulates many features of the romantic fiction of the Great War—Nelly's lament

[1] Mrs Humphry Ward, '*Missing*' (London, 1918), 48–9.

for her gender, the two lovers' effusive emotions, the colloquialisms—but, in George's description of life at the Front, illustrates how books, and novels in particular, were a source of distraction and amusement. Joseph Hocking's hero Bob Nancarrow in *All for a Scrap of Paper* (1915) similarly notes how reading was also an essential part of convalescing from war wounds: 'Literally tons of periodicals, novels, and other light literature had been forwarded ... evidences of the fact that millions at home, although they were unable to fight, were anxious to help those who could.'[2] In these wonderful examples of intertextuality, both Ward and Hocking demonstrate what was already obvious to the then public-at-large: the demand for books was not diminished by the outbreak of war.

The sheer numbers of novels and their subsequent reviews in periodicals like *The Bookman*, the *Times Literary Supplement*, and *The Athenaeum* demonstrate that 'wartime not only served to perpetuate existing reading habits but appeared to encourage new readers'.[3] In the *Daily Mirror* in 1915, the publisher Herbert Jenkins declared:

> 'What a boon new novels are to the man at the Front, the wounded, the bereaved. I have received many very touching testimonies of the gratitude of those who want to forget things occasionally for an hour or so'.[4]

This is certainly a case of the publisher touting his wares, but as Chapter 2 has shown, books had their role to play in the war effort, and novels were no exception. Although memoirs and personal accounts by combatants or non-combatants (such as nurses) sold well, the demand in *fiction* was not for realistic war stories, but for romantic tales and detective thrillers that may or may not have had war as a backdrop. Even Wilfred Owen, while at training camp, was found by his brother Harold to be reading a popular novel, *Rest-harrow* (by Maurice Hewlett): 'I asked him if he was enjoying it; giving a little shrug, he replied, "It distracts me most pleasantly."'[5] Popular novelists like Mrs Humphry Ward saw themselves as providers of entertainment and amusement in a war-weary world, but

[2] Joseph Hocking, *All for a Scrap of Paper: A Romance of the Present War* (London, 1915), 243.

[3] Joseph McAleer, *Popular Reading and Publishing in Britain, 1914–1950* (London, 1992), 72.

[4] Ibid.

[5] Harold Owen, *Journey from Obscurity: Memoirs of the Owen Family, 1893–1918*, vol. III, *War* (London, 1965), 152

> there is something faintly disingenuous about her emphasis on '*délassement* and refreshment' because, even at their most undemanding, the novels never allow the reader to forget the consuming importance of the war effort. Their subject-matter may be far removed from the front, but their tone is almost always proselytizing and their language is the language of moral conflict.[6]

This may describe the kind of novel of which Owen later complained. Having been to the Front and while convalescent in hospital he groused in a letter to his mother, 'one of the sisters brought me some novels, about as palatable as warm water to a starving jaguar'.[7] The poet's view was surely not unique among soldiers or even civilians and many found romantic fiction tedious and uninspiring. However, the sheer volume of such novels indicates that there were others who thought differently. This chapter will consider only a fraction of the hundreds of 'light fiction' books published between 1914 and 1918: *My Heart's Right There* (1914) by Florence Barclay, *Khaki and Kisses* (1915) by Berta Ruck, *Richard Chatterton, V.C.* (1915) by Ruby M. Ayres, *A Girl Munition Worker* (1917) by Bessie Marchant, *Before the Wind* (1918) by Janet Laing, and *Good Old Anna* (1915) by Marie Belloc Lowndes. It will demonstrate that the Great War was a fertile subject, providing ample opportunity for melodrama, adventure, and complications to and resolutions of love affairs. Some of the novelists considered here, like Marie Belloc Lowndes, were well-established and familiar names by 1914. Others, especially Berta Ruck and Ruby M. Ayres, built lifetime careers on the success their wartime writing. Although my focus is on women writers in the genre, this chapter will highlight, by way of thematic and character comparison, novels by men. Popular and prolific male authors such as William LeQueux, Joseph Hocking, and Herbert Strang (the pseudonym of George Herbert Ely and James L'Estrange) wrote with equal vigour and enthusiasm for the war effort. Their use of language and plotlines mirror those of their female colleagues. Their novels, as I will show, are as melodramatic

[6] Helen Small, 'Mrs Humphry Ward and the First Casualty of War', in S. Raitt and T. Tate (eds.), *Women's Fiction and the Great War* (Oxford, 1997), 21. Small argues that in *'Missing'* Ward was voicing concerns about truth-telling, which she suppressed in her propaganda writings for the government: 'unflagging though her endorsement of Britain's role in the war was, she was also troubled by a sense of the aesthetic and ethical cost of her own passionate militarism'.

[7] Wilfred Owen, *Selected Letters*, ed. John Bell (Oxford and New York, 1985), 230.

and effusive as any composed by a supposedly 'overemotional' woman writer.

Novels that exploited the Great War were much more than the 'distracting' tales praised by George Sarratt and Herbert Jenkins. They were part of the public's fantasy investment in the War. As Chapter 1 pointed out, although the reality of warfare was very different, there was a continuing demand for stories that brought order where there was chaos and allowed the reader vicariously to experience life as she would like it to be lived. Freud, of course, believed that the adult 'phantasy' or daydream, indeed art generally, was escapist wish-fulfilment, but psychoanalysts that came after him argued that fantasy arising from the creative imagination is 'a vital aspect of man's adaptation to the world'.[8] Far from disengaging with reality, the fantasy/daydream is 'an imaginative story or internal dialogue that . . . transcribes our hopes'.[9] This is certainly true of the novels this chapter highlights. Moreover, although they may conform to the stereotypes of breathy romantic fiction and be deemed 'light reading', such novels, in providing encouragement in the face of loss and uncertainty, were, in effect, vehicles for the dissemination of patriotic ideals and models of appropriate wartime behaviour.

All their heroines are virtuous, all their heroes manly. The heroes are manly even when and—it can be argued—*because* they are wounded. In fact, wounds are actually sought, not so much because they represent the 'blighty' that will take them home and permanently out of the War, but because they are badges of honour: 'the receipt, stamped and signed upon their bodies, from God and their country'.[10] With the ever-increasing numbers of war wounded, it was essential that the attitudes attached to physical disability and disfigurement be refashioned, at least for those injured in war. Although civilian disablement (either from birth or accident) continued to be stigmatized, 'the wartime mutilated were regarded as the responsibility of the nation'.[11] Lost limbs, blinded eyes, wounds

[8] Anthony Storr, *Freud* (Oxford, 1989), 83.

[9] Ethel S. Person, *The Force of Fantasy: Its Roles, Its Benefits and What It Reveals about Our Lives* (London, 1997), 7. For a discussion on the importance of fantasy in the Great War writings of Ford Madox Ford, Rudyard Kipling, and HD, see Trudi Tate, *Modernism, History and the First World War* (Manchester, 1998).

[10] Robert Valentine Dolbey, *A Regimental Surgeon in War and Prison* (London, 1917), 246.

[11] Joanna Bourke, *Dismembering the Male: Men's Bodies, Britain and the Great War* (London, 1996), 41.

'in a mentionable place', to quote Sassoon, were lauded. Novelists went out of their way to show that the loss of a limb was no bar to manly/sexual performance. Wounds, which were increasingly visible in everyday life, became increasingly normalized in popular fiction.

The *character* imperfections of the heroes and heroines in these novels serve to make them more human and therefore more identifiable to the reader. In fact, the reader is often more aware of their flaws and how to resolve them than the characters. This is intentional, for what Kate Flint argues is true for the woman reader of sensation novels is also true for the woman reader of Great War romantic fiction: she 'is habitually acknowledged as possessing a wider, more subtle interpretative system than that granted to the heroine. The ability to read literature carefully is equated . . . with the ability to read life'.[12] So in addition to imparting patriotic values, these novels also encourage the reader to cultivate her own discerning taste and morality. She may choose similarly to the heroine, but at the same time she anticipates the pitfalls her fictional alter ego does not. She may feel superior. The choices made by the characters in the novels are meant to parallel the choices made by the reader in everyday life, choices made for love and for their country, both of which should be determined by their patriotism.

Values, therefore, are blatantly obvious; very little in these novels is left to interpretive chance. Even the dust jackets contribute to the implicit messages the prose communicates. There is a clear moral component in every novel that

> generally accrues round the narrative elements of False and Revised Perception; it has to do with not judging by appearances, with 'trying to understand', with your responsibility to others, with seeing where your duty and your happiness lie. The moral message goes step by step with the narrative structure, and is never challenged, as far as the reader is concerned, by any ambivalent or conflicting circumstance in the fable.[13]

The high-minded moral message is explored and communicated by equally high-minded and 'traditional moral language'.[14] The stories are littered with Biblical references, literary allusions, and patriotic cliché, but their writers also employ more technical

[12] Kate Flint, *The Woman Reader, 1837–1914* (Oxford, 1993), 293.

[13] Walter Nash, *Language in Popular Fiction* (London, 1990), 12.

[14] Paul Fussell, *The Great War and Modern Memory* (London, 1975), 23.

'lexical-semantic devices', such as 'upgrading' and 'agent-shift'. Upgrading can apply to situations where the novelist rejects the basic vocabulary, such as the verb 'go', for the more specific or stronger word, such as 'dash'. It can also involve the inclusion of metaphor to aid a more emphatic or forceful expression. 'Emotions' become 'whirlwinds', for instance. Agent-shift 'occurs when the apparent agent in the clause—commonly the referent of the grammatical subject—is either non-animate or is part of the human body': panic throttled her; a clamour of desire rose in her, destroying her cool control.[15] These elements help to create the characteristic tone of romantic fiction and become even more highly charged when coupled with the 'great romance' that is the War. A mystery—usually involving a spy whose pro-German, and therefore 'evil', plans of sabotage and destruction must be thwarted—often complicates the love story. The novels follow what Vladimir Propp identified in the 1920s as the underlying trajectory of fairy tales in which the hero embarks on a quest, encounters obstacles to his progress, overcomes these impediments, is transfigured by his experiences, and ultimately generates the story's happy ending.[16] The working out of the mystery and/or the transformation of hero or heroine brings order to where there was chaos. In the same sense, the love story acted as 'a life-enhancing counterpoint to the brutalities and degradations of war. . . . Romantic love seemed to offer both soldiers and civilians some continuity and order to their lives.'[17]

Popular or middlebrow fiction stressed tradition and links with the past in direct opposition to the fragmentation and discord expounded by the avant-garde and modernist writers.[18] In fact, such *non*-traditional movements are criticized both implicitly and explicitly by the books I shall consider. All the novels share the eugenic anxieties about physical, mental, and spiritual deterioration, highlighted in Chapter 1, that emerged in Britain towards the end of the nineteenth century. If society was suffering from a 'degenerative'

[15] Nash, *Language in Popular Fiction*, 48–9.

[16] Vladimir Propp, 'Fairy Tale Transformations', in *Readings in Russian Poetics*, trans. Ladislav Matejka and Krystyna Pomorska (Cambridge, Mass., 1971); and *idem*, *The Theory and History of Folklore*, trans. Adriana Y. Martin and Richard P. Martin (Minneapolis, 1984).

[17] Sharon Ouditt, *Fighting Forces, Writing Women: Identity and Ideology in the First World War* (London, 1994), 89.

[18] Rosa Maria Bracco, *Merchants of Hope: British Middlebrow Writers and the First World War, 1919–1939* (Providence, 1993), 18.

disease, 'a falling-off from original purity, a reversion to less complex forms of structure',[19] then war was a means of regeneration and purification. It was a eugenic *good*. The 'conservative polemic of popular fiction'[20] had a number of 'unfit' targets. Among them were exotic and erotic artistic tastes such as aestheticism and *art nouveau*. A further threat to both men and women was the suffrage movement. It was blamed for desexing women, encouraging them to become pseudo-men, and causing them to lose all touch with their 'true' feminine natures. Such were the ideas that abounded in the press and various sections of society.

That there was actually a cohesive set of values is a 'myth': 'the arguments in this polemical war were various and by no means consistent with each other: the attackers shared only a general sense of who their enemies were.'[21] Class differences were often glossed over by novelists, but the values to which they ascribed themselves and lauded in their writing were solidly middle class. The heroines in these books are primarily of genteel upbringing. When women of the working classes are portrayed, they are lauded for their 'pluckiness' and 'down-to-earth' outlooks, like Emma Brown. Whatever their class, however, women are never shrinking violets; they must draw on hitherto unused reserves of strength and courage to see them through the hardships presented by the War. Like the nurses who will be discussed later, they are made 'better women' in the end, for 'the war is presented as a test, which assures the permanence of womanly values, rather than as an agent for their disruption'.[22]

Florence Barclay's novel, *My Heart's Right There* (1914), bears all the hallmarks of a patriotic romance in both its physical form and its narrative (Fig. 10). It describes the first few months of the War as they affect the life of a young couple, Jim and Polly. A slim book, its deep purple cover is embossed with the Union Jack on an oval shield, the title and author's name stamped above and below in gold. Contemporary readers would have recognized the flag-emblazoned shield as that held by the seated Britannia on every penny piece in their purse.

[19] David Trotter, *The English Novel in History, 1895–1920* (London, 1993), 111.
[20] Ibid., 118.
[21] Samuel Hynes, *A War Imagined: The First World War and English Culture* (London, 1990), 59.
[22] Ouditt, *Fighting Forces, Writing Women*, 90.

FIG. 10. *My Heart's Right There* (1914) by Florence Barclay, embossed cover

The title of this short novel would also have been familiar to any of its wartime readers, taken as it is from the song *Tipperary*, which quickly became one of the most popular marching tunes and an anthem for departing soldiers. On the title page, Barclay includes the musical notes to assert the associations with this resonant song and, at different places throughout the text, repeats the titular phrase. A characteristic feature of the novel is Barclay's tendency to diverge from the specific storyline to give a general appraisal (sometimes two or three paragraphs long) of the causes and implications of the War.

First published in December 1914, *My Heart's Right There* is dedicated 'to our men at the front', and must have been written in haste soon after the outbreak of war. The *Times Literary Supplement* commented that Barclay, well known for her earlier novel *The Rosary*, 'has poured her usual full draughts of highly sweetened sentiment' into this 'tale of home and family life of a soldier at the front in the present war'.[23] Her message is unambiguous: be steadfast in the face of all suffering and sacrifice; the War is a righteous one. Her hero is Jim, a 'stalwart soldier who, having passed unscathed through the South African War and a long term of foreign service, had returned . . . faithful, and eager for banns', and his wife, Polly, a wholesome beauty and a former nurse-maid to a cleric's family.[24] The 'heart' of the novel centres on Jim's wounding at the Front and his return home. Such a scenario provides Barclay with ample opportunity to discuss morality, duty, and sacrifice.

Men and women have clear roles to fulfil. We are told that, before the War, Jim would not allow Polly to go out to work, saying, '"I shouldn't have married you, if I hadn't known I could keep you, without you lending a hand. Your work's in the home"' (13). Both as a soldier in 'the Eastern desert' and as a working man in England, he agrees with the song, 'Be it ever so humble, there's no place like home.' His description of coming back to an empty house recalls a familiar anti-suffrage postcard entitled, 'The Home of a Suffragette', in which a man sits slumped at a messy table, his head in his hands while a baby wails on the floor amidst clutter and dirt:

[23] *Times Literary Supplement*, 10 December 1914.

[24] Florence L. Barclay, *My Heart's Right There* (London, 1914), 8. Numbers in parentheses throughout the text refer to pages in the cited editions.

'suppose I came home from work and up the garden path, tired and glad, and found the house dark, the door locked and the key gone. And suppose the neighbours called to me: "Your wife ain't back from work, yet." What sort of a "no place like home" would that be, d'you think? That's the kind of thing that drives a man to turn and look for lights and welcome, where they keep open house.' (14)

Women going out to work, then, led to moral decline—'lights', 'welcome', and 'open house' denote pubs and brothels, and therefore, sins of an intemperate or sexual nature. Like the Victorian Angel in the House, Polly can only assert her moral force within the home. Her dependence, however, is presented as a service of 'perfect freedom' not unlike a Christian's devotion.[25]

In addition, women learn much of their wisdom from their men. Just after their marriage, Polly muses how, 'in one short week, her soldier-man had taught her many wonderful things' (10). A love-match, she says, is a 'safety-match' because 'it makes a woman feel safer than she ever thought to feel, in this world of ups-and-downs'. Virtuous Polly keeps an ideal home, which is clean to the point of sparkling; she is a good cook; and a patient, loving mother to her daughter, Tiny.

This model of domestic bliss has important implications for the events to come. It provides the stability that survives the upheaval of war: 'just before Tiny's third birthday—the senseless demoniacal ambition of one man decreed that peace and prosperity should be things of the past, in tens of thousands of happy homes' (15). Using a Biblical scenario, the cadences of a sermon and propagandistic rhetoric, Barclay provides a scathing condemnation of Wilhelm II:

Ambition Incarnate led the Kaiser striding to the summit of the Mount of Imagination—that 'exceeding high mountain' from which can be seen 'all the kingdoms of the world and the glory of them.' The Tempter of men then whispered in the Imperial ear: 'All these things I give thee . . . if thou wilt fall down and worship me.'

Unlike that Kingly One, long centuries before, Whose right was world-wide sovereignty, yet Whose answer was to choose the lowly place of obedience and of service—the Kaiser fell down and worshipped; the ministering angels of Love, Joy, and Peace, veiled their faces and fled away; the Devil entered into him, and set Europe in a blaze. (15–16)

[25] Bridget Fowler, *The Alienated Reader: Women's Popular Romantic Literature in the Twentieth Century* (New York and London, 1991), 8.

This is one of a number of instances where Barclay diverges from the specific storyline to give a general appraisal of what the War means, but in Biblical typology that obscures historical reality and analysis. Joseph Hocking, a minister as well as an author, frequently used such language in his novels set during the War. In *All for a Scrap of Paper*, for instance, Bob Nancarrow eschews his Quaker principles to join the army because the Germans have twisted the religious message: they see 'war as the faith of the nation'. Bob enlists declaring '"It's service for Christ!"'[26] Just as Bob Nancarrow is Hocking's exemplar of the righteous Christian, Polly and Jim are Barclay's exemplar of the perfect British couple; their story is applicable to many, even if real people could not live up to the sanctity displayed by the protagonists. In fact, this kind of story is meant to

> take [the reader] out of [herself] by confirming an idealized self-image. Thus, the protagonists of formulaic literature are typically better or more fortunate in some ways than ourselves. They are heroes who have the strength and courage to overcome great dangers, lovers who find their perfectly suited partners.... Formulaic literature is generally characterised by a simple and emotionally charged style that encourages immediate involvement in a character's actions without much sense of complex irony or psychological subtlety.[27]

Barclay's patriotic purpose is certainly transparent, for elsewhere, Jim's example is a springboard for celebrating the average British Tommy and the 'noble part [he is] playing in the making, to-day, of history for all time'. What is most endearing, she says, is that these men 'do not know they are heroes; [they] daily do fine deeds, without for a moment dreaming that their deeds are fine' (19). Such self-effacement and modesty are key characteristics of the average soldier, as the memoirs discussed later highlight especially.

War also makes civilians reassess their outlook on life: 'Hitherto we have been too selfish, too self-centred' (25). The all-encompassing tragedy has meant that 'national life' and the 'needs of others' are becoming priorities. History is a teleological force. God is working out His purpose: 'the eternal good which is going to work out from this apparently intolerable evil' (25). No hint of disillusion

[26] Hocking, *All for a Scrap of Paper*, 137.

[27] John G. Cawelti, *Adventure, Mystery, and Romance: Formula Stories as Art and Popular Culture* (Chicago and London, 1976), 18.

is allowed to creep into this novel. Barclay goes on for another three paragraphs (in a book of only 61 pages) in equally melodramatic language about how the thoughts of 'our brave men in the trenches' must not 'depress us'; that to 'yield to overwhelming sorrow' is useless 'to win back the crown of joy'; and that 'earnest sympathy should make us bright and brave' (25).

This is the lesson that Polly must learn when she welcomes home her wounded 'soldier-man'. She first learns of his fate in a letter written from a convalescent hospital in England. Wounded not once but twice (a familiar badge of the hero of Great War romance novels)—he has been bayoneted in the shoulder by a German and hit in the leg by shrapnel—Jim sings the praises of the nurses who care for him, while longing to 'come limping home to my own dear girl' (31). He describes how he represents to the Sisters 'the entire British Army': '"While they're doing me, they're thinking of all the other chaps, still fighting in the trenches, or lying helpless and wounded on the battlefields. Ay, and some of them are thinking of quiet graves, left behind . . . of lips under the sod, they'll never kiss again"'(30).

He is equally effusive about a visit from the King and Queen. Tired and worn, he wakes from a stupor to see them 'looking down at me'. George and Mary are portrayed as kindly grandparents, asking questions about his home and his family:

> 'Polly—it's one thing to read in print on a placard, YOUR KING AND YOUR COUNTRY WANT YOU; and quite another thing to hear it from himself, as man to man, so to speak—straight from him to you.
>
> 'After They had gone, though I hadn't been able before to do much more than whisper, I felt as if I must lie and shout "God Save the King" right through, from beginning to end. And I wanted to be up and out at the Front again, to start "scattering his enemies," right away. Then, all of a sudden, I found myself up on my elbow, laughing and cheering and singing, in a shaky kind of voice: "See how they run! See how they run!"' (35–6)

The sovereign is thus conflated with God by the capitalizing of 'They' and the use of the Biblical phrase 'scattering his enemies' (*Numbers* 10:35 and *Psalms* 68:1).

Polly's pride in Jim's wounds for King and Country still cannot prepare her for the first sight of her returning husband: 'she had known his left arm would be in a sling; she had known he would limp when he came up the garden path. But she had not expected him to be so gaunt and worn' (42). It was already becoming common to describe the men from the Front as having what Kate Finzi, in her memoir, discussed later, would call 'the trench-haunted look'. Not only is Jim 'gaunt and worn', but he has a brooding countenance, 'a look in his sunken eyes which suddenly told Polly more about what battles really mean, than anything she had read in the papers, or gathered from his letters' (42). The written word, therefore, is not the best source. Seeing the reality for oneself is what communicates the truth. Barclay may be said to be implicitly commenting on her own profession as a novelist—she too is incapable of truly communicating the reality of what soldiers have been through. She admits a certain inadequacy, that seeing is believing: until you have been there, you cannot know. Whereas she may be admitting her own inadequacy as a writer, as a woman and a non-combatant, Barclay carves out a particular niche for Polly, rather than condemning her or castigating her through Jim. Polly's perspective, her imaginative picture of the 'reality' of war can be said to represent that of most British women at this time. Images of 'forced marches, hard fighting, days and nights in the trenches' brought on by the thought of Jim in his 'stained worn suit of khaki' become less romantic when confronted with the living example. It further reinforces Polly's (and other civilians') exclusion from the experience of war. Her isolation 'almost made her afraid of her soldier-man. And yet he was so much to her; she could not bear that any thought of his should be beyond her sharing' (46). Jim, reluctant to speak of the trenches, explains to her why she—and every other woman—cannot possibly understand:

> 'there are things in these past weeks which a man can't speak of to anybody at home—least of all to the woman he loves best. He could only speak of them to the chaps who've been with him in the trenches, who've marched through the ruined villages, who've seen—God help them!—what he has seen; who know what he knows. You would have cause never to forgive me—I should never forgive myself—if, to ease my own mind by sharing them, I passed on to you the ghastly things I've been forced to know and to see, away where the Devil has been let loose to work his will on defenseless women, and on little children'. (48)

This highlights a particularly crucial point about the so-called ignorance of the home front. Although it is true that many men were *unable* to put into words the extremity of what they had experienced, it is also true that many were *unwilling* to describe events that would have further worried or frightened their loved ones. Whereas Owen and Sassoon wanted to disabuse the public of their ignorance through graphic representations of the horrors of warfare, there were those who were reluctant to pass on the 'ghastly things' they had seen. In isolating them even from the tales of war, Barclay places women in an altogether separate sphere, but one that carries its own particular duties: letting the men go and keeping the home fires burning. Polly stands for the antithesis of all that is ghastly, horrible, filthy, and deadly, and exemplifies the kind of world the men are fighting to protect. The closing paragraphs elide the ideas and tropes of romantic fiction with patriotic rhetoric:

> He put his arm around her, and caught her to his breast.
>
> 'Oh, Polly,' he said; 'it's for King and Country and Home!'
>
> Polly held him close. She knew she must let him go again; she meant to be brave about letting him go. But, anyway she had him now.
>
> Then she remembered the first part of his prayer: 'If I am called upon to die, let it be a bullet through my heart, swift and clean.' Ah, thank God, it had not been that! She slipped her hand under the sling, and laid it on his breast. She could feel the steady beat, beneath her palm. . . .
>
> 'Yes, Polly,' he said; 'there's no doubt at all about it. "My heart's right there!"' (60)

This intimate moment is intended to be both touching and symbolic. The passage asserts that Jim's heart is unscathed not only by bullets or unfaithfulness but is untouched by disillusion and remains true to the patriotic trinity of King, Country, and Home. As with the other novels discussed in this chapter, Barclay's book 'reveals the reality and the strength of the resistance against an ironic interpretation of the war'.[28]

Effusive patriotism is also an overriding feature of *Khaki and Kisses* (1915) by Berta Ruck. A heart dominates the centre of the paperback's khaki-coloured cover (Fig. 11). Inside the heart is an illustration of a blonde woman in a powder-blue dress holding a pink rose. She is held in the embrace of a dark-haired man in uniform. It is an image that is, even today in romance novels, touted as the fantasy of every woman—a tall, dark, handsome, manly man (manly by virtue of his soldier uniform). The cover description says that the book contains

[28] Bracco, *Merchants of Hope*, 3.

FIG. 11. *Khaki and Kisses* (1915) by Berta Ruck, cover illustration (25611 e.4561), Bodleian Library, University of Oxford

A series of delightful love stories closely associated with the Great War. On the reverse side of this—the greatest tragedy of all time—is comedy to be found which this work faithfully portrays.[29]

The stories, however, are not just simple tales of love set against a backdrop of war. Like Barclay's novel, they contain explicit lessons about the role of women and appropriate feminine behaviour. Moreover, *Khaki and Kisses* says a great deal about avant-garde artists, militant suffragettes, slackers, Germans, and soldiers' sweethearts. In fulsome language, each story reproduces stereotypes that assert the particular propagandistic theme. The prose is often punctuated by exclamation points as characters parade their beliefs in sermon-like fashion. Imagery is blatant. Subtlety is not a hallmark of *Khaki and Kisses*.

The opening tale, 'Infant in Arms', depicts the transformation of 'She' from flippant coquette to serious lady, and 'He' from feeble artist to heroic soldier. Obsessive concerns about degenerate youth permeate the story, particularly in relation to the 'hero'. Neither character is given a specific name other than 'He' or 'She', as if to reinforce the idea that they could be any man or woman in Britain at the time—any middle- or upper-class man or woman, that is. The first part opens at a party in June 1914, a glittering scene of 'men and women in fantastic costumes—Harlequins, Nautch-girls, Vorticist Princesses, Futurist Follies, Caliphs à la Bakst'.[30] Facets of the avant-garde, and Vorticism in particular, were labelled 'Junkerist' by some conservative elements in society for what they saw as Prussian—and therefore, ominous—influence.[31] A similar threat appears in the sinister figure of a German waiter who lurks in the

[29] 'Delightful' was a common epithet for Ruck's fiction. Her series, 'The Years for Rachel', ran in Annie S. Swan's magazine *Woman at Home* during the latter half of 1918 and is lauded as 'our delightful new serial' that 'deals in Miss Ruck's perfectly charming manner with a question that is always interesting, from whatever standpoint we view it'. An advertisement announcing the first instalment contains a photograph of Ruck with her two little sons (both dressed in sailor suits) and declares that 'the reader who does not like Berta Ruck's stories does not exist. Publishers and editors clamour for anything from her clever pen, so that your Editor thinks she is very lucky indeed to have secured "The Years for Rachel." Order your copy of next month's number *now*, or you may not be able to secure one. Owing to paper shortage the number cannot be reprinted' (*Woman at Home*, edited by Annie S. Swan (April 1918), 236).

[30] Berta Ruck, *Khaki and Kisses* (London, 1915), 7.

[31] Hynes, *A War Imagined*, 63.

background at this 'unconventional theatrical Costume-Ball'. The German waiter/spy was a familiar trope in the fiction of the early 1900s and Ruck's minor character would have immediately sent alarm bells ringing in the minds of her readers.[32] Her costume party—like her characters—are meant to be symbols of a national disease, 'part of the brief, grotesque phase in English History when dancing and masquerading seemed affairs of national importance' (8).

'She' is dressed as Nijinsky's Spectre de la Rose, 'He' as a Black Panther. The sexual overtones are obvious. The waltz in which they take part is more like a risqué tango with the couple 'moving together with a voluptuous swing and zest' (9). Their movements are alluring, seductive, immodest. Under the decadent modern influences, seemly behaviour is flung aside. Even more shocking is the charade of sexual activity in which She is the dominant partner. In what might be seen as an attempt on his part to 'make an honest woman' out of her, He proposes marriage, shyly, with reticence, in a pleading fashion. She refuses even to 'care a little', saying that she will eventually marry, not for love and commitment, but 'for frocks and a setting, and that sort of thing' (10). She has a rebellious, cold modernity with more concern for show and glamour than affection as

> they walk up and down; black, graceful, free-limbed, silhouette against the frieze of the sighing willows and the star-spangled sky, leaving a trail of cigarette smoke (hers) and a deep-voiced mutter of appeal (his) upon the night-breeze (9).

The romantic beauty of their shadows and the summer evening are set against the inversion of gender stereotypes: *she* smokes, *he*

[32] Trotter, *English Novel in History*, 168. See also Panikos Panayi's *The Enemy in Our Midst: Germans in Britain during the First World War* (Oxford, 1991), which analyses the paranoia and anti-German sentiment in the years preceding the outbreak. Waiters were especially singled-out, perhaps due to their large numbers in the capital: in 1911, Germans made up approximately 10% of waiters and waitresses in restaurants in London, at a time when Germans made up only 25% of the population of England and Wales (Panayi, 25). 'The Hun invasion would be facilitated, so the stories went, by thousands of German bakers, barbers, and waiters who were quietly awaiting the opportunity to assist the Fatherland.... Stories circulated about German waiters and butchers poisoning food, German watchmakers constructing bombs, German barbers cutting customers' throats' (Gerard J. DeGroot, *Blighty: British Society in the Era of the Great War* (London and New York, 1996), 191).

appeals. To her, He is a child, feeble, and 'predictable', which She claims is 'fatal' to a woman's opinion of a suitor:

'I look upon you as such a baby. You and your sculpturing! It *is* just like a baby with its box of bricks. Yes; one couldn't look upon you as a *man*. I tell you what you are. You're just an infant-in-arms. A girl can't want to marry a man when she *knows* she knows much more than he does! Sorry. Sorry for myself, too. It would be more amusing for me if I weren't too wide-awake, too spoilt, too sophisticated to fall in love! But I am'. (10)

Although there is scorn for her spoilt sophistication, it is He that is most culpable. If He were only strong-willed, assertive, and dominant, not taken in by the insipidity of the avant-garde, She would not feel so spoilt. The modernist world has encouraged men to be shades of Wildean aesthetes, just as it has encouraged an unnatural interest in sex and sophistication in women. Such corruption of Britain's youth has consequences for future generations: her declaration that '"Infant, that makes a woman utterly impregnable. *Not in the* mood!"' suggests that the procreation of the race may be in doubt. The male writer F. Frankfort Moore makes a similar comment on women's assertiveness. The heroine of his novel *The Romance of a Red Cross Hospital* (1915), Angela Inman, is respected in her community but

She was a little too confident in the accuracy of her judgments.

As a matter of fact, she would have been more universally liked if she had been more frequently astray; and that is only another way of saying that she would have been accounted more womanly. Stern accuracy of judgment is not esteemed as a womanly trait by men. It is not that men regard it as an exclusively masculine trait; it is simply that men know perfectly well that, if it became universal in women, men would have a poor chance with them. Men know there's no use wooing a woman who can see through them. They know that the flexible feminine judgment is their best friend; so they call it womanliness and love it.[33]

For Ruck the War begins before such nonsense can take a firm hold. The story switches to the spring of 1915, and a better London has bloomed as a result, showing what England is really made of:

London's gayest finery of lilac and laburnum seems put on in special honour of the khaki boys that throng her streets; London's sons departing for the Front, or returning, snatching a few days' leave from the trenches. For the soil

[33] F. Frankfort Moore, *The Romance of a Red Cross Hospital* (London, 1915), 21.

of slackness that produced those gay and bizarre blossoms of decadence has not proved so deep after all; there was British bed-rock beneath it! (11)

The artificial decoration of the summer party is transformed into a scene of natural goodness. The blossoms of decadence seem limp in comparison with the solid, gritty elements of soil and bed-rock. Fecundity and 'manhood' in every sense have been restored.

Transformed, too, is our heroine. We see her on her way to hospital, this time not in teasing 'Nijinsky rig' but a sensible 'long, belted coat'. He, in hospital, is also different. Gone is the Black Panther costume as he lies under a 'black panther rug', drained, but (of course) still handsome: 'He was a dilettante sculptor once, but looks a thorough soldier now. He answered the Call to Arms at the beginning of the War; gained his commission and lost his leg at Ypres' (12). This simple profit-and-loss account expresses little pity for the casualty because the loss of a limb becomes the sign of his manhood, the evidence that He is no longer an aesthete.

As he tells his tale to her, the reader realizes that the German sniper who wounds him is actually the waiter seen lurking at the costume party. The Prussian threat to un-man the nation, physically and militarily, seems to have been carried out, but tragedy is transformed:

She looks at him and her heart swells with pride for him. It sinks with shame for herself. And she had thought herself so much wiser, so much better than the infatuated boy at whom she laughed—What folly! . . . A new thrill runs through her. She had thought herself 'sophisticated' out of that. But again she thrills, glowing and shy at the thought of what had left her flippant and indifferent last year. Can it be that this War, which has cut all life in half for our nation, has worked another miracle in her? (13)

She is put in her place, but 'thrills' at such an outcome. The war is seen as a miracle, as something positive, even when—and perhaps because—it has 'cut all life in half for our nation'. She rejoices in his wounding because it proves that He risked his life in manly pursuit for the good of the Empire and the nation.

He has, it seems, regained his manhood in another way. Whereas before he only appealed for a kiss, Ruck records that there is 'an uneasy movement under the panther rug'. We are left to speculate what this might be, for although it could be a spasm of the stump of his amputated limb, the sexual overtones are present nonetheless: He might be missing a leg, but he is not emasculated. She parries his concerns that He is simply the object of her pity:

> The radiant, kneeling girl beside him laughs and sobs together. 'Oh, can't you understand that this has made everything different? You're just twice as much of a man, now that you'll have to get on with one leg, as you were when you were dancing and fooling about on two! As for me, I'm not even a woman unless you'll help make me one.' (15)

Her physically subservient position (kneeling) and her gushing sentiments about womanhood make Ruck's theme clear: the social order and future of the nation are based upon men as the masculine defenders and women as yielding, mothering partners. The War has transformed this once avant-garde couple into perfect models of romance. They have been purified. 'He' was parading, 'fooling about', as a man before, dressed-up as a war-like brave animal, wearing a pelt. Now, because he has been a soldier, and sacrificed a limb in the process, he does not have to dress up. Like his contemporaries, the bed-rock manhood (in every sense of the term) was there underneath the aesthete all the time. 'She', too, has been purified, not only of a flippant outlook but also of an unseemly, teasing sexuality.

In many ways, however, their roles have not really changed. His handicap means that, in some ways, He is still the infant in arms of the title. She remains the physically dominant partner: mother to his infantilized state. However, as Ruck seems to want to make clear, She surrenders her sophistication, and 'wide-awake' outlook to his guidance. He will make her a woman, and in that sense, She becomes the infant in arms. They each have a master–child role to play.

The same is even more blatantly expounded in the story 'Wanted—A Master'. The title, again, plays a dual role: to whom does it refer? Is it the dog, named Sydney, owned by a soldier going to the Front, or is it the heroine, also named Sydney, who answers the advertisement to look after the pet? Both have masculine-sounding names, but they are spelt in the feminine way; both human and animal are females who act like males.

Sydney Ellerton, the heroine, was once 'aggressive' and every man was her enemy for she had been 'the most uncompromising Militant Suffragette who ever embittered the life of a policeman—or of a politician'. In time of war, however,

> it all seemed very long ago and trivial now. In these days Sydney grudged every penny of the money that she had once thrown recklessly away on subscriptions to The Cause, and on petroleum and pamphlets and other

inflammatory propaganda, for now her small independent income was being stretched to the uttermost to help a Belgian orphan. (205)

The suffragette becomes reformed and, even as a single woman, performs a mothering role by sponsoring a child. The War has clarified her values, and shown her the error of her aggressive ways and her political pretensions. The romantic tale becomes another propaganda tract, this time against Votes for Women, for although the Pankhursts and their supporters transferred their energies from working for the franchise to canvassing for enlistment, they did so only temporarily—'for the duration'. Ruck's heroine completely changes her political outlook.

Once the dog's owner gets over his amazement that Sydney Ellerton is a woman, he recognizes her from a suffragette rally where she had berated him in his pre-war occupation as an MP opposed to the female franchise. Sydney herself admits that she was the activist who set his house on fire, burning it to the ground. He takes this information with amazing composure, forgiving her and saying, in much the same way as 'His' loss of a limb is recorded, that the house had nothing of value in it: '"This war seems to show one which are the things one really does care about—which are things that count"' (209). Sydney has realized this as well, but as she renounces her militant past, calling it 'criminally silly' and adding that '"it was wrong even to try and merge the differences between women's work—and yours"', she does not actually blame women but *men*:

'don't you understand, in those days one didn't particularly see any point in the average man, as such. Why should we? Did he appear particularly intelligent? No. Was there anything particular which he did, in everyday civilian life, that one didn't feel a woman couldn't or might do as well? No.

'All those lady-like young men who used to sit about on lawns and settees, prattling about Art and Socialism, and Russian Operas and Politics, what had they done to deserve the Franchise? What had they, in short, done? Nothing! except make girls with healthy brains and healthy instincts into Suffragettes,' declared Sydney, only half-laughing. 'How could one help despising them—as they were? It was those slackers who made us lose all sense of proportion. But now these same people are working as Territorials and enlisting as Kitchener's men and making brilliant charges, as the London Scottish, and one feels so different about them!

'It's taken war, and the sight of man doing a man's old job as a woman's protector, to put all these things in the right places.' (210)

Delivered as if she were on a podium at a suffrage rally, Sydney's speech makes clear what Ruck means by the 'natural' roles of men and women. Women want to be manly because men have failed to be men, preferring instead to be effeminate—perhaps homosexual—artists and slackers of duty. The health of the minds and the bodies of young women has been adversely affected by the kind of contamination associated with such degeneracy. Women must pick up the pieces, but it is unnatural for them to do so. This contradicts the argument made by some feminist critics that women desired a gender inversion and revelled in the chances to become pseudo-men.[34] Even those who did not become involved in the war effort, but worked for peace, called upon the feminine and, as they saw it, less-warlike side of women's nature to lead in the movement for an end to fighting and for a conciliatory future.[35] For Ruck, the War, which combatants and rescue workers alike described as chaos, is actually a stabilizing force for the real chaos—a gender inversion—at home.

Not only have gender roles become confused, but also moral and social values. In the story 'P.P.C.', contempt for the intellectual circle of 'Camford' is encouraged, especially Evadne and her donnish father, to whom 'all wars and violence and soldiering were distasteful' (82). They are 'roused at last' but for the wrong reasons:

> Not by the cutting up of our glorious Cavalry in the early days of this War. Not by the sacrifice of the countless young and promising lives that might have been saved if England, for the last ten years, had been preparing the Army that was needed. Not these thoughts had converted them to War; but the thoughts of ruined architecture and of smashed stained-glass. They had wept tears of anger—over cathedrals. (82)

Ruck dramatically enhances their folly first by listing 'appropriate' reasons to be 'roused' and then by isolating the intellectuals' motivation from the end of an archaically phrased sentence, 'Not these thoughts'. The rhetorical suspension of 'over cathedrals' reinforces the intended satire and irony.

[34] Sandra Gilbert and Susan Gubar, 'Soldier's Heart', in *No Man's Land: The Place of the Woman Writer in the Twentieth Century*, vol. 2 (New Haven and London, 1989), 258–323.

[35] C. K. Ogden and Mary Sargant Florence, *Militarism vs. Feminism* (London, 1915).

It is, of course, assumed that the reader will automatically recognize the absurdity of the artists and intellectuals Ruck portrays. The reader—most probably a woman—is in on the joke. She laughs with Ruck at the pretensions of these unpatriotic and misguided classes, and she can flatter herself akin to the reformed individuals or to the characters held up as heroines. It is hoped, for instance, that the reader will identify with the indignant nurse in the story, 'Tommy Doll'. She is employed by Ruck's *bêtes noires*, the eccentric artists, to look after their son, Hilary (an androgynous name suggestive of gender confusion). The mother will not let him have a Tommy Doll because she believes it will make militaristic 'impressions' on him. Equally, she insists on dressing him in 'Peter Pan suits' rather than 'little man o' war' outfits he prefers. His Nurse is the daughter of a soldier and 'agreed with Kipling that the army was the Lordliest Life on Earth' (54). She becomes increasingly incensed with her employers' attitudes, especially after the outbreak of war. They claim that it is '"Really too frightful!—it's *fantastic*!.... That we should be actually *fighting* an intellectual, civilized cultured sister-nation like Germany!"' (57). Nurse's assertion that the Germans 'have been preparing for it for years and years' is met with incredulity, and scorn is poured on 'brainless Army type[s]' and those 'militarists' who supported 'National Service or whatever it was'. Nurse controls her anger outwardly, but the reader is let in on her (violent) thoughts:

> But for what *that* brainless type is doing now, your own 'brains' would be getting spattered at this moment over all these Morris wallpapers of yours! And it's people of your type who shut their eyes to the danger, and who wouldn't prepare—it's you principally, that we've got to thank for our unreadiness for the War! It's you—*you* that were the alien enemy in our midst! (57)

Hilary eventually gets his Tommy Doll and Nurse meets her own Tommy in the Park, so the world is put to rights again, but not before Ruck has made a clear distinction between the patriot and the enemy-alien.

Other female characters make similar declarations that prove their 'correct' outlook. In 'The Eleventh-Hour Lover', a parlour maid berates the butcher's young man for not enlisting: '"*No gun, no girl*.... I'm rather *particular* about who I'm seen about with in time o'war! ... *no khaki, no kisses* ... That's *my* motto!"' (32). In the same story, the heroine Gladys tells her lover that she will not hold him back from his duty and, pleading asks '"Oh, Fred, you are *my* recruit for the Army, aren't you?"' (36). Angela Hart, in 'O.H.M.S.', responds with 'blushing' anger at the suggestion that the War should be stopped:

> 'Surely no one with a grain of manhood in him dreams of anything but a fight to the finish in this War? One comfort being only a woman these days is that one *can* walk about the streets without needing to feel sick with shame that one isn't carrying a rifle or wearing khaki!' (132)

Sybil Cory's indignation at men still in civilian clothes is defended in the story 'The War Film':

> Woman is accused of 'loving the uniform'. Why be ashamed of the fact? Whether consciously or not, her glance is held by something with an inner meaning scarcely ignoble. Does not the uniform seem to hide the shortcomings, the irritating 'little ways' and ugliness of the individual? Doesn't it merge him into a type with every fighter who was ever brave and chivalrous and enduring and handsome and all that a man should be? Doesn't it mean that upon every pair of shoulders in khaki or blue serge there has fallen some fold of the mantle of our Country's honour? (188)

In Ruck's scheme of things even Quakers, normally pacifist, do their duty, becoming soldiers 'in the face of everything that Nature intended for [them]' (259). Here natural instincts are resisted, which seems to contradict what has been asserted throughout *Khaki and Kisses*—namely, that men lean instinctively towards the martial way of life. However, what distinguishes such an individual is that he is not an artist, an intellectual, or a shirker, from a lack of commitment, but a 'man of Peace', one whose convictions are sincere and strong. He is not simply a seeker of pleasure like the pre-War 'He' of 'Infant in Arms' or Hilary's father in 'Tommy Doll'.

Berta Ruck continued to produce love stories in a similar patriotic vein in *The Girl at His Billet* (1916), *The Bridge of Kisses* (1917), and *The Land-Girl's Love Story* (1918). As many propagandists had done before her, she did not question the reality of killing, but used it to justify the cause. *Khaki and Kisses* cannot be claimed to be simply light entertainment. It is a didactic work and a strong piece of propaganda for the war effort directed specifically at women. While publishers must have catered to the public demand, as evidenced in Ruck's case by the citation of her previous success, 'so great was the demand for Berta Ruck's last novel, "His Official Fiancée", that ten editions were required, and this book bids fair to become equally popular', George Robb rightly notes that 'a popular work [by Berta Ruck] had a much wider readership than the work of a "serious" (critically respected) writer, such as H. G. Wells's *Mr Britling Sees it Through*.'[36] Chapter 2 has shown how commercial publishing houses were involved in the work of the government-sponsored propaganda machine. Ruck's publishers for *Khaki and Kisses*, Hutchinson, and her publisher for her later novels, Hodder & Stoughton, were two of the many purveyors of works for Wellington House. Although it is unlikely that Ruck herself had anything to do with official government propaganda, it is certainly true that her books fitted well into the national effort of reinforcing popular support for the War. She prescribes an acceptable code of behaviour for women counter to the trends of feminism, pacifism, the avant-garde, and intellectual elite that could undermine enlistment. Her heroines free men to do their task of fighting, extol masculinity, and rule out-of-order any questions as to the 'why' of the War.

Ruby M. Ayres's *Richard Chatterton, V.C.* (1915)[37] concentrates on one man's metamorphosis. The title is surely meant to call to mind the 'marvellous boy' poet Thomas Chatterton, who died young, a connection that heightens the novel's sense of a doomed but romantic—and quintessentially English—youth. The cover illustration shows a uniformed man crouching, alert in No Man's Land, the sky above him alight with shell-fire (Fig. 12). Over the picture is written 'A laggard in love, and a laggard in war. What did they give him his manhood for?', lines adapted from Lady Heron's Song about young Lochinvar in Walter Scott's *Marmion*.[38] In Ayres's novel, 'manhood' connotes virility and heroism.

Richard Chatterton's 'gift' of manhood is wasted because, when the novel opens, he is an effete lay-about: he spends his days at his club dozing, disturbed only by the marching of recruits in the

[36] George Robb, *British Culture and the First World War* (Basingstoke, 2002), 2.

[37] Numerous novels and memoirs published between 1914 and 1918 used the accolade 'V.C.' in their title. Ruby Ayres appears to have been the only woman amongst the male authors, who included R. W. Campbell, *Sergt. Spud Tamson, V.C.*; Escott Lynn, *Oliver Hastings, V.C.*; and John Alexander Steuart, *Cupid, V.C.*

[38] Walter Scott, *Marmion*, Canto V, *The Poetical Works of Walter Scott* (London, 1878), 103–4.

FIG. 12. *Richard Chatterton, V.C.* (1915) by Ruby M. Ayres, dustjacket illustration (25611 e.3974), Bodleian Library, University of Oxford

streets. The members of the club and Sonia, his fiancée, begin to berate him for his failure to enlist: 'he was a laggard—a weakling, content to stay at home while others cheerfully offered their lives in the sacred cause of freedom'.[39] Though less censorious, his friend Jardine, who represents the older generation, continually exclaims: '"If I were only twenty years younger!"' The idle, comfort-seeking 'slacker' was a familiar character in the work of both male and female popular novelists. When the pleasure-seeking Geoffrey Canavan in Joseph Keating's *Tipperary Tommy* (1915) decides to enlist because the War will provide him with the opportunity to make something of his 'worthless life', his equally idle friend who 'had the weak, white face of a poltroon' tells him, '"It makes me feel all greasy and crumpled to think about it."'[40] Those around Chatterton, however, only highlight his weakness. He is shown up in particular by Carter, his valet. Anxious to join the ranks, this young man has a recruiting poster ('Will they ever come?') pinned to his bedroom wall 'surmounted by a row of little flags' (20). Sonia echoes Ruck's heroines (and quite a number of war posters) in her enthusiasm for the War and in her complaint:

> 'Oh, if I were only a man! . . . Because if I were I shouldn't be here dressed up like a doll—idle, useless! Because if I were I shouldn't have to stay at home and let others go out and fight for me. Oh, how can they be content not to help—all those men who might so easily go?' (30)

Chatterton is her prime target. Her 'bitter disappointment and disillusion had beaten down her love—her pride in him' (28).

Though she wishes for an active role, Sonia's sentiments are seen as romantic enthusiasm for the War and do not go unchecked. Lady Merriman, her guardian, is realistic and insightful: 'she'd worship any man who came back wounded or disabled', and mocks Sonia's fervour as 'stuff and nonsense', saying: '"Take it from me, my dear, that mothers and sweethearts don't give a fig for the country when they hear that their sons and lovers have been butchered by those German savages"' (81). Although Lady Merriman has something to say about empty and idealistic patriotism, she expresses the prevalent belief that the Germans are evil.

[39] Ruby M. Ayres, *Richard Chatterton, V.C.* (London, 1915), 28. All extracts reprinted by permission of PFD on behalf of the Estate of Ruby M. Ayres. © Estate of Ruby M. Ayres [as printed in the original volume].

[40] Joseph Keating, *Tipperary Tommy: A Novel of the Great War* (London, 1915), 6.

When Sonia exclaims, '"I don't find the War at all depressing ... It's the most wonderful, greatest thing that's ever happened in all the world, I should think. I'm never tired of hearing about it and reading about it"' (126), Mr Courtenay, a young friend just returned from the Front, tells her:

'You wait until you've lost a friend or someone out there ... That'll make all the difference, Sonia. There doesn't seem anything very grand or wonderful about it when someone you've known all your life is finished off by a German bullet or killed by a gun' (126).

Courtenay presages the disillusion and the calls for a more realistic attitude to conflict that came to characterize post-war writing, but although he stresses how war is not 'very grand or wonderful', he believes it is still necessary. For Ayres and for others, awareness did not necessarily go hand-in-hand with cynicism or pacifism.

Disgusted with Chatterton, Sonia breaks off their engagement and becomes attached to Montague. Like Walter Scott's fair Ellen (Chatterton even thinks of Sonia in similar terms: 'her fair name' (276)), she nearly marries this 'dastard'. Lamed in a motoring accident, Montague is unable to enlist. Although his disability is the result of manly activity and allows him honourable exemption from fighting, it is not accorded the same status as the injury incurred by Ruck's hero in 'Infant in Arms' or Barclay's Jim, both of which result from the *supreme* manly pursuit of war. There is a hierarchy of disability: Montague has a 'picturesque lameness' not a heroic one. As a result, it seems, he gradually becomes a scheming antagonist, 'quite a nasty enemy' (334).

Attempting to throw off his derisive nickname 'laggard' with its particular wartime implications of slacker and coward, Richard Chatterton finally enlists, unbeknownst to Sonia. Once in uniform as a Tommy (he refuses to wait for a commission), he is a changed man. Like Ruck's transformed feeble artist, the donning of the soldier's uniform is the donning/dawning of manhood:

Where had his manhood been all these weeks that he had not rushed to do his bit in the fight against murder and militarism? He felt himself the veriest pigmy of a man, a coward of giant proportions. No wonder Sonia had despised him ...

After all, there was still something glorious in life, even though it were shorn of love; something glorious in the knowledge that he was at last one of the hundreds of thousands of men rushing out to swell that thin brown line of khaki which was all that would ultimately stand between Germany and the freedom of the Channel.

With a new pride and confidence in himself, Richard Chatterton squared his shoulders and lifted his head. They had called him a laggard—they had laughed at him, well, he would show them...

The fighting instinct had struggled uppermost at last through the enveloping slackness and inertia born of long years of indolence, and as eager and loyal a soldier as ever drew a sword in defence of King and Country walked proudly through London's dimly lit streets in the person of Richard Chatterton. (99)[41]

The jargon of Empire ('do his bit'; 'in defence of King and Country'), the rhetoric of degeneration debates ('the enveloping slackness and inertia born of long years of indolence'), and the clichés of schooldays fiction ('he would show them') all come into play in this passage. The repetition of phrases such as 'something glorious' in the second paragraph is a feature of Ayres's omniscient narration, particularly when she communicates the thoughts of her main characters. Richard and Sonia, in particular, think in this fulsome and melodramatic way.

In the pygmy-versus-giant comparison, Chatterton is both a little, stunted man, and a larger-than-life coward. Both images are derisory. The reference to pygmies also intimates savagery and regression. He has somehow reverted to a lesser state of development in the imperial eye that sees the white race as superior to those in 'primitive' societies. The hyperbolic, romantic language ennobles both the event of war and the character that participates in it.

Wounded during his first twelve days in France (a testament to his courage in face of the enemy), Chatterton is sent to convalesce in London. Here he is spotted by Sonia, who seeing him in uniform, finds 'her whole outlook on the war had changed...it turned her cold to think of him out there "somewhere in France", fighting for his life—perhaps badly wounded—lying, alone in shot-riven darkness, with no one to help him, no one to care' (213).

[41] Henry Gervis, in his memoir, *Arms and the Doctor: Being the Military Experiences of a Middle-Aged Medical Man,* expresses a slight reservation at donning his khaki uniform, feeling that at his age he is being 'theatrical', but as he 'marched boldly forth, endeavouring not to look self-conscious', he is spotted by a little boy walking with his mother. When the child exclaims, '"Look, mother, a soldier!"', Gervis 'swelled with pride; never in my wildest dreams had I expected to live to be a soldier' ((London, 1920), 11).

Lady Merriman's admonitions have proved correct as Sonia is transformed, not by donning khaki herself, but by *observing* it on the man she loves. Her sentimental and catastrophic visions of the 'imaginary horrors that awaited Chatterton' (213) are typical of those of other women in novels and in memoirs: Olive Dent in *A V.A.D. in France* describes how she conjured scenes of 'fire, slaughter, dripping bayonet, shrieking shell', and Barclay's Polly had imagined her Jim amidst similar horrors.

Ayres also paints a familiar and well-exploited scene of the War—soldiers departing from Waterloo:

> She had *never* seen anything like this before; she had often read of the farewell scenes at the different stations as portrayed by the picturesque pen of a newspaper man or lady journalist, but somehow she had *never* imagined it like this. She had *never* realised the vivid reality of it all; *never* dreamed how its finality came home to one; *never* properly understood the thrill of mingled pride and anguish that every woman in that crowd must be experiencing. (221; italics mine)

The repetition of 'never' reinforces the extent to which Sonia, like Polly, is disabused of her second-hand notions and experiences the particular 'woman's' reality for herself—it has become personal. She continues to think romantically about the War, but the meaning of the words has altered from abstract to concrete.

Later in this scene, Sonia begins a conversation with Nurse Anderson, who looked after Chatterton during his convalescence in London (she is unaware that Sonia has observed them together):

> The little nurse was full of the war and her work; she told Sonia many incidents of pluck and patience that had come under her own care. She had boundless enthusiasm for the soldiers she had nursed; she spoke as if she considered it a privilege to help them.
>
> . . . 'Some of the men like to talk to us,' said Nurse Anderson. 'But others say very little. It depends on the temperament I suppose . . . but I often think that the less a man says the more he feels. . . . The women are so brave, too,' she went on. 'Some of them come to the hospital to see their sons and husbands, but they never show what they are feeling—or they try very hard not to. They smile and try to be cheerful. . . .' (246)

Nurse Anderson's 'boundless enthusiasm' mirrors her real-life counterparts, as the next chapter will demonstrate, but she is more sympathetic to hospital visitors than some memoirists like Pat Beauchamp and Enid Bagnold, who have scathing things to say. It indicates the investment that Ayres, as a romantic novelist, had in the opinion and feelings of her readers. She tries to put everyone in a good light. Real-life active service women such as Beauchamp and Bagnold had no such investment.

In their attitudes toward the Germans and Tommy Atkins, however, the memoirists and novelists are in agreement. Though they are 'brave as lions' (273), the Germans are generally represented as giant vermin, supernaturally strong: 'earth seemed to breed those swarming, grey-clad figures' (275). Compared with the mud-stained and exhausted British troops, they seem 'as fresh to-day as when they started' (273), a warning that the enemy will not be easily overcome: 'it doesn't do to underrate it.... We shall win in the long run, because we've jolly well got to, but there'll be the very devil to pay first' (274).

Tommy, by contrast, is above reproach. As Chatterton becomes a man-of-action at the Front, his heroism comes to represent that of the British army as a whole. Standing for eight hours in the liquid mud of the trenches, he 'had seen men dropping all around him—seen broken limbs and shattered bodies, witnessed the bravery with which Englishmen can bear agony' (261). Even such an 'inhuman war...does *not* dehumanize him'.[42] He goes out fighting: 'shouting, swearing, even singing snatches of song, they leapt the parapets of the trenches and rushed forward'. Tommy also goes down fighting:

> Men were dropping like flies around him as he ran; some falling with a laugh, and using their last drop of vitality to struggle to their feet again; some went down without even a moan, and lay where they had fallen, shapeless, huddled masses, their khaki uniforms one with brown, riddled earth. (268)

War, here, as in Ruck's stories, strips away the false surface to reveal the 'bed-rock'. The metaphors of surface and depth are potent for they attest to the belief, or the hope, that underneath frivolous exteriors there lies a serious interior that will be revealed in time of crisis.

Not surprisingly, Chatterton's heroism exceeds even this fearlessness in the face of death. Ayres's prose, then, creates a kind of 'moral synthesis whose pivot [is] the nobility of individual choice and

[42] Bracco, *Merchants of Hope*, 4.

action'.[43] The hellish scenes reinforce Chatterton's worthiness to be called a hero. They are not meant to repulse, for nothing in the novel is 'stomach-churning', to use Fussell's phrase. Indeed, Ayres conforms to the idea that 'events had to be tidied up for presentation'.[44] The battle-scenes are written in the language of high adventure, intended to excite the reader. They are what Cawelti calls 'effective melodramatic incident[s]' expressing 'direct and immediate emotion [with] an arsenal of techniques of simplification and intensification'.[45] Ayres's 'arsenal' of metaphor, ellipses, and repetition reinforce Richard Chatterton's 'moments of crisis'.[46] And he has a number of these.

Thinking that Sonia has married Montague (she has not; Carter, his valet, was misled by that 'dastard'), her rejected lover is spurred on to reckless, do-or-die action:

> A sort of mad exuberance seized Chatterton. The blood was hammering in his veins. As he ran he shouted and yelled with the rest. It was like hell let loose. Fear was forgotten—left behind with the mud and death in the trenches....
>
> At one time even the thought of bayoneting a man had turned Chatterton sick, but now each time a grey-clad figure went down before him the exuberance grew in his veins....
>
> This was vengeance; this was the wiping out a little of the heavy score of the earlier days of the war; he was striking a blow for England, and each blow went home.... (276–7)

Angry with Montague and Sonia, as well as the Germans, Chatterton's 'primitive savagery', his regression, is acceptable because it is harnessed to defeat the enemy of England. It is important that Ayres stresses vengeance, not just blind violent aggression. Chatterton is not like the Germans who instigated the War. He is a defender, an agent of a kind of divine retribution. He is allowed an 'exuberance' as each bayonet thrust strikes the enemy.

Ayres's metaphors, a salient feature of her prose, rely heavily on colour and the natural world to bring the unnatural effects of the battlefield into sharper focus: 'his face had gone as white as the clumsy bandage which bound his forehead' (272); 'his limbs felt as if they were weighted with lead' (272); 'a grey sky was gathering

[43] Ibid., 42. [44] Fussell, *The Great War and Modern Memory*, 178.
[45] Cawelti, *Adventure, Mystery, and Romance*, 264. [46] Ibid.

overhead like a drab curtain' (274); searchlights 'swept earth and sky like the eyes of a demon from which it is impossible to hide' (275); 'the sickening fear of death stalked about like a maniac, laying a clammy hand on the shoulder of old and young alike' (275); bullets 'whiz past...like a swarm of angry grey hornets' (280). The text is also littered with compound adjectives: 'shell-smitten darkness' (275); 'earth-stained, khaki-clad figures' (276); 'blue-spurting flame' (276); 'shrapnel-swept ground' (279); 'drawn-out eternity' (279); 'pain-twisted face' (280); 'death-spattered field' (281). Although 'sanitized', these are sinister and eerie images of a 'troglodyte world'.[47]

Similarly, action sequences are vivid and dramatic. Ayres heightens the tension between her (often short) paragraphs with frequent use of ellipses, a technique employed by Enid Bagnold in *A Diary without Dates*. The sense of dreadful monotony—'day after day the same partial victory had been maintained; day after day the same fight for the same row of trenches was enacted' (278)—is mingled with 'the heart-breaking, hopeless scene' of the dead and the dying her hero observes around him. While surveying the field, Chatterton notices a young lieutenant, 'whose fair hair had made him think of Sonia, trying painfully to drag himself back to the lines....'(278). The young lieutenant 'lost his cap, and his fair, curly hair looked almost like a girl's in the mingled glare of grey dawn light and gunfire....Something in the boyish excitement of his shaven face reminded Chatterton of Sonia a little' (277). We are reminded of the language of Owen's poetry when Ayres refers to the young officer as 'that huddled, boyish figure' and 'the poor lad' with 'white lips' (279). Elsewhere a young gunner appears 'with a dead boyish face' (278). However, any homoeroticism is quickly rejected by the author, and by her manly protagonist, with his assertion that

> actually there was no resemblance [between the young lieutenant and Sonia], but his brain was a ferment of pain and madness, and in such a mood a sentimental streak of moonlight on the floor of a barn would have made him think of the woman he loved. (277)

There is to be no suggestion that he is anything other than heterosexual. The feelings of attraction to this boyish figure and the degeneracy they recall are countermanded by Chatterton's thoughts

[47] Fussell, *The Great War and Modern Memory*, 36–74.

of a woman, Sonia, and by the statement that in this deadly environment he is half-mad—any romantic image like the moonlight would recall his beloved. He loves men in comradeship, in the brotherhood men feel in war, but he does not love them sexually. His exploits on the battlefield are to leave no doubt as to his masculinity and heroism. In the penultimate act of heroism, Chatterton leaps over the 'trench-head in a single bound' to try and save the boy:

His action had drawn the rifle fire towards himself; there was something revengeful and venomous in the volleying ping, ping!—a hundred bullets missed him as he ran: someone from the trenches at his back shouted after him. . . .

'Come back, you fool . . . come back, you d——d fool!' . . .

Chatterton laughed and ran on. . . . For the moment he was drunk with excitement; the strength of a giant seemed tightening the muscles of his weary limbs; he ran on with the splendid foolhardiness of utter recklessness.

But the hundred yards seemed a thousand; the few panting moments which it took him to run the distance seemed a drawn-out eternity. . . .

A bullet struck the heel of his boot and tore it away; another ripped the shoulder of his coat. . . .

But he was there now, and on his knees beside that huddled, boyish figure, raising it with strong, capable arms. . . . And then the return journey began. . . . (281)

When he reaches the trenches, his comrades 'swarmed over the earthworks' to cheer and to help him. As they do, a bullet strikes Chatterton, but his heroic exploits do not stop. Carrying the young lieutenant to safety, he sees his valet Carter wounded on the battlefield, 'the man who, all unconsciously, had been instrumental in changing a slacker into a man' (280). Using his name 'Carter' like a mantra—he repeats it three times on two separate occasions—Chatterton 'knew what he meant to do. . . . He was going back' (281). As before he is 'greeted with a chorus of dissuasion. . . . "It's madness—you'll never come through again . . . Chatterton, don't be a fool."' Being the hero that he is, 'he hardly heard them'. Richard goes out again in search of Carter, and engages in the ultimate manly fight, *mano á mano* with the enemy:

Chatterton was unarmed, but he saw them in time, and, standing astride Carter's helpless body, he faced them with blazing eyes and clenched fists.

. . . . he stooped and snatched up a revolver that had fallen from the inert hand of a dead officer a stone's-throw away; a sort of wild prayer that it might be loaded rushed to his lips; he levelled it at the foremost of the oncoming Germans and pulled the trigger... it snapped harmlessly—the last cartridge had gone....

It was too late to try for another weapon; Chatterton lifted his injured arm and brought the revolver smashing down with butt-end in the man's face.... A last mighty effort and he was up again. A last desperate smite—right and left... his knuckles struck one man's jaw and the other man's temple. The pain in his body was agonising; the world began to swim before his eyes into a sea of blood... he knew that he stooped, groped for Carter and tried to raise him....

But it was not possible... his strength was giving out fast—fast....

But he could still crawl... and crawl those remaining yards he did, with his sound arm hooked around Carter and his whole body seared and tortured with pain unutterable.... (282–3)

The laggard, become the Man of Action, is ultimately awarded the V.C. and, after a lengthy convalescence, survives with little more than a limp—a 'picturesque lameness'—a wound in a 'mentionable place' for Sonia to enthuse over.[48] Despite containing elements of the adventure story—a male protagonist, perilous situations, heroic acts—*Richard Chatterton, V.C.* is nevertheless a romance novel: the 'dangers function as a means of challenging and then cementing the love relationship'.[49] By the end, Chatterton becomes the 'woman's man', as Elaine Showalter has called the heroes of many female-authored romances. In one way he is feminized by his wound, excluded now from the manly pursuit of war, just as Sonia is, an 'infant in arms'. That Ayres's central character is a man in many ways follows Showalter's further assertion that the woman's man 'was often a more effective outlet for the "deviant" aspects of the author's personality than were her heroines'.[50] Her assessment of the Victorian hero is equally applicable to his Great War counterpart:

The model hero was even less the product of adulation than of ignorance. To a considerable degree, he was the projection of women's fantasies about how they would act and feel if they were men, and, more didactically, of their views on how men *should* act and feel. It is customary for critics... to see the women's heroes as fantasy lovers, daydreams of romantic suitors.

[48] Siegfried Sassoon, 'The Glory of Women', *The War Poems*, ed. Rupert Hart Davis (London, 1983), 100.

[49] Cawelti, *Adventure, Mystery, and Romance*, 41.

[50] Elaine Showalter, *A Literature of Their Own: British Women Novelists from Brontë to Lessing* (London, 1978), 28.

> Critics have been rather slow to perceive that much of the wish-fulfilment in the feminine novel comes from women wishing they were men, with the greater freedom and range masculinity confers. Their heroes are not so much their ideal lovers as their projected egos.[51]

With this in mind, Sonia's exclamation—'if I were only a man [instead of] a doll—idle useless'—may be seen from a different angle. She wants Richard to act as she would act. In the end all her hopes are fulfilled and, with them, the hopes of the country as a whole. The love story and tale of one man's metamorphosis becomes a vehicle for expressing particular moral and societal values especially important at this time of crisis:

> Writing about the experience of war necessarily involved the authors in an act of reflection about grave and great matters which often transcended the power of their literary skills, but which were matched by their earnest enterprise of singling out and representing what was truly valuable in national life.[52]

Chatterton earns the noble epithet of Walter Scott's hero: 'So faithful in love, and so dauntless in war, | There never was knight like the young Lochinvar'. By invoking Scott's world, and the ideals upon which much of his work is based, Ayres aligns her novel with the chivalric tradition and suggests to her readers that Chatterton is the latest in that line of heroes, and that the Great War, the agent of his transformation from laggard to modern knight, is itself part of that legacy of noble conflict.

The Athenaeum reviewer was restrained in his assessment of Ayres's contribution to the 'large crop of inevitable "war novels"'. Judging *Richard Chatterton, V.C.* 'good of its kind', the plot and characters 'adequate', he concludes that 'the language and sentiment are sufficiently restrained to avoid the dangers that usually attend the feuilleton made to order'. Yet the profit and loss ledgers of Ayres's publisher, Hodder & Stoughton, reveal a more excited reception by the reading public at large. The initial print-run of 8,000 copies was eclipsed the following year by one of 25,000. Another 19,000 copies were printed in 1917 and a staggering 34,750 rolled off the presses in 1918.[53] Surely this is not simply a case of creating but rather feeding a public demand. Ayres quickly

[51] Ibid., 136.
[52] Bracco, *Merchants of Hope*, 39.
[53] Publishing ledgers of Hodder & Stoughton, Ltd., Guildhall Library MS 16310.

followed *Richard Chatterton* with a sequel, *The Long Lane to Happiness*, also in 1915, which sees Sonia and Richard married, though their blissful marriage takes some time to get going, as a series of misunderstandings, rather than war action, constitute the plot.

Whereas Barclay, Ruck, and Ayres extolled what may be called the passive heroine, other novelists lionized young women characters who performed daring and patriotic acts. *Irene to the Rescue* (1916), *Adventurous Anne* (1916), *Pickles: A Red Cross Heroine* (1916), and *An English Girl in Serbia: The Story of a Great Adventure* (1916) are just a few examples. These books were often penned by those who, before the War, made up the pantheon of writers of schoolgirl fiction: May Baldwin, Evelyn Everett-Green (Edith C. Kenyon), Dorothea Moore, and May Wynne. Of them all, Bessie Marchant was perhaps the most famous. Dubbed 'the girls' Henty', Marchant wrote numerous stories between 1894 and 1939 in which adventure was by no means confined to boys or men.

Deborah Lynch, Bessie Marchant's eponymous heroine of *A Girl Munition Worker* (1916) (Fig. 13), takes part in what the *TLS* review called 'the stirring plane of action . . . contained neatly in a three-and-sixpenny volume. . . . And it makes a good story, too, more readable at the moment than the same author's "Unknown Island," which deals with shipwrecked children in the far Seychelles.'[54] *The Bookman* was full of praise for the way in which Marchant surpassed other writers who have 'exhausted [the] epithet and aspect' of 'the girl munition worker'. Deborah, it says, is a 'lifelike and loveable character' who is 'no common heroine' with her 'quick faculties and address of mind':

> No reader with a patriotic verve or a true sense of fiction would desire anything but a favourable ending for Deborah and condign punishment for the spy, and here the author shows her right instinct, for she satisfies both respects . . . a truly topical and likeable book.[55]

With her 'fiery zeal and red-hot patriotism',[56] Deborah follows in a line of characters who perform exciting deeds for the Empire in Victorian and Edwardian adventure tales. Moreover, with 'a will of

[54] *TLS* (14 December 1916).

[55] *The Bookman* (Xmas Supplement, 1916).

[56] Bessie Marchant, *A Girl Munition Worker: The Story of a Girl's Work during the Great War* (London, 1916), 17.

FIG. 13. *A Girl Munition Worker* (1916) by Bessie Marchant, cover

her own' but with 'the blessing of tact to keep the will from appearing a nuisance' (13), she also fits the mould of the New Girl, a personality created by and lauded in such novels as *The Fortunes of Philippa* (Angela Brazil, 1907), *A Plucky Schoolgirl* (Dorothea Moore, 1908), *The Girls of Merton College* (L. T. Meade, 1911), and *Schoolgirls and Scouts* (Elsie Oxenham, 1914). These heroines are 'an amalgam of patriotism, good-heartedness and naivety'.[57] Whereas in boys' wartime adventure tales such as *With French at the Front* by Captain Brereton, girls and women present unwanted distractions, in Marchant's world females take charge. 'Forgery, embezzlement, smuggling, and detection—the kind of mystery later formulated in girl detective stories'[58]—are key elements in Marchant's narrative, but commentaries on the roles of patriotic people in wartime are also embedded in the plot of *A Girl Munition Worker*. The subject of munitions work is not a common one in popular novels of 1914–18. Sharon Ouditt posits that this may have to do with 'the usual problems of relating to the articulation of working-class experience and the fact that there was only a small number of middle-class women employed'.[59] *Munition Mary* by Brenda Girvin resembles Marchant's novel, but neither book 'challenge[s] stereotypical class assumptions. Like Berta Ruck [Marchant and Girvin] reproduce popular ideologies in the setting of a developing, if troubled, romance that leads to marriage'.[60] Certainly, the steadfast attitude towards the War and its consequences in *A Girl Munition Worker* is far from radical or challenging.

Deborah exhibits all the qualities of a child of the army extolled by magazines like *The Girl's Realm*. She constantly strives to measure up to the example of her father, who, on the outbreak, resigns his post at the War Office to serve in the Dardanelles; and her brother Bobby, serving 'with his regiment in Flanders' (21). He has already been mentioned twice in dispatches for conspicuous bravery, we are told. Deborah prays 'earnestly' for them daily and restrains her 'aching for distraction' from the 'fixed round of work' by reasoning: 'if her father and her brother could bear the hardship

[57] Mary Cadogan, *And Then Their Hearts Stood Still: An Exuberant Look at Romantic Fiction Past and Present* (London, 1994), 158.

[58] Sally Mitchell, *The New Girl: Girls' Culture in England, 1880–1915* (New York, 1915), 117.

[59] Ouditt, *Fighting Forces, Writing Women*, 85.

[60] Ibid., 85.

of a soldier's life without making a fuss, she was certainly not going to complain of anything that she might have to do or bear' (17). Colonel Lynch has taught her that discipline is 'the great essential of a soldier's life' (45), and Deborah applies this when looking after her elderly aunts, the stereotypic fictional spinsters. Agatha, frail and languid, loathes '"this horrible and wholly unnecessary war"', while Beatrice, 'tall, horsey-doggy looking', vigorous and ten years younger than her sister, believes that '"no one need be idle in these terrible times"' (14). However, Beatrice '"simply will not tramp from door to door to beg for cast-off clothes, old boots, and all the rest of it"', as she has been asked to do by the Red Cross.

Three days a week Deborah makes tents at a munitions factory, 'though she would have preferred something much more dangerous' (17). This desire is fulfilled when Gladys, her brother's fiancée, loses a foot in an explosion: 'poor heroic Gladys, who had chosen the most dangerous work she could find, because her soldier must perforce be in danger too!' (110). As if to compound the tragedy, Deborah learns that her brother is missing. The exhortation of a hospital matron to Gladys, '"with hope in your eyes, and cheerful words on your lips"'(115), is no doubt also meant for the reader who might be in a similar situation of grief and despair.

Deborah volunteers for Gladys's post, resolving to be a 'soldier-daughter' to her father: 'She looked upon her overalls as a uniform, and her throat swelled to think that she would henceforth walk with death as closely as her soldier father. She, too, belonged to the British Army now' (132). Like Richard Chatterton, the uniform is transformative, a symbol of belonging, a source of pride. She is taught by her co-workers how to face the danger entailed in making munitions: '"the only way to bear the strain is to lose sight of one's self in the doing of one's duty. Better still, try to feel that you are giving yourself to your country.... If you are blown to pieces to-morrow, it will not really matter to you"' (135). Stark words from Kate M'Masters who has lost her father and three brothers in the navy. She works her '"very hardest all day long at doing [her] bit to pull down the German Empire. The purpose dwarfs the peril"' (136). Her patriotic rhetoric is directed not just at Deborah, but also at the reader. Self-sacrifice and courage are the bywords of the novel—and of the propagandists' mission.

Kate's declaration—'"What a lot of wasted endeavour used to mark the old days!... I don't think it will ever be the same again, though. When the war is over we shall look out on the world with clearer vision"' (141)—anticipates a sentiment common in the memoirs. Deborah remains slightly more censorious, for she 'had not much faith in a wholesale regeneration of the human race' (141). It is likely that she doubts the capacity of the Germans to change, but Marchant's choice of words is striking and familiar: 'clearer vision', 'regeneration'—the effects of a just, necessary, and even timely war.

Marchant pontificates further through the character of Miss Wickham who, having been caught in the gear of the drying-fans, is dying. She exhorts Deborah '"to tell the girls I am not afraid to die; it is not dreadful at all, and it is light all the way through. Tell them they must not slacken because of accidents like this"'. With her dying breath, she exclaims, '"We shall win through!"'(255).

Deborah takes it upon herself to 'win through' when she uncovers a plot by the German spy Max Daubrechten to blow up the munitions factory. She knows she must warn the sentries immediately, so at one o'clock in the morning, she makes the rough and precarious journey on foot from the workers' hostel to the factory. Nearly stumbling over the huddled form of Dick Ferris—love-interest and unlikely hero of the novel—lying on the path, unconscious, she assumes he is 'drunk and incapable while on duty!' (167). In disgust but also excitement, she picks up his rifle and carries on towards the sentry's shed, in a role- reversal characteristic of Marchant's frontier adventures:[61]

> On and on she went. The dark had no terrors for her now, that is to say she had no sense of personal danger, being wholly engrossed with the fear of something happening to the nightshift. It was dreadful to think of what might come. Her ears strained to catch the slightest sound, her eyes were peering from side to side as she ran. (169)

Finding no guards at the shed, and bewildered, she begins to hear a distant 'faint hum . . . swelling louder and louder'. She fires upward in order to attract help, but no one comes. Like Richard Chatterton, 'a wild panic seized Deborah', as she runs 'with leaps and bounds', shouting as she goes, back to where Dick is lying unconscious. She realizes that the sound of the motor is the sound of an approaching Zeppelin, and that it is being guided by 'a blue light of intense brillancy which shone from the marsh'. Knowing that its bombs

[61] Mitchell, *The New Girl*, 133.

would strike the cordite factory and kill hundreds of girls on the night-shift, Deborah acts in the only way she can:

> she could shoot. Ah, yes, she could shoot! Dropping on one knee beside the unconscious figure of Dick, she took careful aim at the blue light that burned so brightly, and she fired. She had missed, for the blue gleam still showed. Again she fired, and again she missed.
>
> A terrible despair dropped upon her. The whirring of the motor had grown so loud. . . .
>
> 'Oh God, don't let me fail this time!' she cried, her whole soul going out in pleading. . . .
>
> The desperate character of the situation served to steady her nerves. Her hand did not tremble now, and her sight cleared. Again she fired, and— and—oh joy, the blue light had disappeared! (173)

Not only has she distracted the Zeppelin from its course, but she shoots off the signaller's finger, found by soldiers to be 'still warm and bleeding'. Deborah, 'for the very first time in her life', faints. As in other tales of women's derring-do, 'strict limits [are placed] on girls' aggression',[62] and, as if to reinforce the unnaturalness of such aggression, Deborah concedes, '"it was a terrible time. I don't think I shall ever feel really young again. Something seemed to snap in my heart whilst I knelt there trying to shoot that light out"' (246).

Despite her outward modesty over her actions, she is self-righteous in her attitude towards Dick, even when she learns he was not drunk, but drugged with chewing tobacco (which he is taking for a toothache) by Daubrechten. He gives her a dressing-down:

> 'In your intolerance you have no thought for the other side of the question, and it doesn't concern you a rap that I nearly lost my life by chewing that filthy stuff. It concerns you less that my pride has been humbled to the dust, and that it is as much as I can do to go on bearing things from day to day. You are what is called a good girl. You are so eaten up with pride in the fact that your life is such a success, and that you have performed a deed that ought to bring you a V.C., that it is only natural you should have no space in which to pity a fellow who is down and out.' (247)

When she later reads in the newspaper about Dick's heroic deeds on the battlefield, she regrets even more her treatment of him. It transpires that he 'crept through a cloud of poison gas' to destroy

[62] Ibid., 132. Mitchell goes on to point out Marchant's 'empire adventures altered significantly between 1900 and 1915. In the earliest books girls listened and watched while men acted. In Marchant's later books girls have adventures and courageously rescue men' (137).

a German 'machine-gun that had been dealing death and destruction in British trenches' (273)—more perpetuation of 'the fantasy of war as individual combat'.[63] Deborah sinks 'her pride in the dust' and writes 'a contrite letter' (274), which she knows he may never get: 'the correspondence of soldiers so often went astray. He might even be dead' (275). However, this being a story of romance as well as adventure, the two are brought together again to be 'lifted to the heights of bliss' (282). The ending is neatly tied together: the taxi in which Deborah is riding with her father knocks Max Daubrechten down and kills him in a perfect twist of fate and timing; Daubrechten is revealed as the German spy/signaller whose finger Deborah shot off; Bobby, though a prisoner, is alive; Gladys slowly recovers; Elsie finds 'her vocation at last' in nursing Gladys; Dick is granted a 'special leave' because 'he had suffered so badly from poison gas'; and Deborah returns to work at the munitions factory 'to do her bit, and to do it to her very best' (287). Writing in wartime, Marchant necessarily ends on an uncertain note, for Dick must return to his regiment and Deborah still faces danger at the factory:

> They would have to wait for their happiness, but it would be all the sweeter when it came. A thing worth having is worth waiting for.
>
> They parted in London, looking their last at each other in that Hall of Farewell at Victoria Station. If death passed them by, they would come together again when their work was done.
>
> If not—well, then, for them there would be the fadeless summer in the land where no night is.
>
> In either case it was well with them. (288)

Hope of a spiritual reconciliation is what sustains them—and, by extension, *should* sustain the reader—in the face of death and grief. Once again, heroine and hero are transformed by their war experiences.

Fred Lorimer's actions in Janet Laing's *Before the Wind* (1918) are every bit as courageous as the deeds of Richard Chatterton and Dick Ferris, but he undergoes a different sort of transformation. 'Severely wounded at the battle of the Marne, where he showed conspicuous gallantry' (324) and received the V.C., he provides part of the intrigue as he goes 'undercover' to root out a suspected thief and spy from a small Scottish community. (There are unmistakeable echoes here of John Buchan's wartime thrillers *The*

[63] Mitchell, *The New Girl*, 130.

Thirty-Nine Steps (1915) and *Greenmantle* (1916).) As in Ayres's novel, the danger that accompanies his mission is the means of challenging and cementing the love relationships. In its short review of *Before the Wind*, the *TLS* praised the 'varied entertainment' provided by the various storylines and Ann's 'soldier romance' with its 'very piquant developments'. It remarked that 'the whole is light and amusing enough to keep one swimming contentedly on with the current of events and with the coming and going of new streamlets of interest'.[64]

Its opening sequence bears many of the hallmarks of a Gothic novel: 'It was a dark November night' and Ann Charteris is making her way through a chaotic London to St Pancras and the train which will carry her to Scotland.[65] This 'tired young woman' is to take up a post as companion to two elderly women. In doing so, she follows in a long line of fictional heroines who, being left without money or family, take up employment in occupations that suited their genteel status: 'Behind her lay seventeen sunny years of youth and one more which had been as the valley of the shadow of death to her' (1).

Melodrama, hyperbole, and rhapsodic rhythm characterize Laing's prose. When Ann falls in love with Fred Lorimer, 'she gloried in the splendour of his devotion' (6); 'his eyes had held hers prisoners for one great moment' (129); and 'she cried and cried and cried for happiness' (328). In addition to these staples of

[64] *TLS* (7 February 1918).

[65] Janet Laing, *Before the Wind* (London and Toronto, 1918), 1. The original title of the novel was 'The Windlestraws'. Laing wrote to J. M. Dent that it was 'a slight thing which has behind it the tremendous background of the war.... I have come through some training since I last sent you a book. I have seen a lot of life and come face to face with death, and I feel that I have at least more to say than I had then.... I feel somehow as though I had only really begun to write *now*! I used to be keen always, but now a book takes hold of me and possesses me as never before.... Is it mad to think that in my forties I can begin again?' (Janet Laing to J. M. Dent, 18 June 1917, Dent papers 11043, Fol. 953, Manuscripts Department, University of North Carolina at Chapel Hill). Dent seems to have been concerned that Laing may have drawn too heavily on the people she knew and observed in the relatively closed community of St Andrews and suggested that she use a pseudonym. Both Laing and her husband rejected this idea: 'My husband is anxious for me to stick to my own name so I shall just do it. I never photograph people. I merely take characteristics, mix them up and turn out a type. If people think they recognize themselves I can't help it. There will never be anything to offend anyone in any of my books' (Janet Laing to J. M. Dent, 9 September 1917, Dent papers 11043, Folder 953, Manuscripts Department, University of North Carolina at Chapel Hill).

romantic fiction, Laing laces her narrative with contemporary slang: 'pluck', 'jolly', 'you're a brick','it was ripping'—trademarks of the school novels and adventure tales of the Edwardian period.

She consistently contrasts the imagery of darkness and light, dreams and nightmares in her tale of love during the Great War. The author of the darkness is, not surprisingly, the Kaiser:

> A man who, but for the accident of his birth, would have cut a grotesque and insignificant figure on this planet, was sitting in Berlin carefully guarded from intrusion, dreaming fantastic dreams of world-empire.
>
> Because of those dreams thousands upon thousands of better men, out to materialise them, were sacrificing all that they once had held dear and sacred; flames from desolate homes were lighting up the gloomy heavens; fair lands were lying waste under the cover of the darkness. (1)

This evil man's 'fantastic dreams' have provided Ann's share of tragedy. She leaves school after the outbreak of war to look after her infirm parents when her brother, Jim, enlists in the army. Rising to the occasion

> turned the schoolgirl into a woman, changing her affection for her two charges into a passionate devotion. They were so helpless and so dependent upon her. It broke her heart to think of her inadequacy. But she spent herself in their service to the last ounce of her capacity. She was everything that she could be to them. (4)

Evincing all the characteristics of virtuous, self-effacing womanhood, Ann feels 'despair... at the thought of her powers as compared with those of her brilliant brother' (2). Being the grateful sibling, he commends her devotion: '"You're a brick, Ann... I want you to know that it's all the world for a man to have—anyone like you to back him"' (5). This firmly defines her position: to be the support, the encourager, the keeper of the home fires. Their exchange of sentiments before Jim returns to the front is cliché-ridden:

> 'Try if you can not to cry,' said Jim. 'I—I can't bear it.' Ann dashed away her tears.
>
> 'I'm not crying, dear,' she said. 'I only wish I was going with you. It's grand for you to be a man.'
>
> 'Yes. Isn't it?' said Jim all aglow again in a moment. 'Isn't it?' (6)

Like her fictional and real-life counterparts, Ann laments her enforced passivity: 'Why was she not a man that she might pass triumphantly out from all this and offer up her empty life on the field of honour?'(230). Some women did not 'watch in silence' as they took up jobs left vacant by men, and in recognition of this, Laing notes how a post-*girl* brings Jim's eagerly awaited letters. However, Ann's misfortunes are soon compounded: after the death of her mother ('the thought of [Jim's] going [to the front] helped to kill her' (4)), he is killed in action, her father dies, and she is left penniless and in debt. In a scene of high melodrama, 'a terror seized her of what she must now suffer' and, despite a hurricane, she leaves the house,

> hatless, coatless, with her hair loosening behind her, she struggled down the pathway to the gate.... A sense of utter impotence and insignificance overwhelmed her.
>
> What was the good of battling on? she asked herself. She would have to go under at last. Even Jim had had to, and what was she in comparison? They had all gone—all her loved ones in to the darkness.... blinded, maddened, like a creature at bay, she hurled back a wild defiance.
>
> 'I hate You—hate You—hate You, God!' she shrieked aloud into the universe... (18–19)

The wind of the title is now a tempest. Ann's frenzy, however, is only temporary. She ultimately does apply 'courage'—the byword of the novel—to her despair. Mr Charteris continually admonished his daughter to 'rise to this new occasion' (4) and to have 'thoughts of courage' (10), and later in the novel, her employer will assert that '"Our courage is intact".' (343)

This being a romance novel, however, it is love that is Ann's primary salvation. She is initially 'rescued' from her early despair by accepting a marriage proposal from Dr Warren, the family physician, twenty years her senior. The imagery of darkness and light is again employed: 'He stood between her and the power of darkness, the terror, the horror that had almost driven her frantic. He had come out of the all-surrounding cruelty and folded her to his breast for shelter' (22). Ann vows to pay off her debts before becoming Mrs Warren, and so begins her life as a 'companion' in the Scottish village of Bartonsmuir.

Her 'training in sorrow' has given her not only insight, but also a sensitized awareness of the war that is at odds with the complacency of Caroline and Emily Barton, her employers. So angry does she become at one point that she attempts—much like Ruck's Nurse in her story 'Tommy Doll'—to shock them with newspaper details of fiendish outrages and sickening horrors. It was a relief for her to do so. She wanted to make their blood run cold, to fling the fearful facts and happenings down before them, to see their mild old eyes grow awestricken. She longed to tear asunder the web of self-complacency that peace and affluence had woven about them. (41)

However, just as she does not give into despair, neither does Ann resort to cruelty. She believes they are to be pitied for their apathy, and she has a 'strong maternal affection' for the Bartons: 'It was not their fault that they lived immune from sorrow, that they looked from afar on the agonizing world beyond their little domain with a regret which was mostly bewilderment' (38).

Laing then has her opportunity to comment on what it is exactly that people like these can do for the 'war effort'. Ann decides to quit their employ after reading about the need for war workers: '"Don't you see how you and people like you—good, kind, dear people—are keeping back hundreds of workers?"' (49). In response, Caroline observes how she and her sister are 'wrack-straws', flying before the wind, of no use. Their only service can be inviting other such elderly women to live with them so as to free up their maids, cooks, and chauffeurs for *national* service. Ann agrees to organize this venture and to stay with the 'Wrack-Straws', as they come to be known, 'for the duration'. The group includes six women—and one man, Mr Tosh, an author, who before the War published a book entitled 'The Utter Impossibility of a War with Germany'. (His name is perhaps meant to reinforce the folly of his outlook.) At Bartonsmuir, he has had to revise its content and title to 'The Utter Impossibility of Annihilating Germany' (206).

Love triangles complicate the plot. We learn, for instance, that Lottie Alleyne of the neighbouring village of Rathness is the former love of Dr Warren, and at the same time as they begin to rekindle their relationship, Ann is having second thoughts about her engagement: 'Paolo and Francesca—what had her feeling for David [Warren] in common with a mad passion such as theirs?.... The harbour was safe certainly, but what of the ocean outside—boundless, mysterious? What if the harbour-bar were also a prison-bar?' (165). Ann's burgeoning sexual desire is internalized, portrayed as an emotional rather than a physical need, and is described with high-flown and erotic metaphor.[66]

[66] Jan Cohn, *Romance and the Erotics of Property: Mass-Market Fiction for Women* (Durham and London, 1988), 25.

The reader is aware, even though Ann is not, that one of the reasons for these misgivings about Dr Warren is that she is in love with Fred Lorimer. Her relationship with him follows the familiar and 'rudimentary' storyline, 'three unvarying segments':

> an initial meeting with the hero and heroine, which incurs the heroine's hostility to the hero; a long period of armed truce in which the hero and heroine are thrown together to work toward some mutually accepted goal; and a final episode of danger, rescue, and exile leading to the declaration of love.[67]

Ann knows Fred only as James Green, his assumed disguise, and believes him to be a conscientious objector. Though enraged at this idea—'he was evidently educated and a gentleman . . . who preferred valeting to fighting, preferred holding fur overcoats to drawing swords'—Ann feels drawn to him and defends him to the Wrack-Straws: '"not one of us can go to fight. None of us, therefore, have the right surely to sit in judgement on any man"' (146). This is an interesting comment, since all the novelists considered in this chapter offer a gendered judgement of man and manliness.

The reader knows how fine a man Fred really is. When he comes to visit Lottie Alleyne, his aunt, he rejects her offer of a celebratory party : '"I can't be bothered with [strangers] just now. They get on my nerves somehow and make me feel idiotic"' (31). Robert Graves and his comrades could have identified with these feelings of Laing's hero—the alienation and the frustration at being made the 'star attraction'.[68] Lottie goes ahead with her plan anyway: 'fourteen people are coming tonight to meet the V.C.' (31). Fred is not simply being awkward, for he believes that he has done very little to deserve his commendation:

> 'I've done no more than thousands have done, and very much less than thousands have done really. . . . It is not a question of heroism, it's chance and brute violence and brute instinct of self-defence, and conceit that makes you willing to die rather than appear a coward before company—that's why I hate and loathe this V.C. business. "Look at me," I seem always to be saying, "how brave and noble I am!" Pah! It's monstrous.' (112)

[67] Ibid., 20.

[68] Home on leave in April 1916, Graves is coerced by his parents to attend a church service and he feels 'a slight suspicion that they were anxious to show me off in church wearing my battle-stained officer's uniform' (Robert Graves, *Goodbye to all That* (New York, 1985), 199).

Such self-effacement is meant to be seen as admirable as is his acceptance that he must love Ann from a distance. Knowing she is engaged to Warren, his wish is only that 'he might do service for his beloved before going out to the front again and making there a decent exit' (128). The word 'decent' is charged with meaning. It connotes the 'fitting end' the hero envisages on the battlefield and the honourable manner in which he treats the woman he loves. It reinforces Fred Lorimer's worthiness not only to be called 'hero' but also to be accepted as Ann's husband. In this way, *he* evinces a characteristic of the romantic heroine who 'must seem to seek *nothing*, as if to confess to desire in any form were to confess to the deeper, the vengeful and aggressive, desires that are forbidden'.[69]

'Vengeful and aggressive' are words that could be used to describe the characters' attitudes towards the Germans who are, as in Ruck's stories, pilloried. 'Wretched *Hohenzollern!*'(216) is an insult, and it is believed that if someone '*is* a German, he or she will be a person who has no sense of shame to appeal to and no gratitude to be aroused' (329). Though they and their evil leader in Berlin are the source of the darkness that is the War, they are not the prime movers of the mystery the story unfolds. It is hinted that spies are at work in Bartonsmuir, but it transpires that more run-of-the-mill villains are causing trouble.

Albert is a thief who exploits his position as valet to Mr Tosh to steal the jewels of the Wrack-Straws. He enlists the help of Jane, a housemaid, and discovers the secret of Japp, the last remaining male servant of the Bartons who reluctantly guards a cache of petrol and bombs hoarded by his uncle in a tunnel beneath the Lodge:

> 'My uncle was [a German spy], and I always hated him. I hate him now though he is dead for getting me into the mess I'm in. . . . He was the worst of spies. . . . Oh, he was a hateful traitor!. . . . My uncle said that this was my post and that there were Germans all about and that they would know if I left it. He said it would be known in Berlin, too, and that to desert would be as much as my life was worth'. (102)

Excited by this knowledge, Albert decides to use it for his own purposes, not because he is pro-German or a spy, but because, as he says, '"for me there exists only two peoples in the world—the

[69] Cohn, *Romance and the Erotics of Property*, 5.

Rich and the Not Rich. . . . I appropriate superfluous wealth"' (103). He convinces Japp to enlist, to get him out of the way, but plagued by a guilty conscience, Japp continually tries to warn the residents of Bartonsmuir of imminent danger and the nefarious intentions of Albert.

As in detective stories, *Before the Wind* has its own policeman who suspects that something is amiss. Captain Piffard enlists the help of the convalescing hero, Fred, who, in disguise as James Green, is able through various complications and twists and turns of plot to bring the intrigue to the anticipated exciting conclusion in the explosive-laden tunnel. The danger it poses 'thrilled him with the once-familiar thrill of the trenches' (270), and is heightened by a Zeppelin that appears overhead sounding 'like a threshing machine'. Ann herself dives into the tunnel to warn the man she still believes to be a conscientious objector and for whom she cannot help but feel an attraction. A bomb from the airship traps them together. Mrs Gellanty, a Wrack-Straw, is frightened but exhilarated when this is realized: '"to think . . . of those two down there! It's a romance. The brave soldier and the lovely maiden"' (336). For Fred it is the opportunity to reveal his true identity and declare his love to Ann:

> 'Miss Charteris', he said, 'striving to speak steadily, I must say one thing in case—in case I do not get through in time—and—we go out together. The man you love is not here to be with you, but I have loved you from the very first moment I saw you, and shall love you till death, and after death if God wills. If—if there is anything at all beyond, you will not pass alone into the darkness'. (324)

They eventually find their way out of the tunnel—from literal darkness to light—through a passage to the beach, and are welcomed home by shouts of joy from the Wrack-Straws. In the sitting room of the house, more is revealed about Albert's dealings and Jane's disguise as the Wrack-Straw Mrs Dodsworth. Ann is engaged to Fred and Dr Warren to Lottie Alleyne. Everyone is overcome with emotion for 'what we *have* gone through and [are] all the better for it' (343): 'The cook had wept over the scrambled eggs as she thought that there might have been no one alive to eat them' (340). The two couples then ride off into the sunset—in a motor car rather than on horseback—since this *is* 1915. Sitting together in the *back* seat, the two women watch 'the men in the front seat [who] talked hard till the last moment of the war and being in the thick of it and driving the Boches over the Rhine' (344).

The reader is meant to be left entertained by the 'drama and intricacy' in which, as Nicola Beauman points out, 'the hero and heroine endure tests of endurance which would crush ordinary mortals, but the reader has the satisfaction of knowing that they will come through with flying colours'.[70] The reader also is surely meant to be empowered by the patriotic sentiments. There are lessons to be learned. It goes without saying that all fit men should enlist. The elderly may follow the example of the Wrack-Straws, and do their bit by sharing a house and servants. Lottie Alleyne provides the example of what middle-aged women can do. She is constantly busy running canteens, organizing prisoners' parcels, mending soldiers' clothes, and supervising entertainment for those on leave. At one point she delivers a panegyric on the War:

> 'What a splendid chance this war—terrible as it is—is giving to us middle-aged women. One's heart bleeds for the young girls who many of them are losing so much and for the wives and mothers whose men are in the trenches, and for the very old who can only look on and wait. But for us middle-aged and unattached ones—why it's nothing but pure luck.... You see us at Rathness—old girls of 40 and 50 and 60—how the Kaiser has renewed our youth for us. We've no time to get old now, or to have nervous breakdowns. We have no time for too much bridge. We have no time for rest-cures. The lonely ones of us who before were cut off from the world of men are now set in the midst of it at the hospitals and canteens. Born mothers without sons and born sisters without brothers can find any amount of them among these soldier lads... Oh, I can tell you it has been a new life for them. It has renewed their good looks too. You should see even the plainest ones with their Queen Mary's Guild head-dresses on. Why they look like Madonnas! You wouldn't know 'em again. Yes, we middle-aged of this war-time will never grow old I think, or at least when we do we shall have had a double share of youth first'. (294–5)

Dr Warren heartily agrees on behalf of middle-aged *men:* '"By Jove, this getting called-up has a wonderful effect. We had begun to have the too-old-at-40 feeling—a lot of us.... Now look at us—even the ones who were invalids, in the trenches and better often than ever they were. This war has made us ordinary men extraordinary"'(295). The War, it is implied, not only purifies and reveals a

[70] Nicola Beauman, *A Very Great Profession: The Woman's Novel, 1914–39* (London, 1983), 183.

truer identity, but actually increases an individual's ability and worth. It elevates the esoteric status of middle-class men, who are already gentlemen, just as for Sister Martin-Nicholson, it elevates the status of Tommy Atkins.[71]

Patriotic and didactic notions are sandwiched between the intrigue and romance embedded in Laing's novel. *Before the Wind* has 'at its centre the moral fantasy of showing forth the essential "rightness" of the world order'.[72] In its complex plot and cast of characters, 'we see not so much the working of individual fates but the underlying moral process of the world.... Melodramatic suffering and violence are a means of testing and ultimately demonstrating the... ultimate triumph of the good.'[73]

It is surprising, then, to find that in Marie Belloc Lowndes's novel of 1915, *Good Old Anna*, not all the resolutions are so 'comforting' and 'the triumph of the good' (in this case a literal reference to the title) is far more ambiguous. The reader may be deceived by the cover illustration showing a woman in full bridal regalia holding the hand of a man propped up in a hospital bed, the couple observed by a benevolent-looking cleric (Fig. 14). Such a romantic resolution indeed takes place between the heroine Rose Otway and her wounded soldier-lover Jervis Blake, and there is a marriage between Rose's widowed mother and Major Guthrie, but no such happy ending awaits the title character. Anna Bauer, Mrs Otway's German housekeeper, is unwittingly caught up in a spy network and her fate is shocking. Claire Tylee calls it 'typical of the paranoid vision of espionage fiction, [in which] the British characters were impossibly heroic and the Germans bestial'.[74] A review published in *The Outlook* on 27 November 1915 proclaimed that this novel showed 'There is only one way to treat Germans as there is to treat snakes—to scotch them.' The *Times*

[71] Martin-Nicholson's memoir is discussed in Chapter 4.

[72] Cawelti, *Adventure, Mystery, and Romance*, 45.

[73] Ibid., 46.

[74] Claire M. Tylee, *The Great War and Women's Consciousness: Images of Militarism and Womanhood in Women's Writings, 1914–1964* (Iowa City, 1990) 104.

In *How We Lived Then 1914–18*, Mrs C. S. Peel describes how spy mania gripped the nation: 'Even before the war was actually declared, this burst out and gave rise to absurd and some cruel occurrences. In some cases the lives of foreign governesses and maids who had grown old in the service of British families were made a burden to them. It became necessary to obtain a permit for an alien member of any household. A child, hearing some discussion on the subject, asked anxiously, "Oh, mummie, *must* we kill poor Fräulein?"' (Mrs C. S. Peel, *How We Lived Then 1914–18: A Sketch of Social and Domestic Life in England during the War* (London, 1929), 39).

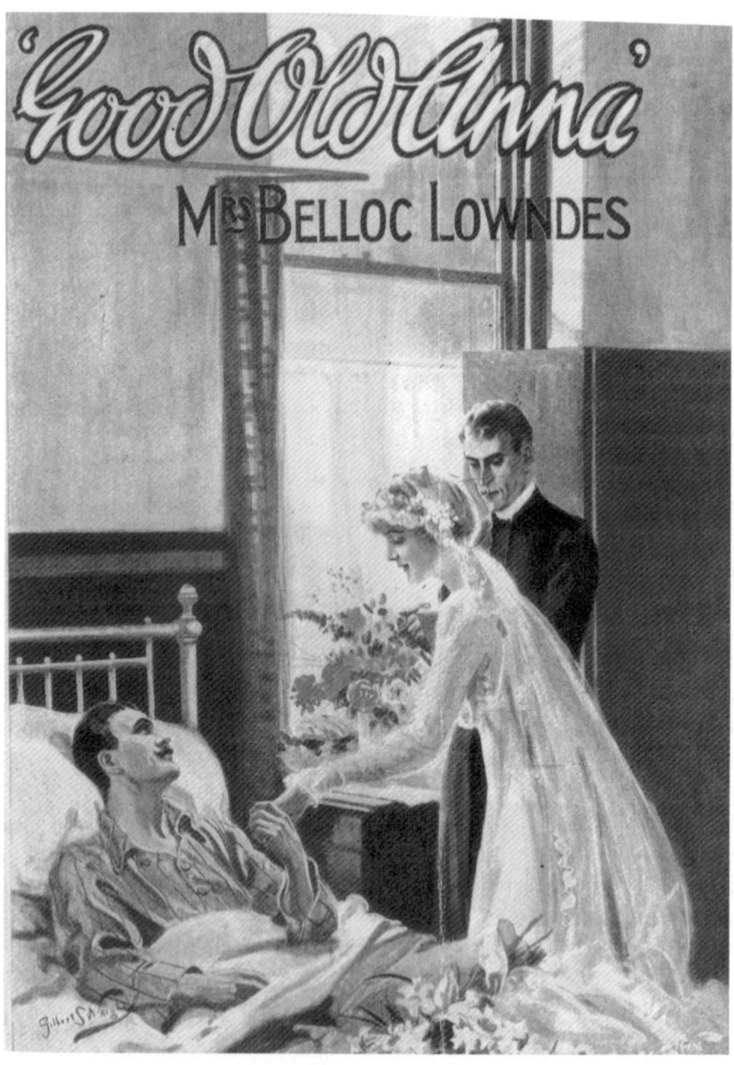

Fig. 14. *'Good Old Anna'* (1917) by Marie Belloc Lowndes, dustjacket illustration (25611 e. 4462), Bodleian Library, University of Oxford

Literary Supplement review (11 November 1915) was a little more tempered in its admiration, calling the book 'credible from start to finish'. It complained that 'most authors of spy-stories lead their tales up with wild doings in which no one can believe, and which have the effect (if they had any effect) of persuading one that there are no German spies in England' but, it asserted, 'that is not Mrs Lowndes's way'. Her skill as a writer, it is argued, means that not only do her characters seem 'real', but the novel paints 'a faithful picture of the general reluctance to face the truth, the bland assumption that the war would make no difference to life in English Cathedral cities and pretty little homes in the Close'.

Mrs Otway is advised by a number of people in Witanbury to send 'good old Anna' back to Germany now that war has been declared. Elderly Miss Forsyth tells her that the town is viewed as '"a spy centre for this part of England"' (312). However, Mrs Otway remains staunchly loyal to her housekeeper and makes a distinction between martial Germany and 'civilised' Germany—a theme that runs throughout the novel:

> 'Why, because the powers of evil have conquered—I mean by that dreadful German military party—should I behave unjustly to a faithful old German woman who has been with me—let me see—why, who has been with me exactly eighteen years? With the exception of a married niece with whom she went and stayed in Berlin three autumns ago, my poor old Anna hasn't a relation left in Germany. Her whole life is centred in me—or perhaps I ought to say in Rose. She was the only nurse Rose ever had'.[75]

Furthermore, because Mrs Otway lived for two years in Berlin, she finds she can love both countries: '"after all, you may hate the sin and love the sinner!"' (135) She insists that '"Anna has all the virtues of the German woman; she is faithful, kindly, industrious, and thrifty"' (3). However, sometimes her housekeeper exhibits what Miss Forsyth calls 'typically German' vices: arrogance, stinginess, bigotry. She is also fat. It is obvious that Anna maintains an allegiance to the Fatherland. On the dresser in her 'cosy bedroom' is a pair of white china busts of Bismarck and von Moltke, 'her heroes' (253). She 'hated Belgium and the Belgians' (242); 'terrible, barbarous' Russia is sneered at alongside 'prosperous, perfidious' France. For the British, 'as a people,

[75] Marie Belloc Lowndes, *Good Old Anna* (London, 1915), 2.

Anna Bauer cherished a tolerant affection and kindly contempt' (26). England

> had no army to speak of—no *real* army. She remembered the day when France had declared war on Germany in 1870. How at once every street of the little town in which she lived had become full of soldiers—splendid, lion-hearted soldiers going off to fight for the beloved Fatherland. Nothing of the sort had taken place here, though Witanbury was a garrison town. The usual tradesmen, strong, lusty, young men, had called for orders that morning. They had laughed and joked as usual. [No one] seemed aware that his country was at war. The old German woman's lip curled disdainfully. (25)

Her impressions of English*women* are no less severe: 'politics were out of woman's province' (29) and she 'laughed aloud' over the idea of women's suffrage (which Rose supports) and 'the antics of the Suffragettes'. 'Wise, masculine Germans' would have committed such females to the 'idiot asylum' (29). Every 'true' woman's motto, according to Anna, should be 'Church, Kitchen, and Children'. Indeed, 'she lived in a chronic state of wonder over the laziness, thriftlessness, and the dirt of the Englishwomen' (240).

Although Lowndes's novel reinforces familiar stereotypes of the Germans and asserts that 'England was going to war...in a just cause' (21), it also calls for tolerance and clear-thinking. Like Mrs Otway, Dr Haworth, the Dean of Witanbury Cathedral, takes every opportunity, in high-minded language, to discourage bigotry:

> it would be wrong indeed for England to allow her heart to be filled with bitterness. It was probable that even at this moment a large number of Germans were ashamed of what had happened last Monday—he alluded to the invasion of Belgium.... The Dean wished to impress on his hearers the need for a generous broad-mindedness in their attitude towards the foe. England was a great civilised nation and so was Germany. The war would be fought in an honourable, straightforward manner, as between high-souled enemies. (22)

The Dean particularly urges a Christian kindness to the naturalized Germans who lived in the town itself. The barber, Mr Fröhling, for instance, has lived in England for forty years, has a son in the British Army, and 'was a German of the good old sort... he did not share Anna's enthusiasm for the Kaiser, the Kaiserin, and their stalwart sons' (32). He is also distraught over '"what a few people have done to my beloved country"' (69). The Dean's confidence and generosity seem misplaced, however, when the reader is introduced to Manfred

Hegner. The biggest retail tradesman in the town, he owns 'The Witanbury Stores' and is an active member of the city council with 'all sorts of profitable irons in the fire' (35), some of which are nefarious. In his room he has a safe where he hoards money and various letters written in German, and he keeps a 'little black book' on his person. His physical description reinforces his sinister role in the novel: 'because of his German birth... and even more because of certain facial and hirsute peculiarities, he went by the nickname of "The Kaiser"' (35).

Hegner's English wife, Polly, bears the brunt of his 'Teutonic' duplicity and cruelty. He is miserly with her and extravagant towards himself. In front of his customers he is all smiles, but in private he berates his wife for her sloppiness, wilfulness, and tendency to speak of his activities. He is enraged, for instance, when she casually tells her sister that he recently went to Southampton on a day-trip. His anger is unbounded as he fears his spying activities will come to light. Polly is thus banished to her room by her husband and bewildered by his anger.

All of Anna's misfortunes—and her ultimate downfall—are the result of her involvement with Hegner, who on the outbreak of war, anglicizes his name to 'Alfred Head'. She receives a 'commission' from him for encouraging customers. In reality, Head/Hegner is paying her for the 'military' information she gleans from Mrs Otway's liaison with Major Guthrie and Rose's romance with Jervis Blake. The information is wheedled out of the naïve Anna in the form of 'innocent' social conversation: 'the old woman thought [Head's] questions quite natural, for all Germans have an insatiable curiosity concerning what may be called the gossip side of life' (152). *The Outlook* reviewer is scathing about Anna's character, concluding that 'If "good old Anna" had been the gentlewoman which the English faithful servant would assuredly have been for all her humble birth, she would not have done the things she did.' The reviewer asserts that Anna is 'that evil thing, the woman of modern Germany, cradled in the mischievous traditions of Prussian militarism until every right instinct in her had become warped.'

There is no doubt that Anna takes delight in the news of the Fatherland that Head passes on to her. When he tells her that the Germans have sunk an English war vessel, 'Good Old Anna's face beamed. It was not that she disliked England—indeed, she was very fond of England. But she naturally felt that it was only right and fair that the Fatherland should win' (149). She learns through the 'German newspapers Mr Head had managed to smuggle through' that 'the women of Belgium had put out the eyes of wounded German soldiers.... no punishment for such conduct could be too severe' (242). The now-familiar stories about German atrocities committed against 'little Belgium' are inverted. Instead of being the innocent victims portrayed by the British press, they are the perpetrators of wanton cruelty. It could be said that Lowndes is further reinforcing the assumed guile of the enemy, Germany's ability to find ways of justifying actions, which have no justification. Certainly *The Outlook* reviewer believed she was doing so: '"Have no truck with Germans", is thus the moral writ large over Mrs Belloc Lowndes' pages.' However, it is also possible she is suggesting that propaganda from either side is not entirely to be trusted. Both governments can turn stories to their own advantage. We are told that Rose and her mother try not to believe the atrocity stories coming out of Belgium, and Mrs Otway is dubious about the rumours of a 'mysterious passage of Russians through the country', 20,000–100,000 men in 'this secret army of Avengers' (179). Tolerance and censoriousness, then, would seem to be the preferred attitudes to have. They form the voice of reason in the novel.

When her character is considered further, especially in light of her epithets 'good old Anna' or 'poor old Anna', it is obvious that the reader is meant to have sympathy for this naïve German woman. (The phrase 'good old' is also used for Herr Fröhling, who is clearly a sympathetic character.) Her love for her homeland is continually exploited. Treachery and espionage are not part of this allegiance, so she fails to see it in others. She equates Head's secretiveness with the countenance of a wealthy big business man: 'it is always well to be in with such lucky folk' (251). Even the mysterious visitors she observes in the shadows do not tip her off to any sinister goings-on.

The intrigue created by Alfred Head and his network of spies runs parallel with the romances of Rose and Mrs Otway and their respective partners. The language of love is effusive, the thoughts of the heroines idealistic. Rose's first love letter is described in familiar purple prose:

> she made a little silk envelope for it, and wore it on her heart. It was like a bit of Jervis himself—direct, simple, telling her all she wanted to know, yet leaving much unsaid. Rose had once been shown a love-letter in which the

word 'kiss' occurred 34 times. She was glad that there was nothing of that sort in Jervis's letter, and yet she longed with a piteous, aching longing to feel once more his arms clasping hers close, and his lips trembling on hers. . . . (175)

(Presumably, Rose would have been unimpressed by the obsession with kisses displayed by Berta Ruck![76]) Male writers could be equally effusive in their depictions of romantic encounters. William LeQueux's eponymous heroine, Annette of the Argonne, is overcome when the spy Charles Lavignac, 'gripped her hand firmly and, placing his strong arm around her neck, bent until she suddenly felt his moustache brush her cheek, until his lips met hers in a hot passionate caress, as he declared, in all the deep earnestness of his manhood, that he loved her.'[77]

Mrs Otway's lover, Major Guthrie, comes from a 'fighting caste'; his father and his grandfather were soldiers. Guthrie himself 'had been through the Boer War and was wounded at Spion Kop' (162). Even though he has 'done his duty by his country', he enlists immediately to fight in the new war: '"It's made me feel like a young man again—that's what it's done!"' (94) Not until he is in France does he declare his love for Mrs Otway in a letter. Just like her daughter, she thrusts it into her bodice to keep it 'close to her beating heart' (200).

The two love stories, however, follow a complicated trajectory. Like other romance writers, Lowndes had 'to manipulate her plot and her characters' desires so that the hero and heroine do not fall too fixedly into each other's arms until the closing paragraphs'.[78] War, of course, provides a perfect vehicle for prolonging the amorous tension. Mrs Otway soon learns that Major Guthrie has been wounded and is missing, but through the Geneva Red Cross she receives word that he is alive though a prisoner in Germany. (Anna is happy that he is in the Fatherland where he will be well treated.) She next learns that the Major has been permanently blinded, but will soon be exchanged for German prisoners and sent home to England.

[76] Mary Cadogan notes how 'kisses and kissing cropped up in several of [Ruck's] titles, from *Khaki and Kisses* (1915) and *The Bridge of Kisses* (1917) to *Half-Past Kissing Time* (1936) and *Quarrel and Kiss* (1942).' Cadogan, *And Then Their Hearts Stood Still*, 60.

[77] William LeQueux, *Annette of the Argonne* (London, 1916), 19.

[78] Cadogan, *And Then Their Hearts Stood Still*, 55.

Rose's fiancé, Jervis Blake, is also severely wounded, but, again, 'due to the wonderful organisation of our Red Cross' (260), gets sent back to Witanbury to be treated by a family friend, Sir Jacques Robey. The eminent surgeon decides that Jervis must have his foot amputated and urges Rose to marry him before the operation takes place. Though overcome with emotions that she has tried up until this point to control, our heroine rises to the occasion:

> She became agitated, tearful—in her eagerness she put her hand on Sir Jacques' breast, and looking piteously up into his face, 'Of course I want to marry him at once!' she said brokenly. 'Every time I have had to leave him in the last few days, I have felt miserable. You see, I *feel* married to him already, and if you feel married, it's so very strange not to *be* married'. (272)

Jervis intends to 'release' Rose from her obligation, but unlike Ruck's hero, he needs no convincing to honour his proposal of marriage: 'This great trouble which had come on him was her trouble as well as his, and he knew she was going to take it and to bear it, as he meant to take it and to bear it' (277). The perfect patriotic couple is married just as the cover illustration promised.

However, all the happiness of two nuptials is overshadowed by the troubles facing 'good old Anna'. Not only has she been receiving a 'commission' from Alfred Head but, since 1912, she has been storing parcels for him in a secret cupboard in her room. Once again, she is duped into believing that 'what had been left with her was connected with some new, secret process in the chemical business. In that special branch of trade . . . the Germans were far, far ahead of the British' (335). Of course the reader realizes that the parcels contain equipment for making bombs. Such a development falls in line with what war soothsayers had been claiming all along—German saboteurs and spies were at work in England preparing for 'the Day'.

Arrested and incarcerated, Anna staunchly claims her innocence. Mrs Otway, now Mrs Guthrie, pleads, '"I appeal to you as an Englishwoman to help us in the matter"' (360). Whilst the Guthries believe Anna, the police remain unconvinced and call in Alfred Head (whom they do not yet suspect). Once alone, he evinces more of his evil nature telling 'poor old Anna' that she has led both of them within 'sight of the gallows' and that should she reveal she received money from him. He tells her 'in a hissing whisper', '"I can tell how it was through you that a certain factory in Flanders was shelled, and 80 Englishmen were killed"' (379). It was at this site that Jervis Blake was severely wounded. Appalled by her 'part' in this and the pain it has caused Rose, Anna believes 'she did indeed deserve to hang. A shameful death would to be nothing in comparison to the agony of fearing that her darling might come to learn of the truth' (387). When he leaves the cell, Alfred Head is arrested on the information given by his wife, Polly—a true Briton—who discovers his secret activities and provides the evidence. Anna, however, remains in despair. She will not eat, but finds that the coffee gives her 'awakened, keener perceptions'. With just enough light to see by, she picks up the

> beautiful band of crochet lace which was destined to serve as trimming for Mrs Jervis Blake's dressing table. The band was very nearly finished; there were over three yards of it done. Worked in the best and strongest linen thread, it was the kind of thing which would last, even if it were cleaned very frequently, for years and years, and which would grow finer with cleaning.
>
> The band neatly rolled up and pinned, to keep it clean and nice; but now Anna slowly unpinned and unrolled it.
>
> Yes, it was a beautiful piece of work; rather coarser than that which she was accustomed to do, but then she knew that Miss Rose preferred the coarser to the very fine crochet.
>
> She tested a length of it with a sharp pull, and the result was wonderful—from her point of view most gratifying!....
>
> Yes, whatever the strain were put on this band it would surely recover—recover, that is, if it were dealt with as she, Anna, would deal with such a piece of work. It would have to to be damped and stretched out on a piece of oiled silk, and each point fastened down with a pin. Then an almost cold iron would have to be passed over it, with a piece of clean flannel in between.... (389)

The tension of the final pages is carefully built up by her mechanical action of unwinding the lace, the consideration her handiwork, and the detailed description of damping, stretching, and fastening. The ellipses lend further expectation of what is to follow; Anna's work has not stopped, but the reader will not to be privy to any more. Instead, we learn of its final product: 'poor old Anna' has hanged herself from 'the old-fashioned iron gas bracket, placed in the middle of the ceiling' in her cell.

The romantic conclusion describing Rose and Jervis, as their 'two figures seemed to become merged until they formed one, together'

(398), is overshadowed by the violent and tragic fate of Anna Bauer. The suicide is an indictment of innuendo, suspicion, and prejudice, for despite all the stereotypes Lowndes repeats about the Germans, she makes the distinction between 'military' (culpable) and 'real' (innocent) Germany. Her heroes, after all, are not left unscathed by the War—Jervis loses a foot, the Major his sight, but these tragedies are never used to question the War in its totality. Rather, as other novelists have also done, Lowndes uses them to justify its continuation.

There is little that is subversive in this or any of the other novels—for even when the women perform 'manly' acts of heroism, they remain feminine and return to the world of romantic companionship at the end of every story. The heavily didactic nature of these tales of suspense, adventure, and romance elides them with propaganda. Nevertheless, the sheer number of such novels, with their emphasis on the regenerative, even spiritual power of war—however flawed, idealistic, or unsavoury to a twenty-first-century audience—suggests that they must have responded to a need in the reading public for reassurance.

Claire Tylee has commented that Mrs Humphry Ward, Berta Ruck, Marie Belloc Lowndes and other romantic novelists 'did not require DORA to achieve the bliss of oblivion.... The very reason for [their] wartime success, [their] idealistic patriotism, may have been sufficient reason for [them] to be so forgotten.'[79] However, if we are to see a more complete picture of the Great War, these books must be examined more closely, for they raise important issues about the needs of a wartime readership, needs catered to by publishers eager to meet the demand. Romantic fiction was a profitable enterprise *and* a patriotic contribution. These 'throwaway' stories illuminate the intricacies of wartime polemics and propaganda. Certainly, a public willing to submit to their messages of steadfastness and sacrifice made things easier for the government and its war effort. A public that could identify with the fictional characters that expounded the righteousness of the cause was a public that could be persuaded to carry on to the bitter end. We must, of course, be careful not to assume that readers at the time could not see the humour or hyperbole in the sentiments and

[79] Tylee, *The Great War and Women's Consciousness*, 151.

caricatures of these stories, but the patriotic ideals and conservative values espoused and celebrated spoke to at least a section of the reading public. This means that these seemingly inconsequential 'light' tales of love, adventure, or suspense, read for amusement, were, in fact, the perfect vehicles for sustaining the hearts and minds of the population. Forget your troubles for an hour or so and become, in the process, more convinced of the effort you are making for the War—be it as a soldier, a sacrificing mother or lover, or a civilian worker. A world of fantasy and escapism where things will come right in the end is a reassuring world. However, it is significant that in the majority of these novels, a happy ending is tempered by the continuing shadow of war. Heroes and heroines may ride off into the sunset but the romantic conclusions may yet end in death outside the realms of the story—just like in real life.

Although it has been argued that romance novels of the kind highlighted here 'bore little relation to women's actual experience',[80] there is a case to be made that however hyperbolic the deeds and however effusive the sentimental utterances of the characters, these novels were popular precisely because they *did* bear a relation to 'actual experience'. If we strip away the fiction, we find embedded in these texts numerous contemporary concerns from the way men should react to 'the Call' to the frustration of women denied an active role. The anxiety of being left to wait for news of loved ones in the war zone is represented in the pages of these books just as is the zeal with which many women threw themselves into war work of all kinds. It is to these texts that we shall now turn.

[80] Angela K. Smith, *The Second Battlefield: Women, Modernism and the First World War* (Manchester, 1999), 12.

4

'I Alone am Left to Tell the Tale . . .' Memoirs by Women on Active Service

> It is quite impossible to keep pace with all the new incarnations of women in war-time—'bus-conductress, ticket-collector, lift-girl, club waitress, post-woman, bank clerk, motor-driver, farm-labourer, guide, munition maker. There is nothing new in the function of the ministering angel: the myriad nurses in hospital here or abroad are only carrying out, though in greater numbers than ever before, what has always been women's mission. But whenever he sees one of these new citizens, or hears fresh stories of their address and ability, Mr. Punch is proud and delighted. Perhaps in the past, even in the present, he may have been, or even still is, a little given to chaff Englishwomen for some of their foibles, and even their aspirations. But he never doubted how splendid they were at heart; he never for a moment supposed they would be anything but ready and keen when the hour of need struck.[1]

In June 1916, *Punch* marvelled, in its inimitable way, at female involvement in the Great War and took its place among other periodicals that praised the ways women were serving their country in its hour of need. As in the Boer War, newspapers and magazines were filled with articles that featured women 'doing their bit'. On Thursday 22 October 1914, *The Daily Mirror* (a Northcliffe paper) ran on its front page a series of photographs entitled 'Treating the wounded in Paris: An all-woman staff at a British Hospital' (Fig. 15). The main picture shows four women 'operating on a wounded

[1] *Mr Punch's History of the Great War* (London, New York, Toronto, and Melbourne, 1919), 95–6.

THE DAILY MIRROR, Thursday, October 22, 1914.

BRITISH WARSHIPS SHELL THE GERMANS IN BELGIUM.

The Daily Mirror

LATEST CERTIFIED CIRCULATION MORE THAN 1,000,000 COPIES PER DAY

No. 3,431. Registered at the G.P.O. as a Newspaper. THURSDAY, OCTOBER 22, 1914 One Halfpenny.

TREATING THE WOUNDED IN PARIS: AN ALL-WOMAN STAFF AT A BRITISH HOSPITAL.

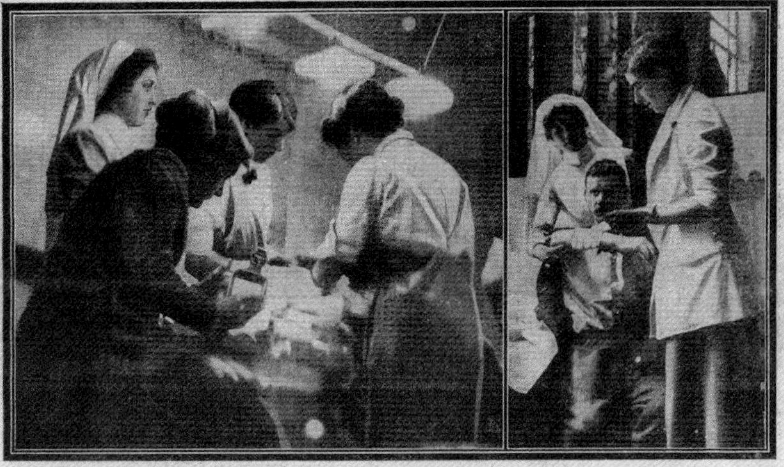

Operating on a wounded soldier. Note the anæsthetist holding the bottle.—(*Daily Mirror* photograph.)

Bandaging an arm.—(*Daily Mirror* photograph.)

The wounded help one another.—(*Daily Mirror* photograph.)

Dr. Garrett-Anderson.

Patient off for a motor-car drive.—(*Daily Mirror* photograph.)

Doctors, nurses, in fact, the whole staff of one of the hospitals for wounded soldiers in Paris is composed of women. The chief surgeon is Dr. Louisa Garrett-Anderson, whose mother, it will be remembered, was one of the pioneers among women in the field of medicine. The institution is fitted with every appliance, and many a British "Tommy" wounded by German bullets or shrapnel is deeply grateful for the treatment he has received at the hands of these skilful women. The hospital is a converted hotel, but dining-rooms, smoking-rooms and lounges have all gone now. They are being made to serve a more useful purpose.

FIG. 15. *The Daily Mirror* (Thursday, 22 October 1914), front page

soldier' and the reader is asked to 'note the anaesthetist holding the bottle'. Depicted in another photograph is Dr Louisa Garrett-Anderson, chief surgeon and daughter of the pioneering women's doctor, Elizabeth Garrett-Anderson, 'bandaging the arm' of a soldier, and helping nurses to put a patient into a motorcar for an outing. The *Mirror* enthuses that 'the institution is fitted with every appliance, and many a British "Tommy" wounded by German bullets or shrapnel is deeply grateful for the treatment he has received at the hands of these skilful women'.

Features in newspapers like *The Daily Mirror* were apt to focus on the dichotomy between the assumed fragility of women and their achievements. In its feature on the '"Quick Change" Nurse Who Escaped', *The Mirror* marvels at how Nurse Dunford, with 'such a frail little body' and 'so weak a frame', could demonstrate such courage and 'strength of mind'. It must be because she has 'the proper British spirit, and is a Cockney to boot', it concludes. (Such commendation echoes that in Northcliffe's other periodicals like *The Girls' Reader*.) She spends 'thrilling days tending wounded in [an Alsace] town that was taken and recaptured many times'. Her patients thus included men from both sides of the conflict. Not surprisingly, the Germans are vindictive and callous occupiers. When fired upon by local inhabitants, they punish the innocent:

> One night in the poor quarters of the town, all the women and children were ordered into the streets, and were kept there all night by guards with fixed bayonets. They were told by a German officer: 'You are all going to be shot in an hour.' Instantly shrieks broke out from the women, and the officer said: 'If you do not stop screaming you will all be shot now.'

German officers are also 'regardless of the lives of their men [who] were literally rushed right up to the cannon's mouth'. Red Cross ideals seem to have no meaning for them as they fit machine guns to the vans and provide ambulance men with pistols so they can 'finish off the wounded horses'. Dunford believes that such arming was for other, more 'awful' reasons. Such flouting of the rules of mercy is one of Germany's chief crimes. Lucky to have escaped occupied territory, Nurse Dunford is said to be keen to return to service with the British Expeditionary Force, 'to do a great work again among her own people'.

These three excerpts are representative of the ways in which women's active service was enshrined in the popular imagination.

They 'play down [the] radical implications' of women's participation in war work by focusing on the needs of the nation, particularly its soldiers.[2] Many male memoirists heap praise on the women who helped them to treat the casualties of war. H. S. Soutar, whose memoir *A Surgeon in Belgium* chronicled his three months of service with the Belgian Field Hospital, wondered 'how many of us realize what Britain owes to her nurses'. After a particularly heavy intake of wounded at Furnes, he marvels

> how the nurses ever managed to look after their patients . . . they were magnificent. They rose to the emergency as only Englishwomen can, and there is not one of those unfortunate men who will not remember with gratitude their sympathy and their skill.[3]

Another surgeon, A. A. Martin, who worked at a Clearing Hospital, asserted that

> the nurse is a welcome sight to both officers and men, and no man nurse can adequately take the place of a trained woman. The presence of nursing sisters in a hospital is good and wholesome, and where they are the hospital work is carried on infinitely better and the patient is well looked after. . . . Our British nursing sisters are splendid women, and work ungrudgingly and sympathetically always. It is good to see a bright-faced, white-aproned nurse amongst the wounded, and she is extraordinarily popular with her patients.[4]

Henry Gervis similarly expressed his 'high appreciation' for the 'keen and intelligent' hospital sisters, who with 'never-failing patience . . . tended the sufferers under their care. . . . They not only ministered to the bodily ills of their patients but helped them in all sorts of other troubles, sympathised with their difficulties and disappointments and often gave them very wise advice.'[5]

Journalists and medical men were not the only ones who chronicled this 'splendid' work of Britannia's daughters. Instead of being simply the 'objects of representation',[6] many 'ministering angels' spoke for themselves. Numerous memoirs by women were

[2] Sharon Ouditt, 'Tommy's Sisters: The Representation of Working Women', in Hugh Cecil and Peter H. Cecil (eds.), *Facing Armageddon 1914–18: The War Experienced* (London, 1996), 739.

[3] H. S. Soutar, *A Surgeon in Belgium* (London, 1915), 17 and 134.

[4] A. A. Martin, *A Surgeon in Khaki* (London, 1915), 139

[5] Henry Gervis, *Arms and the Doctor: Being the Military Experiences of a Middle-Aged Medical Man* (London, 1920), 65.

[6] Sidonie Smith, *A Poetics of Women's Autobiography: Marginality and the Fictions of Self-Representation* (London, 1987), 42.

published between 1914 and 1919.[7] This chapter will consider a representative selection: Kate Finzi's *Eighteen Months in the War Zone* (1916), Violetta Thurstan's *Field Hospital and Flying Column* (1915), Sister Martin-Nicholson's *My Experiences on Three Fronts* (1916), Olive Dent's *A V.A.D. in France* (1917), Pat Beauchamp's *Fanny Goes to War* (1919), and Enid Bagnold's *A Diary without Dates* (1918).

Stylistically, each differs from the others; tone and language vary from the melodramatic rhetoric of propaganda to the austerity and disillusionment of modernist texts, but they are united by their common themes. All heap praise on Tommy Atkins, reproach the civilian slacker, and condemn the Germans; all contain graphic descriptions of wounds and unsanitary conditions; and all express feelings of alienation from the Home Front. The female memoirists reinforce the privileging of battlefront experience and male/warrior supremacy, but they also 'make implicitly subversive claims for the significance of their own experience'.[8]

The 'dominant narrative patterns common in autobiography'—paradise, journey, conversion, and confession[9]—are all to be found in the six memoirs considered in the following. Susanna Egan's elucidation of nineteenth-century male autobiographies provides a useful framework for the war memoirs. With the exception of *A Diary without Dates,* each follows a linear trajectory: pre-war life is represented either as an idyll for the narrator, or a time of (often false) security for the world-at-large; the voyage to the war zone corresponds to the journey; realizations about 'what modern warfare means', as Kate Finzi would call it, usher in the conversion phase; and the ways in which all of these experiences have changed

[7] A survey of the Bodleian Library's pre-1920 catalogue, reveals over 90 'medical' texts published between 1914 and 1919. Included within this number are memoirs, manuals on the treatment of wounds, and reminiscences of visits to hospitals and service units by journalists and other writers. Of these, roughly 50 are memoirs by nurses, surgeons, or ambulance drivers, with women and men being equally represented. Well over sixty journalistic/reportage memoirs by women were also published during the War and in its immediate aftermath. These include *'My Little Bit': A Collection of Articles* (1919) by Marie Corelli; *The Cellar-House of Pervyse* (1917) by Elsie T'Serclaes; *England's Effort* (1916) by Mrs Humphry Ward; and *Germany's Crime against France* (1915) by Jessie Weston.

[8] Dorothy Goldman, *Women Writers and the Great War* (New York, 1995), 43.

[9] Susanna Egan, *Patterns of Experience in Autobiography* (Chapel Hill and London, 1984), 4.

the narrator, physically or emotionally, form her confession. Egan argues that, in autobiographies,

> life as it is lived is transformed into literary events, the autobiographer as a character in a book, and an essentially shapeless life into a life of shape and meaning ... the mechanics of that fictionalizing process [provide] direction for the random events and generally accessible meaning for original subjective experience.[10]

Women's Great War autobiographies transform the intensely personal into the communal. Like the historian, the autobiographer creates part of the national history and consciousness, 'subordinating the historical activity of describing what happened to the poetic activity of conveying what happens, [and] incorporates his facts into a mythic narrative'.[11] It is also true that, in the process of writing, these women become characters in their own literary narratives, for, as Avrom Fleishman argues, 'the book turns the autobiographer into a new being: not the person who lived its events, but the person who wrote it. The events themselves are inevitably transformed from what they were ... to what has been made into literature.'[12] Indeed, all of these memoirs are 'vigorously literary'.[13] They are highly organized and stylized, employing metaphor, irony, allusion, juxtaposition, imagery, and many other literary devices in their attempt to recreate a vivid representation of experience. They are the product of a 'special historical moment' when

> the belief in the educative powers of classical and English literature was still extremely strong [and] the appeal of popular education and 'self-improvement' was at its peak, and such education was still largely conceived in humanistic terms. ... The intersection of these two forces, the one 'aristocratic,' the other 'democratic,' established an atmosphere of public respect for literature unique in modern times.[14]

The women here represented are the 'daughters of educated men', as Virginia Woolf called them,[15] who were steeped in the traditions of the Church of England, well-versed in English literature and

[10] Ibid., 7.
[11] Ibid., 23.
[12] Avrom Fleishman, *Figures of Autobiography: The Language of Self-Writing in Victorian and Early-Modern England* (Los Angeles, 1983), 5.
[13] Paul Fussell, *The Great War and Modern Memory* (Oxford, 1975), 157.
[14] Ibid., 157.
[15] Virginia Woolf, *Three Guineas* (London, 1938), 207.

history, and adept at letter-writing, in an age when letters were 'a basic means of communication and essential to the development of their ideas on paper'.[16] The chaos and disorder that is war is ordered and contained within the memoirs' organization of events, places, dates, and people: 'the artist excels at the transformation of such chaos essentially into a meaningful form that is accessible to all'.[17] The combination of 'feminine power and vulnerability [hinges] on an almost shamanic power to rescue and to heal'.[18] Although telling the tale is intended as an act of remembering the dead, it becomes a medium for coming to terms with experiences that defy all imagining. The act of writing a memoir, then, is an act of self-discovery, 'a process through which the autobiographer struggles to shape an "identity" out of an amorphous subjectivity'.[19]

The driving force behind Kate Finzi's *Eighteen Months in the War Zone* (1916) (Fig. 16) is her compulsion to 'tell the tale'. The phrase occurs three times in the book: in her Foreword, in the main body of the text—an edited version of her diary written between October 1914 and February 1916—and in her Epilogue of May 1916. This tripling effect is a key feature of her style. 'Triples' mostly occur as phrases within paragraphs to give rhetorical emphasis, but they also serve to structure her memoir. Order is imposed on the narrative, on 'what is of necessity a piecy document' (ix). There are three parts, each divided into chapters organized by month and year. Part I, entitled 'As It Was in the Beginning', covers October to December 1914; Part II, 'Order Out of Chaos', the longest of the three, follows Finzi over the twelve months of 1915; and Part III, 'Scrapped', details her final two months of active service in 1916. Utilizing first biblical language and imagery—'as it was in the beginning', 'order out of chaos'—Finzi then employs a colloquial term to sum up her forced retirement from service because of ill health.

The tripartite organization and rhetorical patterning of her book probably derives, subconsciously, from a conventional schooling in the Scriptures and exposure to many Church of England sermons

[16] Tierl Thompson (ed.), *Dear Girl: The Diaries and Letters of Two Working Women 1897–1917* (London, 1987), 4.

[17] Egan, *Patterns of Experience in Autobiography*, 22.

[18] Suzanne Raitt and Trudi Tate (eds.), *Women's Fiction and the Great War* (Oxford, 1997), 9.

[19] Smith, *A Poetics of Women's Autobiography*, 5.

FIG. 16. *Eighteen Months in the War Zone* (1916), by Kate John Finzi, dustjacket illustration (1617 e.69), Bodleian Library, University of Oxford

with their insistent 'firstly... secondly... thirdly' structure.[20] Both the pastoral and the realistic are part of her writing: descriptions of nature delight and soothe whereas catalogues of wounds disturb and sicken. Stylistic contradictions such as these reflect the conflicting emotions engendered by nursing in the war zone.

The development of the narrative is essentially linear, progressing month by month. However, it also doubles back upon itself. Since the act of telling is paramount to Kate Finzi, the Foreword anticipates and the Epilogue returns the reader's attention back to the moment in the diary when she realizes that she *herself* must speak for those who are gone: 'there is no one else'. Significantly, this revelation comes on All Souls' Day after a service for *les morts pour la Patrie*. She is overcome by an awareness that those left behind suffer the keenest pain: 'no passed souls could be so needful of that prayer [*Requiescat in pace!*] as the restless, tortured souls of the living mourning crowd'.[21] The souls of the dead haunt her, however. Following 'an irresistible something', she wanders around the deserted hospital near the quay in Boulogne: 'in spite of the dead stillness that reigned I could feel the throbbing of the many souls who passed away' (204). This repeated reference to the 'souls' emphasizes the force with which their memory assails her. A little later, she perceives a 'spirit':

> A rat ran across the concrete, emphasising the desolation of the scene. Out of the gloom of a certain corner the spirit of a nameless prisoner greeted me. With a last tetanus spasm—a writhe—a death rattle—the jaw relaxed like a gaping fish, and a strange little sigh to betoken a released spirit. . . . A sigh of wind came through a broken pane. Was it imagination, or did it bear with it faintly from afar the old oft-heard cry: "Christ help us!" (204–5)

The drama of the prisoner's death throes is heightened by the triple action of spasm, writhe, and rattle, and the horrific simile of the gaping fish. Yet the unworldly, dream-like nature of this scene is

[20] Fussell compares the relationship between 'the empirical principle of three in military procedure and the magical or mystical threes of myth, epic, drama, ritual, romance, folklore, prophecy, and religion. In the prevailing atmosphere of anxiety, the military threes take on a quality of the mythical or prophetic. The well-known triads of traditional myth and ritual donate, as it were, some of their meanings and implications to the military threes. The result is that military action becomes elevated to the level of myth and imbued with much of its portent' (Fussell, *The Great War and Modern Memory*, 127).

[21] Kate John Finzi, *Eighteen Months in the War Zone: A Record of a Woman's Work on the Western Front* (London, 1916), 203.

reinforced by the continued use of words like 'sigh' and 'spirit'. She rejects actually hearing 'the old oft-heard cry' with one word, 'Bah!', admitting, 'They are gone. I alone am left to tell the tale; and generations to come will never know' (205). No narrative can ever communicate the full extent of the War or of what she has seen or felt.

Such telling is, nevertheless, her mission; she is in a privileged position. Echoing the messenger in the Book of Job—'I only am escaped to tell thee'—and like Edmund Blunden and Robert Graves, Finzi feels compelled 'to go over the ground again'.[22] Along with male memoirists, she and the other women discussed in this chapter follow in the tradition of the poet of the heroic age, who 'was not primarily a warrior. His function was to ensure that his friends did not die unsung. He must escape that he might tell: bear witness.'[23] Finzi bears witness for both the male soldier and the female nurse.

The authenticity of her story is attested to by Maj.-Gen. Sir Alfred Turner, who contributes an introduction praising the nurses that 'softened the horrors of War to our soldiers, who ministered aid to them when they were stricken by wounds or diseases, and mitigated their tortures' (xviii).[24] His praise is coupled with a vehement attack on the Germans, who seem to him the embodiment of evil. He likens the Kaiser to Caligula, calling him 'the imperial braggart' and asserts that Wilhelm himself planned the War, 'the greatest crime ever committed against civilisation and humanity'. According to Turner, Finzi's account, in a 'plain, unvarnished style [is] a terrible and graphic picture' of the savagery of the German troops, as commanded by their officers (xv). Without flowery sentiment—like a solider *not* a woman—she is able to bring home

> the sickening horrors of war and the awful sufferings that our gallant defenders have undergone in doing their duty, in the service of their King and country, for the honour and integrity of Europe, and for the safety and

[22] Edmund Blunden, *Undertones of War* (London, 1928), 223.

[23] Jon Stallworthy, 'Survivors' Songs in Welsh Poetry', Annual Gwyn Jones Lecture, 1982, 6.

[24] Maj.-Gen. Sir Alfred Turner, K.C.B. (1842–1918), joined the Royal Army in 1860, and was, among many occupations, Commander-in-Chief of Ireland from 1885 to 1886, the Commissioner of Police (Cork, Kerry, Clare, Limerick), 1886 to 1892, and Inspector-General of the Auxiliary Forces, 1900 to 1904. He was decorated for civil services in Ireland, for military services, and for being mentioned in despatches (mil. C.B.). Turner published his memoirs, *Sixty Years of a Soldier's Life*, in 1912 (*Who Was Who*, 1916–1928, v. II).

protection of the people in this country in this great war of liberation. [The people at home] are apt to make too light of [German crimes] from want of power to realise them (xvii).

Turner validates this woman's account of a man's war: she is a qualified observer and what she says can be trusted. She follows in the tradition of Florence Nightingale, the archetypal image of female devotion to the wounded soldier, and can be counted in the company of Edith Cavell, that contemporary heroine, the 'ray of glory upon the noble record of our British Nurses'. Finzi and her female compatriots, Turner says, 'showed what they were made of. Hundreds of thousands [of] heroic women . . . face all dangers and hardships for the sake of doing good to others' (xvii). The phrase, 'showed what they were made of', appears time and again in both memoirs and novels, along with such descriptions as 'natural' and 'bed-rock' to emphasize that war brings out the best in people.

Finzi's own 'universal devotion', her war work, begins in October 1914, when as a newly qualified nurse, 'fresh from the statutory discipline of the wards of a London hospital', she embarks at Southampton for France. The 'journey' in Egan's autobiographical schema begins, and it is not long before the 'conversion' phase takes place. Her excitement as 'one of the countless thousands clamouring to "get out" to the scene of action' is checked by the sight of the hundreds of soldiers who embark with her. The image of war as the great game is replaced by the sense that it is, in fact, a 'great slaughter' (5). A. A. Martin echoes these sentiments. When he and his fellow medical colleagues embark on their journey to the war zone, they are anxious 'to see and take part in the romance and adventures of great battles. . . . Romance! Adventure! Very soon we were up against cold facts, and there was no romance or pomp and circumstance then.'[25]

Not all women shared Kate Finzi's awareness, and those like Lady ____, whom she encounters upon arrival in France, receive her critical assessment: 'the chic little woman who, charming though she may be in a London "at-home" is, we fear, liable to give our Allies a false impression of English women in war-time' (7). Such a woman never did any nursing or other work, but went around Belgium hospitals followed by a photographer so that her picture might appear in the newspapers.

[25] Martin, *A Surgeon in Khaki*, 14.

Worse than society ladies, however, are those unlicensed practitioners and young women who come out to France because their fiancés are at the Front (Vera Brittain was one of these). Finzi is scathing about VADs who wear the same uniforms as qualified nurses, and asks

> for what are a number of first-aid lectures or stretcher-drills as compared with the real hospital training. It is ridiculous to imagine that V.A.D.s with their theoretical experience, are competent to run hospitals themselves; it is equally ridiculous to allow the valuable qualified nurses to run themselves to death, doing jobs an untrained woman can do, instead of utilising the many eager workers willing to take over the menial work.
>
> It would not be difficult to sift the wheat from the chaff, the seekers after sensation from the genuine workers. There is no romance in the work of the hospital, no jaunts to the battlefields bearing cups of water to the dying, no soothing of pillows and holding the hands of patients; but ten to twelve hours each day occupied in the accomplishment of tasks so menial that one would hesitate to ask a servant to perform them. (52)

The tripling effect in the second paragraph reinforces her point that the War is not what the uninitiated enthusiast imagines—'no romance', 'no jaunts', 'no soothing of pillows'. It also is meant to emphasize the hardships. To the long hours of unrelenting work with up to a thousand wounded a day and overcrowded conditions are added 'the dirt and bad drainage' of the nurse's quarters. There is no retreat to the comforts of home. The nurse's bunk is a 'white-washed, rat-ridden, ill-smelling partition compartment' (35). Addressing an audience used to servants, she tries to dissuade a privileged class of women—imagining themselves as Florence Nightingales of the Western Front—from coming to France in pursuit of excitement. *Eighteen Months in the War Zone* attempts to convey a more favourable and serious impression of women in wartime. The dullness of some hospital work—and the class hierarchy associated with it—is attested to by Wilmot Parker Herringham in his memoir, *A Physician in France*:

> The alleviation of a nurse's life is the serious case. When there is a great deal to do and the details of nursing are very important for the patient's welfare, nurses never mind the work, however hard and disgusting. But it is depressing to have to take a dozen temperatures, every one of them normal, twice a day, and to have nothing else to do but housemaid's and parlourmaid's work.[26]

[26] Wilmot Parker Herringham, *A Physician in France* (London, 1919), 87.

Similarly, Finzi's scathing comment on inexperienced VADs is echoed by A. A. Martin who complained that when he volunteered for the RAMC in 1914, despite his service both as a Army surgeon in the Boer War and as a civilian surgeon in a leading hospital in New Zealand, he was not entitled 'to hold any rank higher than the young medical man who had completed his training a week ago.... Men with imperfect professional skill and experience were given duties which should have been entrusted only to men fully possessed of those qualifications'.[27]

Although she wants to disabuse her readers of the glamour of wartime nursing, she does not contradict the popular view of the enemy. Along with Maj.-Gen. Turner, she is convinced of Germany's malfeasance and ferocity: 'surely we are pitted against a foe so strong in physique and so brave and cunning, that many years of strenuous training and thrift will be required to fit the united races to withstand the onslaught' (10). Such an assertion reiterates pre-war fears about the physical and moral unfitness of the country that degeneration debates amplified. Elsewhere she aligns herself with eugenics and the theories of race development which, as we have seen, were so prevalent at the time.[28] Those who answered 'The Call' were the 'bed-rock' of Britain, but many remained unrepentant shirkers who should be 'well strafed' in Finzi's opinion:

> Why, after all, should our beautiful island be left with the unfit, the loafers, the "funks" as fathers for the future generations? In every other country the army is representative, not the pick of the land, but of the average male population. We, however, seem bent on committing race suicide. (94)

Stories of war crimes that were becoming increasingly familiar on the Home Front in England through the Bryce Report (1915) and books such as William LeQueux's *German Atrocities* (1914) are echoed here. A Brussels man relates how, when fleeing the city, he and his fellow refugees

> had come across a deserted village where a farmer gave them shelter. His only daughter had been brutally mutilated and murdered before her own parents because, in resisting the embraces of an officer, she scratched out one of his eyes.
>
> 'They cut off her breast and carried away her foot as a trophy.' (15)

[27] Martin, *A Surgeon in Khaki*, 8.

[28] Daniel Pick, *Faces of Degeneration: A European Disorder, c. 1848-c.1918* (London, 1989), 195–9.

The image of the ravaged woman was frequently used as a metaphor for Belgium itself. Finzi's description calls to mind a recruiting poster, where the country is represented by a (presumably) dead female, prostrate beneath the foot of a gorilla-like beast wearing a Prussian helmet and brandishing a bloody-tipped club. A prurient fascination is indulged by both the visual and the written forms of such an image with their none-too-subtle suggestion of rape and the emphasis on the sexual mutilation of cutting off breasts. Mutilating corpses was presented as a German pastime: Finzi recounts how a wounded Scottish soldier told her of his discovery of the desecrated body of a Roman Catholic nurse in a village left by the enemy. His outrage is such that he cannot wait to '"get at 'em again"' (29). Such savagery forms a large part of the incidents recorded by surgeons as well: 'Near a stable built on to a farmhouse we saw a Frenchman lying dead across a manure heap. The top of his head had been blown off, and his brains were plastered over his face. This is the German way.'[29]

The soldiers' zeal to avenge such atrocities is matched by that of their female compatriots. On 30 October, Finzi writes, 'we worked till midnight and were on duty again by 7.30 this morning'. The rush of the hospital makes it possible only to treat the worst cases, such as those who are haemorrhaging. Many men had not had their wounds dressed since the first field station, and there was often nothing to wash them with but red handkerchiefs used to shade lights: 'the worst part of the wounds is the fearful sepsis and the impossibility of getting them anything like clean' (29). The nurses have a half-hour walk from their billets to the hospital, over cobblestones, and often through rain, but Finzi tells us that this has 'the advantage of clearing the haunting smell of the gas-gangrene out of our nostrils' (28). No romantic portrait of Florence Nightingale ever communicated so graphically the sickening reality of wartime nursing:

> fingerless hands, lungs pierced, arms and legs pretty well gangrenous, others already threatening tetanus, . . . mouths swollen beyond all recognition with bullet shots, fractured femurs, shattered jaws, sightless eyes, ugly scalp wounds. (30)

[29] Martin, *A Surgeon in Khaki*, 76.

Other 'manifold horrors of war' include vermin—'the men are alive with them ... even amputated limbs are found to be crawling' (33)—and the condition of the hospital itself. Lack of ventilation means that 'there can be no attempt at asepsis', and supplies such as disinfectant, iodine, and dressings are all at a 'low ebb'. With no lavatory accommodation, the lame are carried to the latrines on the quay on orderlies' backs. 'It is distinctly unhealthy, and the odours in the place are indescribable and never to be forgotten' (38). Such work is not for the faint-hearted, such descriptions not for the squeamish reader.

Despite the work and conditions, Finzi repeatedly declares that she and her fellow nursing sisters become more cheerful as the conditions worsen. They are determined to make the best of it: 'it is strange that all the years we worked hard to amuse ourselves at home not one brought an eighth of the satisfaction of *this*' (40). For all her annoyance at untrained VADs, she can admit that being near the action has an allure:

> No wonder everyone who can afford to be is in France. One feels it in the air, it is the Real Thing; one is no longer a looker-on, but a moving factor of things who can afford to pity those at home whose activities have not yet had occasion to be called into play. (53)

It is not 'until one has felt the clinging of the helpless hand, or run to the call of the feeble voice, [that] one know[s] the greatest of all joys—the joy of service' (58). Here she runs counter to her earlier argument that there is 'no romance' in war-work. What she describes *is* a romantic vision. Although noble, and no doubt sincere, the assertion about the joy of service nevertheless reinforces the more sentimental emotions that elsewhere are renounced. This contradictory stance is a salient feature of women's active service memoirs. The desire to tell, to bear witness to the truth so as to disabuse the Home Front of its apathy and ignorance is coupled with a propensity for sentimental and lyrical reconstruction. Finzi, for one, will never forget a concert at Christmas 1915, the sight of everyone—wounded, nurses, orderlies—crowded together in 'cheerfulness born out of the determination to make the best of abnormal circumstances' (82). Wistfully, she says, 'in after years, it will be interesting to note the music of 1914, the rise and wave of "Tipperary" and "Sister Susie" and a hundred other popular songs that have made life cheery for our warriors' (84). If Peace does not come in the New Year, she asks for 'the strength to play our parts in the great game worthily of our men!' (85).

It is these men, these happy warriors, to borrow Wordsworth's phrase, who are the objects of women's devoted service. Although less maternal in her feelings than some of the other memoirists discussed later, Finzi shares the admiration for Tommy Atkins. She emphasizes the pathos of his situation: 'there is no mistaking a man from the front. They all have it—the trench-haunted look' (50), and their incredible courage:

> what untold misery these crushed bits of humanity mean, brought swiftly to the silent city of suffering! How gladly we would suffer for them! Yet not a moan, not a groan, in those great wards whilst mind and will have the power to cope with the agonies of the flesh! (114)

Like the Scottish soldier mentioned earlier, these wounded only want to recover so as to return to fight the Hun: 'a few are enraged to madness at the sight of a German' (30). Those who must return to the Front are stoic; they know 'it's murder', but they are not 'down-hearted' as they march away (50).

In contrast, civilians at home exhibit a 'slack unpreparedness', the result of a 'slothful system'. Witnessing this while on leave, Finzi is seized by a great anger. She blames the government for keeping the Home Front in ignorance, and aligns herself with the Northcliffe press. People at home are 'utterly oblivious' to the seriousness of the shell campaign, she writes, despite warnings in the *Daily Mail*, which she calls 'the only organ strong enough to bring the truth before the public and combat the weaknesses of a desultory government' (146). Although Finzi acknowledges that the people at home should not know everything about modern war, or 'that vast pestilential graveyard that is Belgium', she does wish that civilians had more sense of the difficulties and the horrors—of the kind she describes—not the 'yarns', which she finds, are in demand. Speaking at a community meeting in Cumberland, she discovers that the audience wants to hear great tales of heroism, of her risking her life with daily shell-fire and the Hun close at hand:

> What they want are descriptions of weeping gas victims and death-bed scenes (that in reality are far better forgotten—if it is possible) and incidents such as a youthful convalescent sapper confided to me recently—of the man who, though his head was blown clean off at midday, was found to be

convulsively clawing the earth with fingers that seemed yet alive at sundown! (149)

Of course, Finzi tells the readers of her memoir some of the very things she derides the Cumberland audience for wanting to know, but she stresses that the real heroism was in the day-to-day work:

maintaining continual cheerfulness in the face of odds like bursting boilers . . . the dullness of buttering endless loaves, of wheedling Primus stoves into working order, of changing French money for English at a varying rate of exchange, of living amongst a strange, heterogeneous crowd of people, far away from one's own friends, and stifling longings for one's *lares et penates*, of the dreadful monotony, and various other details of barmaiding, amateur and otherwise. Therefore, with many a wiser, I seek shelter behind a discreet silence, except when the insistence of the 'Do-tell-me-all-about-it! Have-you-seen-lots-of-horrors?' girl elicits an ironical reply to the effect that most of our time is spent in champagne lunches and moonlight picnics. (149–50)

Here we have what Herbert Read calls 'the compact accretion of details',[30] the rhythm of which imitates the 'dreadful monotony'. She may be perpetuating the image of women's war-work as a 'lark', when she is drawn out of her silence by the insistent story-seeker, but we can appreciate her frustration. She shares with male witnesses the sense of alienation from those at home. Although she sometimes perceives complacency and indifference on the part of civilians, she also, like Graves and Blunden, recognizes that the Home Front was rabid with blood-lust.[31] *Goodbye to All That* and *Undertones of War* were, it is important to note, produced in a post-war world, where time and political, and indeed literary, climate gave their authors the mandate to speak more openly and critically, with reflection, and even embellishment. However, Graves, Blunden, and Finzi all share a discomfiture with the experience of going home, and with the atmosphere they find there. The Front is their true home. What Egan calls 'the conversion phase' is complete as Finzi aligns herself with

a generation that, swept by the great driving spirit . . . from the little ruts in life into the great vortex of war, has already proved its metal. . . . It may be an ironical fate that designs the younger generation to lay down their lives for the political blunders of the older—but the true tragedy is not in the

[30] Herbert Read, *English Prose Style* (London, 1952), 39.

[31] Blunden, *Undertones of War*, 223; Robert Graves, *Goodbye to All That* (New York, 1985), 199.

youths cut down in the flower of their manhood, or the girls broken in health by the magnitude of the task they have tackled; the true tragedy is in the derelict 'dug-outs' vainly hunting for jobs, the aged women wringing their hands, with the cry, 'We are too old to help!' (150–2)

Challenged by such rhetoric, it would be surprising if young women who read *Eighteen Months in the War Zone* were not inspired to become active participants, even with all the criticisms of the idealistic war-worker. To be banded in 'one great unity of purpose' (200) must have held a powerful attraction. In this way, the memoir is more than just a record of one woman's experiences near the Front, designed to bring home to the reader the chaos and suffering of war. It can also be seen as a recruiting tract, for the cataloguing of horrors is outweighed by the lyricism and pathos that characterize its reflective and oratorical passages. The lengthiest, but certainly the most poignant of these (and worth quoting in full) is Finzi's rumination on the meaning of war written on 1 January 1916. Succumbing to failing health, she prepares to be 'scrapped' from active service in the penultimate chapter, the beginning of Book III:

Every now and then one feels tempted to say, "War? What do *you* know of War?

"Have *you* seen men as they came down from the Front during the first mad months, primitive, demented, at their last gasp, ready to face death in any form rather than the hellish uncertainty they had just left? Have *you* heard the groans of the wounded, seen arms rotting off and legs smashed to pieces, and dressed black gaping holes in young boys' sides? Have *you* seen faces blown beyond recognition—faces eyeless, noseless, jawless, and heads that were only half heads?

"Have *you* been round the cold, extemporised wards and covered up countless restless forms on their pallets, smelt the smell of mud-caked coats that were their pillows, soothed their coughs with what was left of tinned milk, hearkening as they cried aloud in their sleep:

'*Great Lord Jesus, help us!*'

"Men who had probably not prayed since their childhood, men who had probably scoffed at the idea of God—have *you* heard them live through their battles again in their slumber or under anaesthetics? '*Get at 'em, lads—now's your last chance—give it 'em 'ot—ah! ah!*'

"Have *you* removed clothes and boots from helpless limbs caked on by seven weeks' mud and overrun with vermin? Have *you* seen forever nameless enemy corpses washed and carried out to the mortuary, and enemy though they were, because of their youth, wished that you could tell their mothers you had done your best?

"When you have seen this . . . and not before, will you know what modern warfare means."

Yet it is all something one would not have missed, although no sane person would face it a second time; for, as an American said recently: "Those who have not participated in this war will be for ever lacking in something which is not to be recaptured later." (227)

This passage contains many resonances.[32] Not only does it exemplify Finzi's use of rhetorical repetition ('Have *you*?'), but it encapsulates the images of modern warfare—the jawless, eyeless, limbless, half-demented, vermin-ridden men—images that would be exploited by poets like Owen. Her phrase 'black gaping holes in young boys' sides' is most Owen-like. She pre-figures Sassoon's 'dreams from the pit' of 'Does it Matter' and Owen's 'smothering dream' in 'Dulce et Decorum Est' when she describes the cries of the wounded as they re-live battles in sleep. The final paragraph turns from these disturbing images to a familiar resolution. In aligning herself with a special generation, Finzi echoes Henry V's speech before the battle of Agincourt:

KING
We few, we happy few, we band of brothers;
For he to-day that sheds his blood with me
Shall be my brother; be he ne'er so vile
This day shall gentle his condition:
And gentlemen in England now a-bed
Shall think themselves accurs'd they were not here,
And hold their manhoods cheap whiles any speaks
That fought with us upon St. Crispin's day.[33]

Though she and her compatriots have 'buried all our youth and most of our vitality' along with the dead,

no doubt one day, when War no longer holds us in its grip, we shall harken spellbound to the strain of some melody that our local band of tin whistles and combs used to play, and mayhap with the divine discontent of

[32] Vera Brittain describes a similar sense of pathetic helplessness, how she had 'to endure the fear and sorrow and fatigue that [the War] brought me, and to witness in impotent anguish the deaths, not only of those who had made my personal life, but of the many brave, uncomplaining men whom I had nursed and could not save' (Vera Brittain, *Testament of Youth* (London, 1933), 471).

[33] William Shakespeare, *Henry V*, IV. iii. 60–67.

humanity, we shall sigh for the good old days of France, bully beef and tin whistles. (222)

Such consolation, however, is far off. She looks forward to the day when 'the odour of Death will no longer haunt our nostrils; mayhap we, too, shall be deaf to the sighing of the many souls in the wind' (251). Visiting a military cemetery 'Somewhere in France' before returning to England, she is again assailed by these 'many souls' and is 'haunted by the cries of the dead and dying I had seen. Not even the most solid edifices of masonry can obliterate the gruesome realities of a vivid memory' (257).

The American Leslie Buswell attested to the omnipresent memory of what he had witnessed in his work as an ambulance driver: 'Sometimes when I get into my bed or am trying to get a few hours' sleep . . . the horrors of blood—broken arms, mutilated trunks, and ripped-open faces, etc.—haunt me.' Like Finzi, however, he is spurred on to continue his service 'when a call comes, and you see those bandaged soldiers waiting to be taken to a hospital' and because 'it has been good to be here in the presence of high courage and to have learned a little in our youth of the values of life and death'.[34] A. A. Martin looked to 'when peace comes again to Belgium, Ypres and its roads, its Hill 60 and its graves will be a place of holy pilgrimage to thousands of English, French, and Germans, for here fell and are buried their bravest dead. But the curious tripper and the Cook's tourist had better keep away from Ypres. Let the friends of the dead and the quiet country folk have the land in their possession for a season.' He adds, 'The memories of the days spent at the front can never be quite forgotten. Time may blunt the clearness of outline of some of the incidents in a hazy mist, but there are others that will stand out clear and undimmed to the last.'[35]

Finzi's Epilogue to Book III and to her diary is not recollected in tranquillity. Not only is she feeling '"scrapped" like the Ford cars, . . . return [ing] home a derelict, a Rip van Winkle' (227), but she pens her last words in a northern town while 'bombs [are] falling on an entirely defenceless city' (259). The War rages on as she makes her confession, a confession that attempts to justify the publication of her diary. She kept it in the beginning 'for purely

[34] Leslie Buswell, *Ambulance No. 10: Personal Letters from the Front* (London and Boston, 1917), 98 and 103.

[35] Martin, *A Surgeon in Khaki*, 246–7 and 277.

personal reasons', but public interest in the work of women at the Base convinced her that 'the appearance of these pages' was warranted. She then adds a more personal reason for publication, one that is not entirely self-effacing in the 'I-publish-only-because-I-have-been-urged-to-do-so' mode. She says, 'seeing as there is no one else to tell the tale, I send my little volume into the world'. This is the third repetition of the phrase 'telling the tale'. Further, she emphasizes that she has told the tale in as much detail as she was allowed. 'If', she states, 'there are many omissions, it must be noted that a War Diary published during wartime is of necessity much expurgated to meet the demands of the censor' (260). By extension, a war diary published in wartime of necessity expresses determination to carry on the fight against the enemy, is effusive in its praise of the fighting man, and is constructed so as to inspire and bolster resolve. Edmund Blunden would repeat such ideas in 1930:

> When the War of 1914–1918 was in progress, of course, an immense output of war-books occurred. Much that was printed has sunk into obscurity. 'Hate' had much to say, which we are happy to forget. . . . It was inevitably a long time before a real account of the War could make its way to light. Loyalty, as we nationally conceived it, co-operated with the censor in enforcing a silence and in trying to indicate by smiles that the war was not a hopeless disaster.[36]

Finzi does not mince words when describing the brutality of warfare. Indeed, *The New Statesman* reviewer asserts as much with the assessment, 'the romance of war fades before tetanus and gangrene.'[37] However, what she witnessed did not lead her to condemn, in the manner of Owen or Sassoon, the politicians and generals who ran the War. Rather, she concludes her memoir with a quotation from Kipling:

> Only the Master shall praise us, only the Master shall blame,
> And no one shall work for money and no one shall work for fame,
> But each for the joy of working. . . .

Eighteen Months in the War Zone is essentially conservative, deeply rooted in the ideals of honour, duty, and sacrifice, and it hinges on a pre-1914 outlook on the world. Claire Tylee is particularly scathing

[36] Edmund Blunden, *A Booklist on the War, 1914–1918*, compiled by E. Blunden, Cyril Falls, H. M. Tomlinson, and R. Wright (London, 1930), 2.

[37] *The New Statesman*, 27 January 1917.

about the way in which Finzi's memoir was 'part of the facile war-propaganda' and finds a 'hollow mockery in [her] stock phrasing' and justifications for the War. Yet in its contradictions, its preoccupation with the souls and the memory of the dead, and its candid descriptions of the horrors of war, *Eighteen Months in the War Zone* prefigures those produced in a very different, post-war climate.

Violetta Thurstan's book, *Field Hospital and Flying Column* (1915), reads like a piece of travel-writing, for it is as much about her peregrinations as about her nursing work. The narrative is propelled forward by the journeys: ten chapters record the active service that takes her from England to occupied Belgium, into German territory to the Dutch frontier, to Poland, and finally to Russia. Not confined to the Western Front, *Field Hospital and Flying Column* provides a wide perspective on the War. Maps visually document Thurstan's movements, recalling nineteenth-century explorations to distant lands, and lending her text a general air of authenticity (Fig. 17). Yet there is also an air of high-society glamour, as she meets and socializes with European royalty and dignitaries: 'a delightful dinner to meet Prince Gustav of Denmark, an invitation to meet Princess Mary of Greece, another lunch with Madame Tschering . . . the "Florence Nightingale of Denmark"'.[38] She is even granted an audience with the Empress Marie Federovna, who 'was absolutely charming to us . . . , such a nice start to our work in Russia' (111). As Claire Tylee notes,

> adopting the narrative form of the travel genre enabled women to structure their books around a journey presented as an expedition, a voyage of discovery across a threatened region, where the unknown menace lurked always over the horizon. . . . The travel genre . . . by granting . . . the authority of class privilege and race-superiority, reinforced the idea of the Germans as the unspeakable Other.[39]

Thurstan shares Kate Finzi's attitude to brutal Germans and the unreadiness of Britain, as well as her antipathy towards excitement-seekers who pose as qualified nurses. Even after her declaration that

[38] Violetta Thurstan, *Field Hospital and Flying Column, Being the Journal of an English Nursing Sister in Belgium and Russia* (1915), 99.

[39] Claire M. Tylee, '"Munitions of the Mind": Travel Writing, Imperial Discourse and Great War Propaganda by Mrs Humphry Ward', *English Literature in Transition 1880–1920*, v.39: 2 (1996), 176.

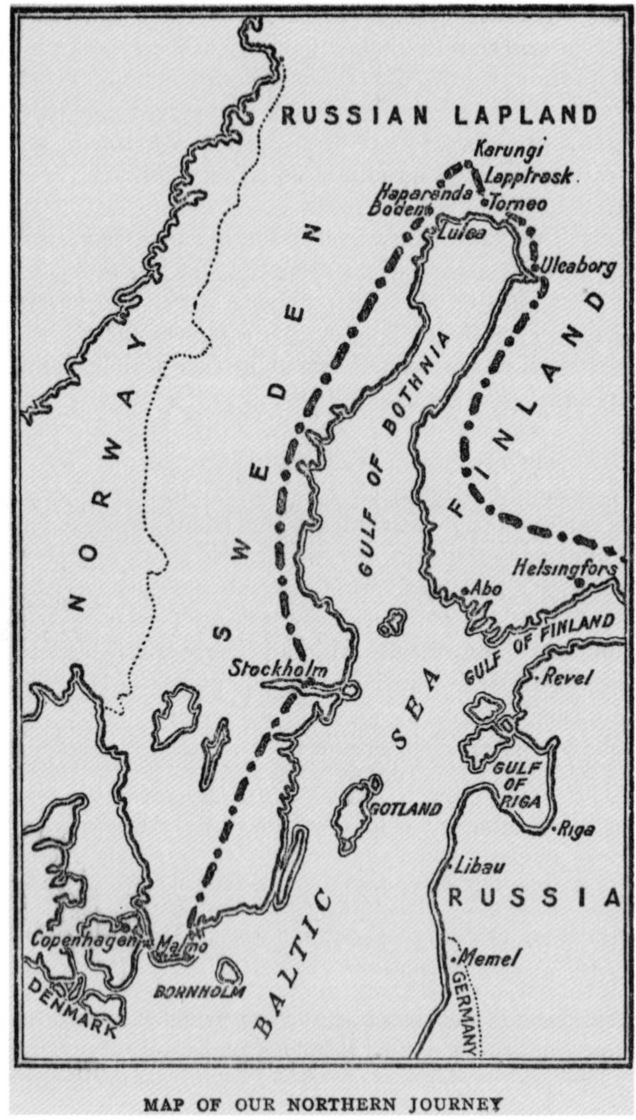

FIG. 17. *Field Hospital and Flying Column* (1915) by Violetta Thurstan, The Hypatia Trust

'this is not a diatribe against members of Voluntary Aid Detachments', she continues to rebuke

> the women who have a few weeks' or months' training, who blossom out into full uniform and call themselves Sister Rose, or Sister Mabel, and are taken at their own valuation by a large section of the public, and manage through influence or bluff to get posts that should only be held by trained nurses, and generally end up by bringing shame and disrepute upon the profession. (5)

Thurstan's tone is generally more buoyant than Finzi's, communicating as it does the sense of movement and impermanency, of confusion and constant activity, indeed, excitement. This nurse is often 'on the go', being sent to another destination—sometimes against her will by the Germans—exploring bombarded villages and positions close to the front line. The multiplicity of places she sees and people with whom she interacts are the focus of her narrative. The reviewer in *The Outlook* (3 July 1915) asserted that 'Miss Thurstan has not the literary skill at command to make her readers realise' the full horror of the miseries she witnesses and that her narrative 'progresses by degrees from the almost holiday air of Brussels to the scenes of ruin and death in a manner which, without intention, almost cloaks these iniquities'. Yet there is underlying praise for the way Thurstan leaves it to the reader to 'supply the pity of it from your own imagination.'[40] She certainly does provide glimpses of the unsavoury details of wartime nursing. We are told about her 'baptism of fire' in the Red Cross hospital outside Charleroi in Belgium:

> The confusion that reigned within was indescribable.... It is a dreadful nightmare to look back at. Blood-stained uniforms hastily cut off the soldiers lying on the floor—half-open packets of dressing were on every locker; basins of dirty water or disinfectant had not been emptied; men were moaning with the pain, calling for water, begging that their dressings might be done again; and several new cases just brought in were requiring urgent attention. And the cannon never ceased booming. (24)

[40] *Field Hospital and Flying Column* received similar treatment in *The Cambridge Review* (26 May 1915) and *The Dial* (24 June 1915). *The Bookman*, which also reproduced a portrait of Thurstan in their 'War Book Supplement', emphasized the 'authenticity' of her story, commenting that 'her book was written at the front, and while she was correcting the proofs the dressing-station where she was posted was shelled out of existence' (October 1917).

The use of short phrases divided by commas and semi-colons in one long sentence emphasizes the constant and frenetic activity. There is hardly a pause for breath. No one image is clearly formed and we are meant to visualize the whole state of confusion. A similar catalogue of horrors is presented to the reader in the chapter entitled 'The Bombardment of Lodz':

> it was more like hell than anything I can imagine. The never-ending processions of groaning men being brought in on those horrible blood-soaked stretchers, suffering unimagined tortures, the filth, the cold, the stench, the hunger, the vermin, and the squalor of it all, added to one's utter helplessness to do more than very little to relieve their misery, was almost enough to make even Satan weep. (136)

Here Thurstan uses more brutal language: 'tortures', 'filth', 'stench', 'vermin', 'squalor', and the accompanying images of hell and Satan create a place of the damned. The reader is forced to associate this scene with the Biblical moment when 'the children of the kingdom shall be cast out into outer darkness: there shall be weeping and gnashing of teeth' (Matthew 8:12). 'Stretchers' and 'vermin' are characteristic images of the Great War, which firmly locate this passage in time, yet the suffering of humanity Thurstan describes has much wider association. This is the case with the opening section of her memoir. Beginning with the dramatic triple repetition of 'War, war, war', Thurstan attempts to communicate the dread and the excitement that characterize the days immediately preceding the outbreak. A 'torchlight tattoo on Salisbury Plain' is described in language that is romantic and high-minded. A scene of anticipation is set. It is also mystical as the military parade unfolds in a kind of arcane ritual:

> It was held on one of those breathless evenings in July when the peace of Europe was trembling in the balance, and when most of us had a certain heartache in case—*in case* England, at this time of internal crisis, did not rise to the supreme sacrifice.
>
> It was just the night for a tattoo—dark and warm and still. Away across the plain a sea of mist was rolling, cutting us off from the outside world, and only a few pale stars lighted our stage from above.
>
> The field was hung round with Chinese lanterns throwing weird lights and shadows over the mysterious forms of men and beasts that moved therein. It was fascinating to watch the stately entrance into the field, Lancers, Irish Rifles, Welsh Fusiliers, Grenadiers and many other gallant

regiments, each marching into the field in turn to the swing of their own particular regimental tune until they were all drawn up in order.

There followed a very fine exhibition of riding and the usual torchlight tricks, and then the supreme moment came. The massed bands had thundered out the first verse of the Evening Hymn, the refrain was taken up by a single trumpet far away—a sweet thin almost unearthly note more to be felt than heard—and then the bands gathered up the whole melody and everybody sang the last verse together.

The Last Post followed, and then I think somehow we all knew. (1)

The sense of other-worldliness is reinforced by the enveloping sea of mist, which not only creates a 'stage' upon which the tattoo may take place but, in cutting the participants off from the outside world, invokes myth and ideas of legendary places such as Avalon, one of the Celtic 'Isles of the Blest'.[41] Further associations with Arthurian legend and courtly romance are suggested by the various regiments who are lauded as 'stately' and 'gallant' (in Fussell's schema, 'earnestly brave'). They could be assembling for a jousting tournament. A strange and exotic air is lent to the scene by the Chinese lanterns. The associations with Stonehenge are surely meant to conjure images of far-older gatherings: remnants of pagan ceremony mix with Christian elements, like the Evening Hymn, to reinforce the tattoo's place in the lineage of English history. This divinely appointed moment is at a juncture between peace and war. Time has seemingly stood still.

Just as the gathering is 'cut off from the outside world' by the diaphanous mist, the words used to describe it, and the paragraphs that contain the images, are cut off from the rest of the memoir by asterisks, literally and figuratively marking a change in scene and in authorial voice. The last sentence/paragraph of the opening section is mirrored by the first sentence/paragraph of the following segment:

The Last Post followed, and then I think somehow we all knew.

* * * * *

A week later I had a telegram from the Red Cross summoning me to London.

The latter sentence heralds the tone of the rest of the memoir, except for an occasional more lyrical interlude. Professional nurse takes

[41] *Oxford Companion to English Literature*, ed. Margaret Drabble (Oxford and London, 1993), 54.

over from wide-eyed spectator. The anticipation of the scene at Salisbury Plain is mirrored by the hustle and bustle of London in the early days of the War, but the metaphysical and mystical calm that is also present is nowhere found in the capital Thurstan describes. She calls it a 'hive of ceaseless activity'.

Such a metaphor is characteristic of the imagery she employs throughout, contrasting unnatural war with the natural world. Belgian refugees appear stampeding like cattle; Prussian commandants are like animals 'often prowling about' in search of rebellious behaviour. German orders come violently, 'like thunderbolts from the blue'; enemy aeroplanes seem like 'birds of prey'; and bursting shells sound 'as animals in pain'. The 'thin stream of dirty water [which] trickled under the door and meandered in little rivulets' over an already filthy hospital floor slides like a snake, silently invading and poisoning. To travel in a car over shelled roads is to feel 'as kernels in a nut', but to experience the relief at journey's end makes the air seem as 'champagne'. She calls the women of her staff 'Red Cross damsels', further invoking the kind of mediaeval imagery she relies on in the opening section. Their appearance, however, can be decidedly *un*glamorous as when, in the initial confusion of the War's early days, she says that she and her staff must have looked 'more like rag-and-bone men than respectable British nursing sisters'; but, generally, Thurstan uses maternal imagery and language to describe the nurses. She is committed to her role as matron, as protector of those in her charge, being forever anxious about *her* nurses and taking responsibility for their welfare. They are constantly referred to as 'my flock', 'my family', 'my brood'. In this way, as Sharon Ouditt comments, 'a maternal discourse ... insulate[s] a narrative that consistently deals with the effects of martial brutality'.[42] The reader's sensibilities are cushioned by the gentle tone and the lapses into lyricism.

Juxtapositions serve to show what Fussell calls the 'ironic structure of events'. By applying 'irony-assisted recall ... to the past ... a rememberer is able to locate, draw forth, and finally shape into significance an event or moment which otherwise would merge without meaning into the general undifferentiated stream'.[43]

[42] Sharon Ouditt, *Fighting Forces, Writing Women: Identity and Ideology in the First World War* (London, 1994), 24.

[43] Fussell, *The Great War and Modern Memory*, 30.

Sometimes these juxtapositions are temporal, comparing past and present, as when Thurstan arrives in Cologne a virtual prisoner of the Germans. She tells us

> an incident happened here that made my blood boil, but nothing could be done so we had to set our teeth and bear it. A waiter came in smiling familiarly, with a bundle of papers under his arm, and put one of these illustrated weeklies beside each plate. On the front page was a horrible caricature of England—so grossly indecent that it makes me hot even now to think of it. (86)

Displaying that stiff upper-lip and control characterized as uniquely British, she hints at the stories of German spies operating in Britain under the guise of waiters or barbers—a trope that romance novelists pick up on and exploit, as shown in Chapter 3. She conveniently ignores the fact that British propaganda was just as 'grossly indecent' and sexually suggestive. In order to show the gentility and decency of pre-war life, she immediately contrasts an earlier trip to the city:

> I could not help thinking of my last visit to Cologne two years before. Then I went as a delegate to a very large Congress and Health Exhibition, when we were the honoured guests of the German National Council of Nurses. Then we were fêted by the Municipality of Cologne—given a reception at the Botanical Gardens, a free pass to all the sights of Cologne, a concert, tableaux, a banquet, I don't know what more. Now I was a prisoner heavily guarded, weary, dirty, humiliated in the very city that had done us so much honour. (87)

Sentence construction and placement effect the same contrast between past and present as do the images. The final two sentences are parallels, juxtaposing honours and niceties with scorn and effrontery.

Other juxtapositions heighten the phantasmic-like quality of the places she visits. In the Polish city of Lodz, she tells us,

> Nothing can express utter desolation much more nakedly than a Grand Hotel that has been through a week or two's bombardment. Here indeed were the mighty fallen. A large hole was ripped out of the wall of the big restaurant, close to the alcove where the band used to play while the smart people dined. An elaborate wine-list still graced each little table, but coffee made from rye bread crusts mixed with a little chicory was the only drink that a few white-faced waiters who crept about the room like shadows could apologetically offer us. (140)

The high-minded diction of 'Here indeed were the mighty fallen' echoes the Bible (2 Samuel 1: 19) and signals a strange vision in which past beauty comes in and out of focus, overlaying the present in an illusory fashion. The waiters are ghost-like with their white faces and creeping demeanour; the Grand Hotel itself like a haunted house, a gloomy pile out of Gothic romance.

Similarly desolate and more conspicuously ironic is her description of nursing in a hospital improvised out of one of the Tsar's private theatres at Skiernevice: 'the scenery had never been taken down after the last dramatic performance . . . and wounded men lay everywhere between the wings and drop scenes' (153). She is literally in the theatre of war.

The irony of such contrasts does not always seem to be apparent to the narrator:

> It was a most lovely day with a soft blue sky, and all the world bathed in winter sunshine. Shelling had ceased during the night, but began again with terrific force in the morning, and we started off under a perfect hail of shells. There were four German aeroplanes hovering just above us, throwing down bombs at short intervals. The shells aimed at them looked so innocent, like little white puff-balls bursting up in the blue sky. We hoped they would be brought down, but they were too high for that. The bombs were only a little diversion of theirs by the way—they were really trying to locate the Russian battery, as they were evidently making signals to their own headquarters. Danger always adds a spice to every entertainment, and as the wounded were all out and we had nobody but ourselves to think about, we enjoyed our thrilling departure from Lodz under heavy fire to the uttermost. And I must say I have rarely enjoyed anything more. It was simply glorious spinning along in that car, and we got out safely without being hurt. (141–2)

Such a passage validates Ouditt's argument about insulating the narrative, 'a dislocation between the severity of the experience and the domesticity of the language'.[44] We wonder whether Thurstan recognizes the incongruity of what she describes. Her glee at the excitement would suggest that she does not. Danger is entertainment.

In much the same way, she deems her final visit to the trenches at Radzivilow 'intensely interesting' because it was accomplished

[44] Ouditt, *Fighting Forces, Writing Women*, 27. Leslie Buswell asserted that 'Those who pretend they like to be in bombardments are either humbugs or have never been in a real one' (Buswell, *Ambulance No. 10*, 135).

during 'a violent German attack'. Occurring as it does near the end of this period of her active service and her memoir, the experience prompts a summation of what she has witnessed:

> I was always loath to leave Radzivilow. The work there was splendid, and there more than anywhere else I have been to one feels the war as a High Adventure.
>
> War would be the most glorious game in the world if it were not for the killing and wounding. In it one tastes the joy of comradeship to the full, the taking and giving, and helping and being helped in a way that would be impossible to conceive in the ordinary world. At Radzivilow, too, one could see the poetry of war, the zest of the frosty mornings, and the delight of the camp-fire at night, the warm, clean smell of the horses tethered everywhere, the keen hunger, the rough food sweetened by the sauce of danger, the riding out in high hope in the morning; even the returning wounded in the evening did not seem altogether such a bad thing out there. One has to die some time, and the Russian peasants esteem it a high honour to die for their 'little Mother' as they call their country. The vision of the High Adventure is not often vouchsafed to one, but it is a good thing to have had it—it carries one through many a night at the shambles. Radzivilow is the only place it came to me. In Belgium one's heart was wrung by the poignancy of it all, its littleness and defencelessness; in Lodz one could see nothing for the squalor and 'frightfulness'; in other places the ruined villages, the flight of the dazed, terrified peasants show one of the darkest sides of war. (175)

She employs familiar war rhetoric, the repetition of the phrase 'High Adventure' reinforcing the sense of imperial mission and patriotic duty. She confirms stereotypes of other nations: 'little Belgium', child-like Russian peasants. The list enhances the romance, and as she says, were it not for the killing, it would be superb. However, it is exactly this element of death and danger that makes war so attractive, this discourse so insidious.

Thurstan is more consciously ironic and even satiric when she tells of 'Poor Madame of the Hotel X' in Belgium who must hand over her 'beautiful beds' to the Germans, who have requisitioned them 'and everything that they wanted from the various hotels'. We learn that the woman had 'wrung her hands over the loss', but then Thurstan interjects her authorial opinion: 'Alas, poor Madame! The next day her husband was shot as a spy, and she cared no longer about the beds' (15). The first half of the sentence presents cold fact, shocking in its brevity; the second contributes the irony.

Authorial interjections such as 'alas!' are a common occurrence in the memoir and signal the author's conscious expression of irony, sarcasm, wit, as in 'Oh dear, what a stampede it was' (12), and in the description of how her expectations are shattered by reality:

Alas and alas! At the end of the week the Germans put in eighty soldiers with sore feet, who had overmarched, and the glorious vision of nursing Tommy Atkins at the front faded into the prosaic reality of putting hundreds of cold compresses on German feet, that they might be ready all the sooner to go out and kill our men. War is a queer thing! (20)

We also see here a characteristic understatement, the cheeriness that was expected even in the most difficult conditions. Instead of being disastrous, these are vexing:

[The Burgomaster] assured us that our things would be sent in a few days—so back to Brussels went my portmanteau with all my clean aprons and caps and everything else, and I did not see it again for nearly a week. But such is war! (21)[45]

Understated and cheery sarcasm is reserved for the Germans. She contemptuously refers to a Prussian officer as 'his lordship' (83), and in the town of Charleroi, where she comes across an inscription written over a doorway reading, '*Vive Guillaume II, roi de l'univers*', she avers 'Not yet, not yet, William' (30).

Thurstan views other enemy activities with less levity. Her description of the German invasion of Brussels can be compared with her earlier description of the entrance to the field on Salisbury Plain:

It was an imposing sight to watch the German troops ride in. The citizens of Brussels behaved magnificently, but what a bitter humiliation for them to undergo. How should we have borne it, I wonder, if it had been London? The streets were crowded, but there was hardly a sound to be heard, and the Germans took possession of Brussels in silence. First the Uhlans rode in, then the other cavalry, then the artillery and infantry. The latter were dog-weary, dusty and travel-strained—they had evidently done forced marching. (14)

[45] Sharon Ouditt refers to this incident as Thurstan 'pouting with distress' and 'concluding with resigned cheeriness. . . . She faces gunfire with the air of a bemused child and indeed relates the incident as if it were a bed-time story. . . . We can see here a governing discourse which sanitises and domesticates the most violent of experiences' (*Fighting Forces, Writing Women*, 24).

The Germans process just as silently as the cavalcade of English regiments, but they have nothing of their stately and gallant veneer.

Thurstan hopes that the scenes she witnesses do not become part of the experience of those at home:

> I have never seen a more pitiful sight. Little groups of terror-stricken peasants fleeing from their homes, some on foot, some more fortunate ones with their bits of furniture in a rough cart drawn by a skeleton horse or a large dog. All had babies, aged parents, or invalids with them. I realised for the first time what war meant. We do not know in England. God grant that we never may. (11)

Such a sentiment is in direct opposition to that of someone like Kate Finzi, and, as Paul Fussell notes, Philip Gibbs's recollection of returning soldiers who 'prayed God to get the Germans to send Zeppelins to England to make the people know what war meant'.[46] Thurstan uses similar language, but to different effect.

The misleading ideas about what war meant must have, in part, been fuelled by books such as *Women Who Dared* by Kent Carr (1920). Carr uses a great deal of text from *Field Hospital and Flying Column* in his chapter on Thurstan, but adds his own opinions in language that heightens the romance of the adventure and his subject's feminine charm:

> If you want to realise how many brave women there are in the world, you have only to talk to Miss Violetta Thurstan. But the last thing that seems to occur to her is that she has been in the very least heroic herself. She has unstinted praise for others; for herself, she just went where she was sent.... Miss Thurstan has the prettiest manner, with a suggestion of shyness about it that is very attractive, and one carries away with one a memory of the haunting sweetness of her smile. She is very fragile in appearance [but] in spite of the flower-like charm of her looks and ways, she has the gift of efficiency.[47]

As Ouditt comments, 'the patriarchal establishment need have nothing to fear... this nurse runs no risk of losing her femininity'.[48]

Thurstan even calls her convalescence after a shrapnel wound an 'enforced holiday'—the cheeriness is still present. Perhaps this is because, unlike Finzi, she knows she will be returning to her

[46] Fussell, *The Great War and Modern Memory*, 86.

[47] Kent Carr, *Women Who Dared: Heroines of the Great War* (London, 1920), 238.

[48] Ouditt, *Fighting Forces, Writing Women*, 25.

'beloved column . . . with its joys and sorrows, its comradeship, its pain and its inexplicable happiness' (177). Returning to the lyricism of the opening section, she concludes her account with a plea for the reader's indulgence: 'Those who are workers themselves . . . will perhaps forget the imperfections in remembering that it had been written close to the turmoil of the battlefield, to the continual music of the cannon and the steady tramp of feet marching past my window' (178). This romantic finish cushions the horrors she has witnessed. The 'music of the cannon' is, of course, oxymoronic, and we know that the 'steady tramp of feet' means more men going off to face the horrors. *Field Hospital and Flying Column*, then, is not only an historical document but also a literary exercise.

Following the same trajectory, but even more consciously literary, is Sister (Mary Eliza L.) Martin-Nicholson's memoir, *My Experiences on Three Fronts* (1916). She and Thurstan served in the same countries, in the same order, and have strikingly similar encounters. In a restaurant during an enforced train journey, Martin-Nicholson is confronted with 'an obscenely indecent paper [which] was laid [on each plate], as if by way of giving insult' (78); in Russia, she is presented to the Empress Marie Federovna, 'a very charming woman with a wide interest in life' (110); and in Brussels, she witnesses the German occupation:

> Many have seen the great Atlantic rollers, sullen, unrelenting, menacing, surging into some quiet, unprotected harbour after a mighty storm. . . . So I likened the entry of the enemy into the happy, smiling capital of neutral Belgium.
>
> Awakened at dawn by the rumble of countless passing batteries of artillery and the shaking of the ground under the tramp of thousands of heavily booted feet, I had gone out to my balcony to watch the never-to-be-forgotten spectacle of the arrival of the German hosts.
>
> . . . the streets were black with people who had come out under the brilliant sky and soft wind of this glorious August dawn. The crowd was clothed almost entirely in black, but the faces were white, some with fear, some with rage which flashed in their hate-filled eyes. . . .
>
> Mile upon mile the invaders stretched, never ending, relentless . . . an irresistible mass of grey-green forms. Unshaven, unclean, with sunken eyes and thin lips, weary from long marching, mechanically keeping step under the stern eye of their officers, they trudged on, wordless, soundless.[49]

[49] Sister Martin-Nicholson, *My Experiences on Three Fronts* (London, 1916), 33.

The image of the storm is used consistently throughout the memoir to represent the menace of war. The sound of marching soldiers mimics the rumble of thunder. Colours are contrasted as the black-clad citizens of Brussels with their white faces stand out in monochrome from the vividness of the bright summer day. Their mood matches their clothing as they desolately watch the arrival of the 'German hosts', ominously portrayed here as walking dead, zombies, acting mechanically at the command of their master-officers.

The passage is indicative of Martin-Nicholson's descriptive capabilities, but even more striking is the vehemence of her language and tone. *My Experiences on Three Fronts* shares the travel-book qualities of *Field Hospital and Flying Column*, but surpasses it in invective, emotion, and melodrama. She writes in a nineteenth-century style that demonstrates what James R. Sutherland called a 'time-lag in literary . . . fashions'. Just as the prose style of the eighteenth century survived, 'with some loss of elegance', well into the nineteenth century, so in the twentieth 'characteristic features of nineteenth-century prose still survive . . . in the writing of those authors . . . whose minds turn naturally to the past'.[50] Martin-Nicholson's memoir is a didactic work containing pages of rhetorical questioning and exclamatory answers; the language is bombastic in its condemnation of the Germans, expressions of outrage at the crimes perpetrated in Belgium, and insistence on Britain's responsibility to fight for freedom. It can certainly be seen as a recruiting tract. This is clear from the beginning, where her principal metaphor, the storm, is invoked:

> How well I remember the 4th of August, 1914!
>
> Clouds hung dark and heavy on the horizon that brilliant, memorable day, dark and heavy, and yet scarcely perceived by those whom the preceding days of peace and sunshine had lulled into slumber.
>
> Thunder growled sullenly in the far distance, and heavier and heavier rose the black pall. Countries already stricken under the crash and flame of the rising storm that was to be the greatest the world had ever known were calling aloud for help, and stretching out their hands in agonized appeal. And here at home laughing men and women, lapped in a sense of security, encouraged by bright summer days, and long years of apparent immunity from all alarms and dangers, punted, sculled, or paddled unheedingly to

[50] James R. Sutherland, *On English Prose* (Toronto, 1957), 82.

their own particular shady nooks, where the sound of the gramophone might stifle the thunder of battle, and the tinkle of ice and the lapping of cool waters allay any slight qualm arising from the green-grey menace on the horizon. (7)

Not only are the clouds a meteorological threat to 'that brilliant memorable day', but they present a perceived metaphorical threat to the security of Europe, representing as they do the possibility of war, the menace of Germany.

The passage is full of juxtapositions: those 'dark and heavy' clouds set against 'peace and sunshine'; countries 'stretching out their hands in agonized appeal' set against 'laughing men and women' at home in England. The alliteration of 'lulled into slumber' enhances the soporific meaning of the phrase. In the same way, the musical 'tinkling of ice' and 'lapping of cool waters' combine with the run-on sentence to reinforce the gentle activities of the happy young people who 'punted, sculled, or paddled'. As in a poem approaching closure, a key phrase is repeated:

Pulling hard against the stream, I steered my light skiff silently through the irresponsible throng towards my goal, a quiet, shady spot beneath the overhanging trees where, far from the noise and laughter, I might find for a space some *peace and rest* before the breaking of the cloud I knew to be hanging so low above our heads.

As I worked my way slowly forward, I could not help thinking how very like life was my passage. Just as on this bright afternoon I pulled hard against the stream for many miles, so in life I had gone through rough and troubled waters until at last I had reached the time when *peace and rest* were at hand. (8, italics mine)

The juxtaposition of literal and figurative—'Pulling hard against the stream'—is hardly subtle. Martin-Nicholson points up the parallel and underlines the irony. This is characteristic of her narrative voice: nothing is left to interpretive chance—she spells it all out for us. Like the ubiquitous exclamatory sentences (twenty-eight in the first twelve pages), her insistence on the symbolic is vigorous and consistent.

As with an actual storm, signs are evident before the deluge. Our author heeds the warnings and is prepared. Others such as 'these happy folk around me might pass away the hours before the storm in laughter and careless, light-hearted merrymaking' (9). Singled out to represent both the crowd around her that day, and unconcerned England in general, is a young man who asks her for some methylated spirits:

> Immaculate as to attire, but stooping of shoulder, resplendent as to hose and tie, but narrow of chest and lack-luster of eye, he was the product of the stool and counting-house. A nice enough, good-hearted enough youth, perhaps, but one to whom cheap cigarettes in flamboyant case, a pretty girl in cheap, pretty clothes, a day up the river, a night in the music-hall, made his sum-total of life, and all through no fault of his own. Brought up with his bumps of observation, judgement, and deduction totally undeveloped, how was he to take heed of the lowering cloud in the west? (9)

Clearly 'lower-class'—'the product of the stool and counting house'—his accoutrements are 'cheap': cigarettes, 'a pretty girl in cheap, pretty clothes'. He finds his entertainment not in a theatre, but in a lowbrow music-hall. As John Carey writes,

> the clerks were hardly equipped to appreciate 'high' culture, which is why an alternative culture was created for them. Northcliffe aimed the *Daily Mail* specifically at clerks.... The periodicals *Tid-Bits* and *Answers*, and the department store Selfridge's, were likewise seen as components of clerk culture. Reviewers denouncing the 'vulgarity'of Jerome K. Jerome's *Three Men in a Boat* pointed out that it was written in 'colloquial clerk's English'.[51]

Indeed, this young man could be a character out of Jerome's novel. He displays all the effete characteristics so denounced by eugenicists, supporters of compulsory military service, and conservative social critics. His ignorance of political affairs, as evidenced by his phrase 'France & Co.' (an echo, perhaps, of Kipling's *Stalky & Co.*), riles Martin-Nicholson in the same way that 'clerk's slang annoyed intellectuals partly because it was flippant and Philistine and trivialized "serious" subjects'.[52] She countermands his flippancy with her own précis of English history and the contemporary political scene. Quoting Sir Robert Borden about the prowess of the German

[51] John Carey, *The Intellectual and the Masses: Pride and Prejudice among the Literary Intelligentsia, 1880–1939* (London, 1992), 58.

Penny Summerfield argues that the music-hall, far from being an escapist form of entertainment, was in fact a site for patriotic inculcation with its songs, melodramas, and extravaganzas that celebrated the imperialist vision. Penny Summerfield, 'Patriotism and Empire: Music-Hall entertainment 1870–1914', in John MacKenzie (ed.), *Imperialism and Popular Culture*, (Manchester, 1986, 17–48).

[52] Carey, *The Intellectual and the Masses*, 59.

Army,[53] she lends authority to her statements. In keeping with current iconography, she depicts Germany as a beast, Belgium as its prey: the 'ravening wolf whose fangs were already buried in the quivering flesh of Belgium! Belgium the neutral! Belgium the sacred!' (12). She repeats the name like a mantra, in a tripling effect reminiscent of Kate Finzi's prose.

Such seriousness or 'mental preparedness for war'[54] is not demonstrated by the flippant young man:

> 'Topping day, isn't it? Shouldn't read those silly old rags on a day like this. Enough to give one the blues. Such bunkum—what? We've decided to stand by old France & Co., haven't we, if there *should* be a real dust up, so why scare the lives out of women and children by headlines a foot long? Thank you very much, and take my advice: send those things floating down the river and go to the Island; they'll dance the tango this afternoon.' (10)

Whereas Martin-Nicholson compares the coming war to a storm, he imagines it to be a 'topping picnic'. Gleefully he tells her, England would

> 'Skip over to France whilst Russia comes along on the other side, catch the Germans in the middle, and make a bally sandwich of them. Christmas in Berlin, and home for the New Year, with "peace on earth," etc. I jolly well hope we *do* declare war; but I don't think so, do you? Russia and France and plucky little Belgium are quite enough to cook any German goose-step, don't you think so?' (15)

Both the literal and the symbolic 'picnic' come to a crashing end, however, as the storm breaks: sirens herald the declaration of war, lightning and thunder herald the downpour that sends people shrieking for cover:

> the sky was rent by a vivid, tearing flash of lightning. For one instant there was an unholy calm, whilst affrighted faces were turned upwards towards the sullen skies, and then crash upon crash, peal upon peal, of thunder shook the earth. Trees bent before the scorching wind which had suddenly arisen from nowhere. Women screamed and hid their heads in silken

[53] Sir Robert Borden (1854–1937) was the leader of the opposition Conservative Party in the Canadian House of Commons from 1901 to 1911 when he was returned as Prime Minister after the General Election. He promoted maximum Canadian commitment to the British imperial war effort, and visited London in July 1915. He represented Canada on the Imperial War Cabinet, 1917–18 (*A Dictionary of the First World War*, ed. Martin Gilbert (London, 1996); and *Who Was Who*, v. III).

[54] Claire M. Tylee, *The Great War and Women's Consciousness* (Iowa City, 1990), 45.

cushions; men sat with useless, empty hands. Lightning flashed and flashed, striking a centuries-old oak, rending it to its stout heart, stripping every leaf from every bough; and then in the midst of strife came the rain. Not in drops or streams, simply in torrents, drenching, flooding, beating upon the unprotected heads, making a noise which, joined to the almost incessant clash of thunder, sounded as though some corner of hell had broken loose. (18)

There are Biblical and other reverberations here. The sky rent by lightning recalls the moment of Christ's death, when the 'veil of the temple was rent in two' (Matthew 27: 51). We are surely also meant to recall the flood from Genesis. The oak, an eponymous symbol of England, is torn asunder by the violent tempest, Lear's 'oak-cleaving thunderbolts' (Act 3, Scene 2). However, Martin-Nicholson also anticipates what we now accept as 'war-torn' imagery, images of a wasteland, visions such as rendered by the artist Paul Nash. The incessant noise of thunder becomes the metaphor for the din of cannons; her talk of hell breaking loose anticipates what Sassoon would call 'the hell where youth and laughter go'. The distressed men and women assailed by the storm should call to mind images of Belgian and other European refugees, and are meant to parallel Martin-Nicholson's earlier images of such vanquished people. She also symbolically reinforces her point about preparedness—she takes heed of the signs and brings with her a mackintosh and a tarpaulin for protection; those careless people who did not are left to hide, run, and exclaim: '"If only *we* had thought; if only *we* had been prepared"' (19).

So determined is this nursing sister to stress her convictions about Britain's unpreparedness, its responsibility to gallant little Belgium, and its superiority once it carries out its duty, that her narrative often becomes a diatribe and reveals a great deal about her prejudices. Her experiences are catalysts for a kind of sociological study of the peoples with whom she comes in contact, and in this way, her memoir is in keeping with so many travel narratives that had at their heart the imperialist vision. She is like the Victorian writer who 'remains unquestionably superior to his readers; if not omniscient, he is at any rate authoritative, self-assured, at times a little condescending, but nearly always willing to make himself generally understood'.[55] Certainly we understand Martin-Nicholson's

[55] Sutherland, *On English Prose*, 90.

point-of-view: each race is categorized and pigeonholed. The idea that the Germans were racially inferior, because they destroyed the physical evidence of Western civilization,[56] is evidenced by Martin-Nicholson's account of her visit to Louvain: 'the University and its marvellous Library, the beautiful Church of St Peter, and street upon street of houses were burned to the ground' (53). Even worse, of course, is their brutality towards human beings. We are given details of the carnage:

> bodies, many charred beyond recognition, lay everywhere, and upon the walls were the dark red splashes of the blood which had been wantonly spilled; there were marks of the same colour on the pavements.
>
> ...
>
> And then, turning a corner some way back from the Place de la Station, I tripped over something lying very still in the summer sun. Golden-haired, with her little face buried in the dust, and her tiny fingers piteously outstretched, lay a little baby girl of about six, dead. Not dead from a passing bullet or falling stone, but dead because between the little shoulder blades shone a knife-edged bayonet. (54)

The discovery of the dead girl is dramatically built up. First, there is general scene of bodies, individually unrecognizable, reinforced by their charred condition, and the random splashes of blood. The sight of the dead child is therefore even more shocking in its distinctness, and the fact that Martin-Nicholson trips over her like a piece of debris. Again, we have the imagistic juxtaposition of the gruesomeness of the body and the golden hair, which seems to reflect the brightness of the summer sunshine. As horror is piled upon horror, the reader is meant to gasp at the final revelation that the child's death was not random but intentional, the image of the bayoneted baby being common in the propaganda war. Martin-Nicholson melodramatically refers to her as a 'poor fragile little butterfly crushed in the coarse Teuton fingers' (54). She misses no opportunity to portray the Germans in the worst possible light. They are likened to 'mad dogs'; in Brussels, she witnesses women being 'provided, like so much cattle, for the German soldiery' (50); the officers, she tells us, are 'brutal, domineering, and ready in every instance to browbeat and insult' (75); and as to their personal hygiene: 'ouff! . . . the sickly stench of their bodies . . . which is best

[56] Tylee, 'Munitions of the Mind', 181.

described as the putrid smell of rotting magnolias' (282). At such moments in the text, 'literature comes rushing in and takes over'.[57]

An equally strong component of her narrative voice is a patronizing note, most evident in the middle section of the memoir, a chronicle of her service in Russia. Having heard much about Russian treachery and cunning, she is surprised to find how gentle and meek the people are. She feels great sympathy for them, as a mother would a helpless child, and believes they will doggedly push their way to victory under the leadership of the Tsar. Yet even as she commends their stoicism, a note of condescension creeps in: 'I grasped the fact that they *do not* understand pain as the people of the West do.... They suffer and forget, putting away their pain as a child will put away a discarded toy' (99). The Russians are 'children' to whose plight the lofty adult responds:

> my heart went out from the first to the people. It was perhaps their childlikeness that appealed to me, who loves all children;... I at once felt at home with these high-booted, wide-trousered, short-coated, befurred children of great Russia. (99)

But they are not the only ones to whom she applies such epithets. Whereas the Russian people are seen as charmingly childlike, the soldiers she cares for have vulnerability forced upon them. The wounded are infantilized, as in the Red Cross poster, 'The Greatest Mother in the World', where a giant nurse cradles in her arms a tiny soldier on a stretcher, 'a bizarre intersection of the Madonna and child and the Pietà'.[58] This iconography comes most into play when Martin-Nicholson describes nursing the English in France. As the final section of her memoir, it is also the culmination of her experiences, the service for which all her previous work has been but a precursor: 'I had tended Belgians, French, Russians, Poles, Austrians, and Germans, and my heart ached for the sight of my own soldiers' (212). This is, in effect, what the memoir is all about—extolling the virtues of Tommy Atkins. Like an indulgent parent, Martin-Nicholson dotingly describes Tommy's idiosyncrasies, including his 'quaint' tendency to 'grumble and grouse'. He may communicate in halting speech, in the Scottish, Irish, or Welsh dialect of his provincial home, but he is far superior to the flippant young clerk on the river. Surgeons and doctors, too, made a point in

[57] Fussell, *The Great War and Modern Memory*, 173.
[58] Ouditt, *Fighting Forces, Writing Women*, 20.

their memoirs to praise the British soldier. Henry Gervis asserted that Tommy was cheery and stoical, 'the best patient in the world' and complained that it was unfair for 'comic papers' and 'serious writers' to 'conspire to malign' Tommy about his grammar and manner of speech. 'As a rule he speaks quite as good grammar as his officers, and it is the rarest thing to come across a man who drops his "h's"'.[59] For Martin-Nicholson, Tommy is always grateful, if at times a little naughty, and she is the strictest of mothers: 'By some great blessing I have always been able to get to the hearts of these soldier-children. Never once have I seen a sign of familiarity, never once, after that first outbreak which sometimes happens, have I to complain of disobedience' (203). As if taking charge in a schoolroom, she brooks no opposition to her rule in the wards.

Many male memoirists confirm the rule, perhaps the attraction, of the nursing sister. Phil J. Fisher, a chaplain, tells us:

> In those wards the doctor is knight, waging incessant war on death, but the 'Sister' is queen. To many of the sufferers who are her charge, fresh from the battle-wrecked wilderness which is 'no woman's land', she enshrined all the tenderness and worshipfulness of English womanhood. They follow her round the ward with wistful eyes; it is so good to look upon her kind again. But after this, she establishes her throne for herself, by her patience, her gentleness, her unvarying cheerfulness, her masterful good humour. Like tired children, the war-torn, war-stricken men resign themselves to her care and acknowledge her rightful sway.[60]

Although Martin-Nicholson spends much time praising British soldier-patients, she nevertheless does not spare us the more harrowing aspects of her nursing experiences. She witnesses suffering in abundance, declaring, 'may you never hear that sound, reader, that scream of fear wrung from one weakened by untold agony' (261). Far from disillusioning her, such scenes strengthen her resolve:

> as I sat with the dying boy's hand tightly grasped in mine . . . I appreciated all the more the heroism and suffering of these grand men who die fighting for their country. For grand men they are, as none know better than we nurses who witness their passing. There is a something—a majesty—which comes into the faces of those who have been in action which one never sees in the face of the ordinary man who has not been tested as the soldier has. (255)

[59] Gervis, *Arms and the Doctor* 13.
[60] Phil J. Fisher, C.F., *Khaki Vignettes: Six Months Chaplain to the Troops in England and Fifteen Months in France* (London, 1917), 35.

This passage recalls not only the idea so prominent in Finzi's memoir about bearing witness, but also the privileged position of those who have served, the 'band of brothers'.

Martin-Nicholson reminds the reader that her assessment is based on her nurse's point of view—'the woman who gets the *man* not the soldier' (277). She sees him at his best and his worst, and adores him all the more: 'We ought to add a new verse to the *Te Deum*: "We praise Thee, O Lord, in that Thou hast seen fit to create anything so fine as Tommy Atkins!"' (283). Not one to restrain her enthusiasm or her opinions, she ends her memoir with a litany of praise:

> I defy any one to enter a ward in the morning or leave it at night without an uplifting of the heart in response to the British soldier's outlook on the day ahead or gratitude for the day just passed. I could write a book on the humour of their sayings and their ways, and I cannot be too thankful that I have been allowed in this terrible time of strife to be with our men under conditions and circumstances which should have nipped every bud of the tree of good humour, but instead has brought forth such wonderful flowers.
>
> Arithmetically I am far from brilliant, but I have learnt to do one sum in the problem of life, and make the answer correct each time. Do it with me: 100 per cent. endurance, courtesy, gentleness, cleanliness, good humour. Divide by honour, multiply by courage, and you will get the finest, grandest total in the world—
>
> TOMMY ATKINS, Gentleman.

To add the title 'gentleman' is to elevate his status, for Tommy was an enlisted soldier, not an officer or a 'gentleman' by birth. Once again *Henry V* resonates: 'be he ne'er so vile/This day shall gentle his condition'. War is seen as an ennobling force such that, inherent within this 'gentling' of condition, there is a blurring of class difference that suited one of the most important needs of war—national unity: 'the pictorial harmony... was to reflect the actual social harmony of a healthy culture representing the civilisation threatened by German barbarity'.[61] The social division, which is described at the beginning of the memoir, is eclipsed, perhaps even rectified, by this effusive celebration of the average British soldier.

Unashamedly strident, Martin-Nicholson is the most vociferous of the memoirists considered here. We are left in no doubt as to her political allegiances and her outlook on life. We see others through her imperial eyes. In the frontispiece photograph, it is her eyes that

[61] Tylee, 'Munitions of the Mind', 183.

grab the gazer's attention (Fig. 18). She looks forthrightly at the camera with her mouth betraying only the slightest hint of a smile, set as it is with a determined seriousness. Her letters to her publisher, Stanley Unwin, reveal that such a personality was not manufactured for the narrative. She comes across in her correspondence just as forthright, opinionated, and determined. In one letter she even asks Unwin, 'Have you joined up yet?' His pacifist principles were no excuse in her mind. Yet, as her portrait attempts to show, she is also feminine, as she wears a white satin and lace gown, her dark hair piled luxuriously on top of her head in the fashion of the day. With hands clasped in front of her chest as she leans slightly forward from sitting position, Sister Martin-Nicholson presents a force to be reckoned with, as nurse—and as autobiographer, who as Susanna Egan points out, 'subordinat[es] the historical activity of describing what happened to the poetic activity of conveying what happens, incorporat[ing] [her] facts into a mythic narrative'.[62]

A V.A.D. in France (1917) presents a very different personality to the reader. The appearance of Olive Dent's book suggests another sort of memoir. The cover reproduces one of the book's fifteen illustrations (Fig. 19). Depicting 'a corner of the nursing quarters with a "wigwam" and two "hen-coops" in the distance', this pen-and-ink drawing shows a demure nurse in white dress and cap standing beside one of the tents or 'wigwams'. The other illustrations are just as charming, picturesque, and non-threatening. Some are even humorous, reminiscent of Bruce Bairnsfather's sketches in the way they poke fun at the life of a soldier or the inconveniences of wartime nursing.

They stand in marked contrast to the photographic illustrations of Finzi's text and the maps interspersed throughout *Field Hospital and Flying Column*. Their aim is not to reinforce the writer's authority to speak about military matters or the scope of her travels, but rather, to complement the jaunty tone of much of Dent's writing. At the outset, we become aware that she is one of the eager young women so criticized by other memoirists, the nonprofessional who, on the outbreak of war, 'resurrects' her nursing books and joins a voluntary aid detachment. Dent has a modicum of training and experience: 'a two-years' course of hygiene and physiology in college, a half-yearly session at advanced physiology

[62] Egan, *Patterns of Experience in Autobiography*, 23.

FIG. 18. *My Experiences on Three Fronts* (1916) by Sister Martin-Nicholson, frontispiece photograph

A CORNER OF THE NURSING QUARTERS WITH A "WIGWAM" AND TWO "HEN-COOPS" IN THE DISTANCE

FIG. 19. *A V.A.D. in France* (1917) by Olive Dent

later, . . . St. John Ambulance work for two or three years' (16), but this in no way measures up to the training that Finzi, Thurstan, and Martin-Nicholson would have demanded. Dent recognizes the hostility with which she is viewed by the nursing profession: 'No doubt we would be despised and abused, considered very raw recruits and given only the donkey-work to do' (15). Yet she will rise to the challenge, saying, 'besides, weren't the regulars, from mildly despising the Kitchener men, veering round to a well-merited appreciation and trust? That might happen in nursing' (16). The patriotic girl is not only aware of her duty, but at the same time optimistic.

She also has great faith in the country's powers-that-be. When Dent does indeed receive the chilly reception she anticipates from the professionals, she prefers to have more 'faith in the knowledge of the Government than the opinion (or possibly the prejudice) of an individual nurse' (30). As Ouditt comments, Dent's 'confidence in her own judgement of the profession into which she has sought part-time entry is, as far as she is concerned, backed up by the patriarchal authority system'.[63]

This faith in authority extends to the printed word. Her memoir opens with an exclamation of disbelief: 'War! *England* at war! It couldn't be. It must be some frightful mistake' (13). Hers is the voice of a dutiful Imperialist daughter:

> War was the prerogative, the privilege, the amusement of the vague, restless, little kingdoms, of the small quarrelsome, European States, and far-distant, half-breed peoples. War was an unreality not to be brought to *our* land, not to be in any way associated with England, with *our* country. (13)

She convinces herself it must be true, since 'newspapers would dare not publish anything untrue which was prejudicial to the common weal' (13). Part of this thinking might come from the fact that sections of this memoir were previously serialized *in* newspapers, among them, *The Daily Mail*, *The Evening News*, and *The Yorkshire Evening Post*.

As belief in authority is integral to her outlook, so also is a romantic sensibility. What she imagines as the characteristics of war, 'fire, slaughter, shrieking shell', come right out of recruitment

[63] Ouditt, *Fighting Forces, Writing Women*, 28.

posters and adventure tales, and when she is moved to view those around her 'with a passion of over-mastering love', she lapses into the language of melodrama:

> One caught one's self looking at strangers in the street, on the bus, and in the railway train,—at that worn little mother with the tired, trouble-haunted eyes, the laughing girl-child with the soft, rounded limbs, the crooning baby with his whole, wondrous future before him. Who was to defend them all? For the first time in a happy, even life one felt bitterly resentful of one's sex. Defence was the only consideration in the popular mind in those early August days. And defence was a man's job, and I, unfortunately, was a woman. (14)

Familiar here, too, is the resentment of gender, the 'if-only-I-were-a-man' attitude that resonates throughout women's writing of this period. The prose rhythm of the passage, its sentence construction, and cliché-ridden diction are typical of *A V.A.D. in France*.

There are similarities between Dent's style and that of the other women, especially in her tendency to wax lyrical on various subjects, but what distinguishes her prose from the others' is her buoyant tone. The 'adaptable girl', she says, 'soon learns to overcome such minor difficulties' (36) as no hot water, no taps, no sinks, no fires or gas-stoves: 'on active service it is a case of improvising, improvising, improvising'. Her daily routine illustrates the monotony of the work described by Finzi: early-morning chores consist of making beds, dusting twenty-four lockers, taking twenty-four temperatures, and tidying the wards. Then there is a snack lunch, a change of apron, and the giving of medicines, inhalations, the applying of fomentations, eusol dressing, two or three doses of castor oil, the cleaning of a linen cupboard, and the distribution of the boys' dinner. The afternoon brings more medicines, the washing of patients, and the making of beds, before going off duty at 5 o'clock. She is kept 'ceaselessly busy', not only with dressings, four-hourly foments, charts, periodical stimulants, and feeds, but with the 'unending, infinitely pathetic call of "Sister, sister, may I have . . ."'. Yet Dent remains enthusiastic, claiming that

> active service nursing, like all other nursing, is intensely fascinating and interesting. The men come practically straight from the trenches, and are deeply grateful for, and appreciative of, the cosy beds, the nicely-cooked food, the absence of vermin, the cleanliness and brightness of the wards, and our attempt to make them comfortable and happy. (39)

The 'boys' are her inspiration, for even when they grumble, they are endearing, and she revels in their 'stumbling expressions of gratitude'.

The memoir is peppered with foreign phrases: '*à la Fauntleroy*', '*blasé*', '*après la guerre*', '*comme il faut*', '*mélange*', '*pour-ma-patrie*', and adverbs such as 'awfully', 'intensely', 'deeply', 'gloriously', and 'marvellously'. These and the often-repeated words 'exciting', 'charming', and 'interesting' lend a schoolgirl eagerness to the narrative voice. Her reader is bombarded by metaphors:

> this morning the rain has come, and we are as glad as the Ancient Mariner to see that rain, for to us it means the passing of the snow. Our camp has looked charmingly picturesque with the surrounding hills receding to a dim blue haze, a Futurist sun arrogant at dawn and sunset, and honey-gold at noon, sentinel trees, tall and gaunt, long, straight roads peopled occasionally by dark lines of passing soldiers, their marching muffled by the snow, their singing dying away as they quickly reach that distance where they look so much like toy soldiers. Poor boys! For their sakes more than our own we are glad to welcome the rain. Picturesque snow it may be, but the practical side of it is cruel. (61)

Scenes and emotions alike are described with a mixture of traditional metaphor and newly formed, wartime imagery. Hyphenated compound words are ubiquitous. Some are the product of grammatical convention of the time, the hyphenation of 'to-day' or 'picture-postcard', for instance (used regularly by all the memoirists discussed in this chapter), but many come right out of the vocabulary of war: 'up-patients', 'dug-out', 'field-card', 'shell-case', and 'shell-shocked'. Some are compound-adjectives used to facilitate an accurate description: 'The clay-covered, blood-spattered surrounding skin is washed' (52); 'the tents are laced closely, blankets are hung purdah-wise over the lacings' (59); 'Bloated, Germanic-looking spiders come up miraculously through the boards in the tent floor' (78); '"Farmer Garge" was a bluff and hearty, beef-and-beer, John-Bull type of man' (110).

Dent's romantic sensibility shows in her many juxtapositions of the beauty of the natural world and the unnatural ugliness of war:

> The country now is lovely.... We have harebells and lovely, blue cornflowers growing wild, and a most delightful, carmine-coloured clover with a conical head which bursts usually into flamingo-pink. The up-patients go out and bring us back armfuls of flowers with which we deck

the tents. Lately we have been going to the forest for lilies-of-the-valley, but they are 'over' now, so we have to content ourselves with Geoffrey Plantagenet's flower, the yellow broom. We get great branches of that,—and in our particular wards it appears to best advantage, in a 'vase' which is made out of the case of a British 18-pounder picked up by one of our R.A.M.C. men after Mons. (76)

Just how much Dent consciously recognizes the irony of this shell-case-*cum*-vase is unclear, but the image presents to the twenty-first-century reader a striking incongruity, almost humorous in its absurdity, but poignant in its innocence.

Such scenes structure her memoir, which follows a loose chronological course from the outbreak of war to the end of 1916. Incidents and snippets of experience order the narrative. Chapters are concerned with such topics as 'Camp Nursing', 'Active Service in the Snow', 'Red Cross Needlework', and 'Night Nursing with the B.E.F.' Two are entitled, 'From my Diary', and contain italicized dates to give the impression of being a journal transcription. Dent employs yet another literary form—a skit—to describe 'The Trials of a Home Sister' (Chapter 10). With speaking parts for the Home Sister and a Cook/Corporal, it is an account of a farcical discussion about the camp's meals.

These entertaining and amusing extracts sit alongside other aspects of her nursing, which are less charming. Although she does not dwell on graphic descriptions, Dent does not avoid telling us about such things as 'evil-smelling gas gangrene', blue-purple trench-feet, and 'ghastly wounds which require dressing every two hours' (278). Lyn Macdonald quotes Capt. Geoffrey Keynes, RAMC, who explains that gas gangrene had 'nothing to do with gas as we knew it later in the war. It was called that because the bacillus that grows in the wound creates gas. The whole thing balloons up. You can tap it under your fingers and it sounds hollow. Even with quite a slight wound, when soil and shreds of uniform are carried in by the missile, it starts up.'[64] A. A. Martin described how 'In many cases of gas gangrene bones were badly shattered and pulverised, splinters of bone were lying in surrounding muscles, or had been driven out through the skin.... The skin was black and lacerated, and muscles were extruded and covered with coagulated blood clots.—Wounds full of blood clots, and containing at times

[64] Lyn Macdonald, *The Roses of No Man's Land* (London, 1980), 24.

pieces of khaki cloth, shrapnel fragments, nickel casing of bullets, gravel.... All the cases of gas gangrene had a very penetrating putrefactive smell, which is quite characteristic.'[65]

When she reassures 'Sister Susies' that they are 'doing some of the most valuable war service' by their making of garments and articles for the wounded, she describes how

> Last night one of 'my boys' died. He had gas gangrene, and he cried continually, 'Where's my lavender bag, sister? My wound does smell so.'... There are dozens of other boys who appreciate the lavender bags, boys who are nauseated by the smell of their wound whilst it is being dressed. (150)

The ghastliness with which she is confronted on a daily basis does not disillusion her, however. Instead, it seems to spur her on to even more patriotic determination. She is consoled by the belief that 'it is better [for death] to have come when doing work that counts, work of national and racial weight, than to live on until old and unwanted' (204), and that 'ours is a country worth fighting for, worth dying for, worth being maimed for' (136). The last sentence exhibits another feature of Dent's prose style (one that mirrors Kate Finzi's): the use of triples. In some highly charged, highly coloured sections of the narrative Dent uses them to reinforce the toll the War has exacted upon her and her generation. Stopping in Wimereux, she visits the cemetery, extended to include a section for the British dead:

> Long lines of smoothed graves, each headed with a little wooden cross,—it is a picture of majestic simplicity, of infinite pathos, *nothing tawdry, nothing trivial, nothing but the grandeur of simplicity.* We think of the poor, maimed bodies, all that remain *of that grace of English youth and comeliness, of the beauty that is consumed away, of man turned to destruction.* We think of Time who unheedingly dims the proud stories of those valiant heroes. Each little smoothed grave means a tragedy, a gap in some home across those dark waters. Our age has paid its price for the nation and the race. Those are the dead who won our freedom. May we cheat Time, and ever retain the thought. May it compel us to *greater patience, greater fortitude, greater forbearance* in the work that is to come. (25, italics mine)

The repetition of 'we think' and 'Time' works with the tripling to create a rhetorical tempo. Threes are also used to convey the

[65] Martin, *A Surgeon in Khaki*, 188–9.

powerful experience of night-nursing with its 'tense anxieties, its straining vigilance, its many sorrows' (270):

> nights when we have shared and suffered with delirious patients *the stench, the choking thirst, the sound of groans*,—all the devilish horror and wracking torture of living again the eternal age with its *waiting, waiting, waiting* in No Man's Land, nights when a dying man on whom morphia has had no effect has persistently cackled ragtime while another,—one of the very, very few who have realised they are in the Valley of the Shadow,—reiterated again and again 'I'm dying, I'm dying, I'm dying' (284, italics mine)

Such repetitions weigh down the usually buoyant voice, and bestow a seriousness and poignancy.

This is especially the case in Dent's description of the aftermath of 'The Big Push' on the Somme (2nd Ypres). She records that everyone at the base hospital knew what to expect, since for days and nights they heard the 'guns ceaselessly cannonading'. The wounded begin to arrive in droves early one morning. Ambulances bring 'stretcher after stretcher' and she is spun into a flurry of activity:

> Tunics had been torn to free wounded arms, breeches had been ripped for access to injured legs, boots had been discarded in favour of huge carpet slippers or bandages, heads were swathed, jaws tied up, bandages stained with dirt and blood.
>
> On and on we worked, forgetful of time and remembering our own meal only as we became exhausted.
>
> [....]
>
> Laughter, tears, immense satisfaction and pleasure, immeasurable pain and disappointment were commingled that day. One lived very many times in a torrent of emotion, *agonised by a flood of pity, racked by an intensity of sympathy, tortured by an exquisite, mental pain,* almost overwhelmed by the passion to help fight for those lives. (330–4, italics mine)

This description, with its cataloguing of emergency nursing, mirrors her earlier description of the dull routine of everyday work. Instead of making beds, tidying, taking temperatures, or applying fomentations, she is now tearing tunics, ripping breeches, discarding boots, swathing heads, and tying up jaws.[66]

[66] A. A. Martin is similarly graphic in his description of the wounded he treats after an enemy attack:

> The first case attended to was that of a young soldier of the Norfolks who had been struck by a shell in the abdomen. His intestines were lying outside the body, and loops were inside the upper part of his trousers. Under chloroform we did what we could. He died painlessly a few hours afterwards. There were many bad shell wounds of the

Dent records one young nurse crying out: '"What a useless wastage of human life . . . a useless waste!"' This anger and disillusion would generally be accepted later, after the War, but in the 1916 of this memoir, such an expression is denounced rather than applauded. Dent records a colleague's impassioned reply:

'How can the gift of those lives be called a "useless waste"? Is it a waste for men to fight, to suffer, and to die for all that they hold dear—their liberty, their ideals, and their loved ones? God made man in His own image, a little lower than the angels. I've realised that fact anew to-day. I've seen that Man can ascend to almost God-like heights, to realms of sublimity unsuspected.

'To-day's stories of the fighting, told to us red-hot from the lips of the boys who have lived them, those stories and the many little incidents we have all witnessed, have shown us that, while war may be a great wastage, it is also a great purifier. It has brought out valour indescribable, patience and magnificent endurance untellable. And are these nothing worth?

'I have heard little scraps of conversation to-day. I have seen little acts of self-sacrifice, kindliness and thoughtfulness between the men, that have made me feel reverent. There may be brutality, bestiality, fiendish recklessness, devilish remorselessness, anguishing mutilation and destruction in war, but to-day I have met fortitude, devotion, self-abnegation, that has brought with it an atmosphere of sanctity, of holiness.

'I am too tired to sleep, too tired to do anything but lie and look up at the wooden roof of the hut, too tired to do anything but think, think, think, too tired to shut out of sight and mind the passionate appeal of two dying eyes, and a low faint whisper of "Sister, am I going to die?"

'But, oh, how glad I am to have lived through this day! With the stinging acute pain of all its experiences raw on me, I say it has been a privilege to undergo these sensations. For the pain will pass, since all pain ultimately dies, but what will endure for ever is the memory of the nobility, the grandeur, the approach to divinity we have all seen. It has made better women of us all; it has brought knowledge to our understanding, life to our ideals, light to our soul'. (337–9)[67]

head; one necessitating a trephining operation. One poor fellow had his tongue half blown off. The loose bit was stitched on. The compound fractures were numerous and of a very bad type, associated with much shattering of the bone. (Martin, *A Surgeon in Khaki*, 97).

[67] A similar plea is made by Capt. Robert Dolbey:

If the truth be told, in spite of the journalists, there is no joy in battle; no fierce delight in conflict, no happiness, no gaiety in the trenches under fire. But the one splendid, precious thing in connection with war is the high sense of duty that takes men and officers back again, time after time. . . . Tommy wonderful? Of course he is wonderful; he is the most wonderful thing in the world. . . . What does his country mean to him that he should make this offering of his life? Is it worth the sacrifice? Who can

With the passion of a sermon and utilizing archaic sentence construction ('are these nothing worth?'), the patriotic nurse's reply is a diatribe against anyone who would waver in their faith in the cause. It contrasts good and evil, celebrates the triad virtues of 'fortitude, devotion, self-abnegation', and promises a kind of resurrection for all those who have suffered. By virtue of their role as agents of healing, women are purified—they heal themselves—of flippancy, irresponsibility, and vanity. They share with the epic hero 'the crisis of war [that] entails descent into the underworld, a trial of the spirit that brings knowledge and wisdom and power to guide others'.[68] The idea of purity or purification is raised again and again by memoirists and chroniclers of women's role in the War. Mary Frances Billington, in *The Red Cross in War*, asserts that 'the ultimate effect of war has been a purifying one—the lifting of a nation to higher issues of justice, of duty, of industry.'[69] Similarly, Hall Caine, in his book *The Drama of 365 Days*, says 'woman's part in this red year of the war has been one of purity, sacrifice, and undivided glory'.[70]

Dent's memoir ends with the order to 'proceed forthwith' to her next posting. She fits Lyn Macdonald's description:

> On the face of it, no one could have been less equipped for the job than these gently nurtured girls who walked straight out of Edwardian drawing-rooms into the manifold horrors of the First World War. It was all a far cry from the old myth of the 'ministering angel'. These girls had to be tough. They worked in flooded operating theatres in Flanders where, in a big 'push', there might be four operations going on at one time, and as many as ten amputations in an hour.[71]

A V.A.D. in France serves to illustrate the ways in which women of Dent's class were able to face the realities of war. It is a sentimental and often romantic account that refuses to be disillusioned and that

doubt it? (Robert Valentine Dolbey, *A Regimental Surgeon in War and Prison* (London, 1917), 245).
Martin is equally 'privileged to be of service'. He asserts he will 'never forget the sight of these poor, maimed, bleeding, dying and dead men' (Martin, *A Surgeon in Khaki*, 107).

[68] Egan, *Patterns of Experience in Autobiography*, 8.

[69] M. F. Billington, *The Red Cross in War: Woman's Part in the Relief of Suffering* (London, 1914), 189.

[70] Hall Caine, *The Drama of 365 Days: Scenes in the Great War* (London, 1915), 117.

[71] Macdonald, *The Roses of No Man's Land*, 11.

celebrates active service for women. Emerging from night-duty, she records seeing 'a pink flush heralding a thousand shafts of ruddy, glowing light, and—rosy as our hopes, radiant with promise—there breaks the Dawn' (287). Such an image is characteristic of the way in which, throughout her memoir, despite grief, hardship, and horror, she uses literary motifs and an idealistic nature to see her through.

Although Finzi, Thurstan, Martin-Nicholson, and Dent admit little if any disillusion with the cause, Pat Beauchamp and Enid Bagnold are less restrained. The final two memoirs in this chapter mark a significant change in tone and in content. Beauchamp's *Fanny Goes to War* (1919) retains some of the high-minded sentiment and patriotic intentions of the earlier four, but chinks have begun to appear in the armour of patriotic certainty. Bagnold's *A Diary without Dates* (1918) is a herald both of post-war sentiment and modernist style.

Beauchamp's memoir is introduced, like Finzi's, with praise from a high-ranking military man. Maj.-Gen. H. N. Thompson, KCMG, CB, DSO, describes the 'intense brotherly sympathy and affection—almost adoration' for women's work in the Great War:

> They have been in situations where, five short years ago, no one should ever have thought of finding them. They have witnessed scenes nerve-racking and heart-rending beyond the power of description.... The free homes of Britain little realise what our war women have been through, or what an undischarged debt is owing to them.[72]

Thompson claims that women were responsible, to a large extent, for keeping morale high. The 'Authoress' demonstrates the heroism of the many: cheerfulness, power to forget danger and hardship, humour, and comradeship. A fine example of the *esprit de corps* of the First Aid Nursing Yeomanry, Beauchamp has two rows of medals to 'bedeck her khaki jacket'.[73]

[72] Pat Beauchamp, *Fanny Goes to War* (London, 1919), v–vi.
Maj.-Gen. Sir Harry Neville Thompson (1861–1925) was born in Ireland, the son of the Rector of Clonmany, Donegal, and educated at Trinity College, Dublin. He took his medical degree in 1883 and became a major in the Royal Army Medical Corps in 1898, rising to the rank of major-general in 1917. He served in Egypt and South Africa and was highly decorated. In the Great War he served with various divisions, and continued to receive honours including the French *Croix de Guerre* with two palms and the American Distinguished Service Medal (*Who Was Who*, 1916–1928, v. II).

[73] Beauchamp, vii.

Beauchamp's memoir is testimony to the fact that, although nursing has taken primary place in the cultural memory of female participation in the Great War, it was not the only way in which women 'did their bit'. *Fanny Goes to War* starts with a history of the First Aid Nursing Yeomanry (FANY).[74] Beauchamp is inspired by a snapshot entitled 'Women Yeomanry in Camp', in the *Mirror* newspaper in the autumn of 1913, depicting a khaki-clad girl on horseback leaping a fence: 'That . . . is the sort of show I'd like to belong to: I'm sick of ambling round the Row on a Park hack. It would be a rag to go into camp with a lot of other girls' (2). After many inquiries and false starts she eventually joins the FANY and completes much of the same training as Olive Dent. On the outbreak of war, the FANY's offer of assistance is refused by the War Office, but enthusiastically received by the Belgian Army. Beauchamp has to wait until she turns twenty-one to be sent abroad, and it is not until January of 1915 that she receives her first posting to the *blessé* ward of a hospital in Lamarck, Belgium. Corroborating other memoirists' assertions about the gratefulness of the wounded, Beauchamp notes how her patients affectionately called the English women 'miskes', a diminutive of miss.

In these early days her excitement knows no bounds; many sentences end with exclamation marks (sometimes two or three to a page) and her diction is full of contemporary (Edwardian) slang. Phrases and words like 'oh so jolly', 'ripping', 'beastly', and 'a rag' appear throughout the text, and Beauchamp often addresses the reader directly with 'I tell you' or 'you can imagine'. Light-hearted incidents that convey a sense of comradeship are related in the manner of schoolgirl fiction:

> Now, if you've never lit a Primus stove before, and in between the time you were told how to do it you had peeled twenty or thirty potatoes, got two scratch breakfasts, swept the Mess tent and kept that field kitchen from going out, it's quite possible your mind would be a little blurred. Mine was. When the time came, I put the methylated in the little cup at the top, lit it, and then pumped with a will. The result was a terrific roar and a sheet of flame reaching almost to the roof! Never having seen one in action before,

[74] Founded in 1910 to supplement the Royal Army Medical Corps (RAMC) in field work, stretcher bearing, and ambulance driving, the First Aid Nursing Yeomanry required that its members be able to ride horses 'bareback or otherwise, as much difficulty had been found in transporting nurses from one place to another on the veldt in the South African War' (1).

I thought it was possible they always behaved like that at first and that the conflagration would subside in a few moments. I watched it doubtfully, arms akimbo. Bridget entered just then and, determined not to appear flustered, in as cool a voice as possible I said: 'Is that all right, old thing?' She put down her parcels, and without a word, seized the stove by one of its legs and threw it on a sand heap outside! Of course the field kitchen had gone out—(I can't think who invented that rotten inadequate grating underneath, anyway), and I felt I was not the bright jewel I might have been. (115–16)

She makes much of her blunders, and Primus stoves are not the only hazards: 'Nothing would make me believe those [tent] ropes were inanimate—they literally lay in wait for me each night! When any loud crash was heard in camp it was always taken for granted it was "only Pat taking another toss"' (117). Convoy work provides similarly amusing scenes:

I was given a little Mons lorry to drive. To say that I adored that car would not be exaggerating my feelings about it at all. The seat was my chief joy, it was of the racing variety, some former sportsman having done away with the tool box that had served as one! 'Tuppy' [the convoy dog] also appreciated that lorry, and when we set off to draw rations, lying almost flat, the tips of his ears could just be seen from the front on a line with the top of my cap. (123)

When her Mons lorry has to be retired, Beauchamp chooses the speediest car on offer: a four-cylinder Napier she dubs 'Susan' (136). Winter frost makes the job of starting the cars a particular problem:

It was no uncommon sight to see F.A.N.Y.s lying supine across the bonnet of their cars, completely winded by their efforts. The morning air was full of sobbing breaths and groans as they swung in vain! This process became known as 'getting her loose'—(I'm referring to the car not the F.A.N.Y., though, from personal experience, it's quite applicable to both.) (191)

Such jocularity and comradeship is further reinforced by the inclusion of poems such as 'A Black Day in the Life of a Convoy F.A.N.Y.' by Winifred Mordaunt.

The jolliness, however, belies the more serious aspects of Beauchamp's wartime experience. She can be the mistress of understatement: when a shell bursts in front of her, she 'felt in an awful funk, and [her] one idea was to flee from that sinister spot' (25); a supply delivery to the Belgian trenches is described as 'rather nervy work'

(36); and turning an ambulance car around on a not-very-wide quay is deemed 'rather ticklish business' (163).

As is the case with the other memoirs, the literariness of *Fanny Goes to War* is attested to by the numerous metaphors: 75's explode with a bang, then go 'swizzing through the air with a sound like a sob' (38); tanks appear 'to be anything in size from a hippopotamus to Buckingham Palace' (165); and shell bursts in the sky seem like 'little round white puffs' (219). German airships hover together like so many 'silver cigars' (71), whereas a 'Zepp' raid is an exhilarating experience:

> It was a bomb. The Zeppelin was still there. The guns blazed away, the row was terrific. Star shells were thrown up to try and locate the Zepp., and the sky was full of showering lights, blue, green, and pink. Four searchlights were playing, shrapnel was bursting, and a motor machine-gun let off volleys from sheer excitement, the sharp tut-tut-tut adding to the general confusion. In the pauses the elusive Zepp. could be heard buzzing like some gigantic angry bee. I wouldn't have missed it for anything. It looked like a fireworks display, and the row was increasing each minute. Every Frenchman in the neighbourhood let off his rifle with gusto. (53)

Beauchamp uses colour, natural imagery, and onomatopoeia to effect a vivid description of this surreal entertainment. Often, however, she comments that what she witnesses is beyond her powers of expression:

> On drawing near we saw that this was the spot where the shell had landed and that there were casualties. We drew up and got down hastily, taking dressings with us. The sight that met my eyes is one I shall never forget, and, in fact, cannot describe. Four men had just been blown to pieces—I leave the details to your imagination, but it gave me a sudden shock to realize that a few minutes earlier those remains had been living men walking along the road laughing and talking. (24)

Why doesn't she describe what she has seen? Other memoirists have been candid, even to the point of sickening detail. Certainly in this excerpt there is the sense that what is left to the imagination of the reader is more horrible than what the writer can spell out; the shock is worse for what is not said. However, in suppressing the reality for the reader, Beauchamp may be said to be suppressing it for herself. It is too awful to contemplate at length. She may also simply be unable to find the words to communicate the gruesomeness of the dismembered bodies. It is easier to wrap up the experience as a nightmare that somehow has not really happened. Things frequently seem 'strangely unreal' and she wonders if 'at times if I was awake' (30).

Beauchamp questions whether her first visit to the trenches 'was a reality or only a dream' (40), and when an air raid occurs as she is reading 'an exciting spy book', she says, 'for a moment I thought that I must be dreaming or that the book was bewitched' (207). Life truly does imitate art in this instance—what she is reading must surely have helped the description of being under fire: 'I had just got to the most thrilling part and was holding my breath from sheer excitement when whiz! sob! bang! and a shell went spinning over the huts' (207). Leslie Buswell described his experience of a German bombardment in a similar way: 'It was rather like a stage scene or a coloured picture show.'[75]

Echoing the sentiments of other memoirists, she praises Sister Susies: 'I thought of the kind hands that had knitted them in far away England and wondered if the knitters had ever imagined their things would be given out like this, to rows of mud-stained men... their words of thanks half-drowned in the thunder of war' (34). Trained sisters, after a time, become 'more human' and cease to make 'remarks or reflections about the defects of the "untrained unit" who "imagined they knew everything after four months of war"' (47). The debris of fighting is turned to practical use: 'we had as many flowers inside our huts as we could possibly get into the shell cases and other souvenirs which perforce were turned into flower vases' (161). Germans are often referred to as brutes, depicted as lascivious, and shown to be wantonly cruel by the retelling of atrocities perpetrated on the Belgians: a German soldier runs his sword through the 'poor old body' of a deaf woman because she served his beer too slowly (65). The ignorance of the British Home Front is lamented as Beauchamp attends a memorial service in *Sacré-Cœur*: 'It seemed so on looking round at those white-faced women... how I wished that *some* of the people in England, who had not been touched by the war, or who at that time (June 1915) hardly realized there even was one, could have been present' (84).

Whereas in the early stages of her active service Beauchamp performs nursing tasks, she later becomes a convoy driver. The great pressure to ease the suffering of the wounded is now put in a

[75] Buswell, *Ambulance No. 10*, 19.

different context as she transports them from hospital barges or casualty clearing stations to field hospitals:

> The journeys back were perfect nightmares. Try as one would, it was impossible not to bump a certain amount over those appalling roads full of holes and cobbles. It was pathetic when a voice from the interior could be heard asking, 'Is it much farther, Sister?' and knowing how far it was my heart ached for them. After all they had been through, one felt they should be spared every extra bit of pain that was possible. (149)

On a 'specially dark night' she is ordered to transport a dying patient from a hospital ship:

> Then followed one of the most trying half-hours I have ever been through.
>
> He seemed to regain consciousness to a certain extent and asked me from time to time:
>
> 'Sister, am I dying?'
>
> 'Will I see me old mother again, Sister?'
>
> 'Why have you taken me off the Blighty ship, Sister?'
>
> Then there would be silence for a space, broken only by groans and an occasional 'Christ, but me back 'urts crool,' and all the comfort I could give was that we would be there soon, and the doctor would do something to ease the pain.
>
> Thank God, at last we arrived at the Casino. One of the most trying things about ambulance driving is that while you long to get the patient to hospital as quickly as possible you are forced to drive slowly. I jumped out and cautioned the orderlies to lift him as gently as they could, and he clung to my hand as I walked beside the stretcher into the ward.
>
> 'You're telling me the truth, Sister? I don't want to die, I tell you that straight,' he said. 'Good-bye and God bless you; I'll come and see you in the morning,' I said, and left him to the nurses' tender care. I went down early next day but he had died at 3 a.m. Somebody's son and only nineteen. That sort of job takes the heart out of you for some days, though Heaven knows we ought to have got used to anything by that time. (189–90)

The questions of this boy-patient are reminiscent of those tended by Finzi and Dent. The stark sentence, 'Somebody's son and only nineteen', is infused with a poignancy that arouses sympathy both for the dead young man and for his bereaved mother. Beauchamp's feeling that she and her comrades 'should be used to it by now' is a common one among the memoirists, its repetition an indication of how they *cannot* get used to the deaths and the suffering they witness. Dent and her fellow nurses offered platitudes to effect a resolution, but Beauchamp is less quick to do so. After another incident, she questions, 'Was the war worth even one boy's eyesight? No, I thought not' (175). This statement ends a chapter—no determined nurse speaks up to offer a contradiction.

Beauchamp continues to work on despite her doubts and her premonitions of personal danger. First felt while on leave in England, these portents are so strong she draws up 'instructions of what I wanted done with such worldly goods as I possessed' (166). In many ways, characteristic of this memoir, a jaunty tone covers real fear. Entitled 'Last Ride' (a nod, perhaps, to Browning's poem 'The Last Ride Together' (published in *Dramatic Romances*, 1863)) Chapter 16 denotes two final incidents: a horseback ride along sands that 'appeared almost golden in the sun' beside 'deep blue waves... against the paler turquoise of the sky' (219), and a lorry supply trip two days later. A similarly perfect day marks this ride:

> I had been up since 5 and was taking a lorry-full of stretchers and blankets past a French Battery to the E.M.O.'s. It was about midday and there was not a cloud in the sky. Then suddenly my heart stood still. Somehow, instinctively, I knew I was 'for it' at last. Whole eternities seemed to elapse before the crash. There was no escape. Could I urge Little Willie on? I knew it was hopeless; even as I did so he bucketed and failed to respond. He would! How I longed for Susan, who could always be relied upon to sprint forward. At last the crash came. I felt myself being hurled from the car into the air, to fall and be swept along for some distance, my face being literally rubbed in the ground. I remember my rage at this, and even in that extreme moment managed to seize my nose in the hope that it at least might not be broken! Presently I was left lying in a crumpled heap on the ground. My first thought, oddly enough, was for the car, which I saw standing sulkily and somewhat battered not far off. 'There *will* be a row,' I thought. (222)

Again, we have the use of contemporary slang and military lingo mixed with intense excitement, but the foreboding of this event is communicated by the sharp, short sentences, which heighten the tension that has been building since Beauchamp first mentioned her 'premonitions'. The reader senses that her injuries are worse than she surmises. The reactions of the French soldiers who tend to her after the crash confirm this:

> I watched them furtively wiping away the tears that rolled down their furrowed cheeks. One even put his arm over his eyes as a child does. I wondered vaguely why they were crying; it never dawned on me it had anything to do with *me*. '*Complètement coupée*,' I heard one say, and quick

as a shot, I asked, *'Où est-ce que c'est qu'est coupé?'* and those tactful souls, just rough soldiers, replied without hesitation, *'La jaquette, Mademoiselle.'*

'Je m'en fiche de la jaquette,' I answered, completely reassured.

I wished the ambulance would come soon. 'I *am* in a beastly mess,' I thought again. 'Fancy broken legs hurting like this. What must the men go through!' (224)

The journey in the ambulance puts her in a position identical to that of the many wounded soldiers she has transported: 'we were into a hole and out again with a bump and the pain became almost too much to bear' (227). Yet her driver is a new recruit and from her stretcher, Beauchamp, knowing 'every hole in that road', ends up giving instructions and directions.

It is over a week before she is told the full extent of her injuries: one leg amputated, the other only just saved. A severed nerve causes her 'terrible involuntary jumps that came so suddenly from nowhere and seized one like a deadly cramp' (230). This 'dreadful demon' is at its worst at night, as are her wakeful thoughts:

I used to lie and think of all the thousands of men in hospital and perhaps even lying untended in No-man's-land going through twice as much as I, and wondered if the world would really be any better for all this suffering or if it would be forgotten as soon as the war was over. It seemed to me to be rather a waste if it was to be so. (232)

The halting criticism characteristic of Beauchamp's outlook turns to bitterness once she is sent home to England and finds her country unprepared to deal with anything so 'unorthodox' as a woman amputee:

the general impression borne in on me was that I was a complete nuisance. There was no recognized hospital for 'the likes of us' to go to, and I was taken to a civilian one where war-work seemed entirely at a discount. (253)

A voice anticipating that of *Testament of Youth* now comes to the fore in the memoir. Nursing sisters are often hostile and dismissive, and visitors, 'whom I had never seen in my life before', gawk as if she were 'a strange animal from the Zoo'. Beauchamp's ear for direct speech and her talent for satire are illustrated by her depiction of one such visitor:

There would be a tap at the door: enter lady, beautifully dressed and a large smile. The opening sentence was invariably the same. 'You don't know who I am, but I'm Lady L_____, Miss so-and-so's third cousin. She told me all about you, and I thought I really *must* come and have a peep.' Enters and subsides into chair near bed smiling sweetly, and in nine cases out of ten jiggles toes against it, which jars one excessively. 'You must have suffered *terribly*! I hear your leg was absolutely *crushed!* And now tell me all about it! Makes you rather sick to talk of it? Fancy that! Conscious all the time, dear me! What you must have gone *through*! (Leg gives one of its jumps.) Whatever was that? Only keeping your knee from getting stiff, how funny! *Lovely* having the *Croix de Guerre*. Quite makes up for it. What? Rather have your *leg*. Dear me, how odd! Wonderful what they do with artificial limbs nowadays. Know a man and really you can't tell *which* is which. (Naturally not, any fool could make a leg the shape of the other!) Well, I really *must* be going. I shall be able to tell all my friends I've *seen* you now and been able to cheer you up a little. *Poor* girl! *So* unfortunate! Terribly cheerful, aren't you? Don't seem to mind a bit. Would you kindly ring for the lift? I find these stairs *so trying*. I've enjoyed myself so much. Goodbye.' Exit (goodby-ee). (256)

In the form of a skit, this society-minded and fashionable woman is parodied with biting sarcasm. Sassoon's 'Does it Matter' comes to mind with the exclamations of callous enthusiasm, and Beauchamp must surely be referring to and sending up the oft-sung tune 'Good-byeee!' The voice, which vividly described the amusing Primus stove incident, is still here, but it has taken on a sharper edge.

She continues to struggle with feelings of isolation and uselessness as she undergoes a series of operations and painful fittings of and adjustments to her artificial leg. Unlike the protagonist in Helen Zenna Smith's *Not So Quiet*, who tells us that 'her soul died on the side of a blood-spattered trench', Beauchamp does not yield entirely to disillusion. Her memoir concludes after the Armistice when she is able to return to France for a reunion of the FANY corps. Travelling along the Ypres–Menin Road, passing Sanctuary Wood, she reiterates not only her previous theme of the indescribable nature of her experiences, but displays the haunting memory alluded to by other memoirists:

Words are inadequate to express the horror and loneliness of that place which seemed peopled only by the ghosts of those 'Beloved soldiers, who love rough life and breath, not less for dying faithful to the last.' (288)

Though doubting the efficacy of language, she has used it in an attempt to come to terms with her own experience. In the end, Beauchamp, like the others, finds solace in patriotic truisms, and ends her memoir with wistful longing instead of emotional numbness:

It was a singular and happy coincidence that on the second anniversary of the day I lost my leg, I should be cantering over the same fields at Peuplinghe where 'Flanders' had so gallantly pursued 'puss' that day long ago, or was it really only yesterday? (290)

Published soon after the Armistice *Fanny Goes to War* merely hints at more familiar post-war attitudes. *A Diary without Dates* (1918) blatantly proclaims them. Enid Bagnold's memoir is characterized by modernist fragmentation of both structure and voice. Along with a frequent use of ellipses, terse sentences and paragraphs are divided by typographical spaces and appear as impressions independent of each other. One follows another in an apparently random manner; in fact, however, they are controlled in a highly organized structure, in much the same way as discordant sounds within modernist scores like Stravinsky's *Rite of Spring*.

The progression of the narrative is not so much linear as circuitous. True to its title, dates are absent. Bagnold's table of contents suggests fluid and illusive meaning: Part I—'Outside the Glass Doors'; Part II—'Inside the Glass Doors'; Part III—'The Boys'. These are more enigmatic than those of Olive Dent's chapter headings such as 'A BEF Christmas' or 'A Big Push'. Bagnold is at once detached from and preoccupied by the hospital and her work, which can be chaotic, appalling, overwhelming, and mesmerizing. That she refers to herself as a 'ghost' further reinforces the surreality of her experience. The hospital itself 'is alive; I feel it like a living being', yet is also 'like a dream. I am afraid of waking up and finding it commonplace. The white Sisters, the ceaselessly-changing patients, the long passages, the sudden plunges into the brilliant wards . . . their scenery hypnotises me' (45).

The shifting form and tone of this record mimic the narrator's shifting sensations. Two kinds of writing style are present—one for the world outside, another for the hospital and work. Nature is characterized as 'cool and wonderful' (3) and lyrically described:

What is there so rapturous about the moon?

The radiance of a floating moon is unbelievable. It is a figment of a dream. The metal-silver ball that hung at the top of the Xmas tree, or, earlier still, the shining thing, necklace or spoon, the thing the baby leans to catch. . . . (68)

Her mood is buoyant, and she is charmed and engrossed by the ethereal qualities of natural elements. She produces sensuous imagery as well: 'How wet and good this new cheese is, and fresh and good the little bits that fall off the edge!' (18); 'Soft sugar, lump sugar, coffee. As one stirs the coffee round the tin the whole room smells of it, that brown, burnt smell' (19). The hospital, on the other hand, is depicted as 'dim', 'half-lit', 'monotone' (3), 'a place of whispers and wheels moving on rubber tyres, long corridors, and strangely unsexed women moving in them.... the white clothes, the hidden hair, the stern white collar just below the chin' (35).

The sterility and routine have their purpose, however. *A Diary without Dates* opens with the assertion, 'I like discipline. I like to be part of an institution. It gives one more liberty than is possible among three or four observant friends' (3). Large and impersonal, an 'institution' will not make her a subject of scrutiny, leaving her mind free:

> Let them pile on the rules, invent and insist; yet behind them, beneath them, I have that strong, secret liberty of an institution that rules like a wind in me and lifts my mind like a leaf.
>
> So long as I conform absolutely, not a soul will glance at my thoughts—few at my face. I have only to be silent and conform, and I might be in so far a land that even the eye of God had lost me. (19)

It is the paradoxical modernist belief that one is more alone in the crowd than in actual physical isolation. Discipline, therefore, is a disguise. It is also, in the routine it demands, the mechanical repetition of tasks, a method of control over the 'everlasting dislocations' of hospital life:

> Sixty-five trays. It takes an hour to do. Thirteen pieces on each tray. Thirteen times sixty-five ... eight hundred and forty-five things to collect, lay, square symmetrically. I like absurd little reflections and arrangements—taking a dislike to the knives because they will not lie still on the polished metal of the tray, but pivot on shafts, and swing out on angles after my fingers have left them. (6)

The prose mimics the action, its control mirroring the speaker's control over her thoughts. When she describes the rebel knives, however, she uses one long sentence made up of a number of phrases to indicate the disruption, the refusal of some elements to be controlled. Thus, the laying of the trays is a metaphor for her emotions. When training a new VAD, she says, 'I did not want to share my trays with her. I love them; they are my recreation' (22).

Other routines in the hospital—such as that which occurs after the death of a patient—are described with equal simplicity:

> When a man dies they fetch him with a stretcher, just as he came in; only he enters with a blanket over him, and a flag covers him as he goes out. When he came in he was one of a convoy, but every man who can stand rises to his feet as he goes out. Then they play him to his funeral, to a grass mound at the back of the hospital. (14)

It is the very lack of embellishment, which gives this passage its poignancy and the dead man his dignity. The order and starkness enable 'the nature of the ordinary wounded soldier to speak for itself'.[76]

Bagnold's descriptions of wounds hold true to this assessment, and other memoirists' clinical descriptions pale in comparison. Of one man's shoulder wound she says:

> It was all very fine for the theatre people to fill his shoulder chock full of pluggings while he lay unconscious on the table; they had packed it as you might stuff linen into a bag: it was another matter to get it out.
>
> I did not dare touch his hand with that too-easy compassion which I have noticed here, or whisper to him, 'It's nearly over' . . . as the forceps pulled at the stiffened gauze. It wasn't nearly over.
>
> Six inches deep the gauze stuck, crackling under the pull of the forceps, blood and pus leaping forward from the cavities as the steady hand of the doctor pulled inch after inch of the gauze to the light. And when one hole was emptied there was another, five in all. (140)

Readers are meant to feel sickened, but they are also meant to experience pity for the man, a more intense pity that arises out of Bagnold's refusal to minimize the horror or to glorify the suffering. In that sense, it becomes 'an act of cultural piety'.[77] It also establishes what Santanu Das argues is a 'bridge, a physical continuum with the male body and experience'.[78] Bagnold may be impotent to assuage his pain or her guilt at such impotence, but she can at least employ her skill with language to bear witness to both.

In another instance, she builds our anticipation for a dramatic, and no less terrifying denouement:

> Round his bed there stood three red screens, and the busy, white-capped heads of two Sisters bobbed above the rampart.

[76] Tylee, *The Great War and Women's Consciousness*, 191.

[77] Ibid.

[78] Santanu Das, *The Sense of Touch in First World War Literature*, unpublished Ph.D. dissertation (Cambridge University, 2002), 169.

> It suddenly shocked me. What were they doing there? Why the screens? Why the look of strain in the eyes of the man in the next bed behind the screens?
>
> I went cold and stood rooted, waiting till one of them could come out and speak to me.
>
> Soon they took away the screen nearest to me; they had done with it.
>
> The man I was to inquire for has no nostrils; they were blown away, and he breathes through two pieces of red rubber tubing: it gave a more horrible look to his face than I have ever seen.
>
> The Sister came out and told me she thought he was 'not up to much'. I think she means he is dying.
>
> I wonder if he thinks it is better to die . . . But he was nearly well before he got pneumonia, had begun to take up little habits of living. He had been out to tea.
>
> Inexplicable, what he thinks of, lying behind the screen. (8)

The reader's anticipation—and dread—of the final revelation of this soldier's condition are heightened by the short paragraphs and staccato questions. The colour of the screens is suggestive of blood; the use of the word 'rampart' not only imitates a barrier, but a military fortification. To peek one's head above a rampart is to expose oneself to danger; for the speaker to look above the hospital rampart is to expose herself to a disturbing spectacle, one that is both a testament to and a reproach of modern warfare. The nurses perform a dumb show; the screens are a temporary cover for their bizarre artistic creation, the wounded man is their grotesque sculpture. Elsewhere Ryan (the soldier) is described as having 'no profile, as we know a man's. Like an ape, he has only his bumpy forehead and his protruding lips—the nose, the left eye gone' (14). He has become animal-like, dehumanized, an uncanny creature. A profound pity is elicited for him when we are told about his taking up the 'little habits of living'; in that one short sentence, 'He had been out to tea', volumes of sadness are communicated, for we wonder how he was received by the world outside. Ryan cannot be kept behind screens, hidden from the gaze of people forever.

The suffering of the men is ennobling, and here Bagnold conforms to the principles of the other memoirists. The final section of *A Diary without Dates* emphasizes this fact with its label, 'The Boys', though she admits, 'they seem to me full-grown men' (98). She makes a distinction between the officers and the enlisted soldiers. Ward provisions vary according to class: 'So now one steps down from chintz covers and lemonade to the Main Army and lemon-water' (97). Instead of having twenty-six lemons per day as she did for the officers, Bagnold must make do with two to squeeze 'into an old jug and hope for the best about the sugar'. Niceties and formality do not exist in a Tommies' ward: 'one can dare ask anything; there isn't the mystery which used to surround the officers' illnesses' (98). The relaxed atmosphere is communicated by her descriptions of these various 'boys'. Characters are vivid and displayed with gentle regard:

> We had a heated discussion to-day as to whether the old lady who leaves a tract beneath a single rose by each bedside could no longer be tolerated.
>
> 'She's a nuisance,' said the Sister; 'the men make more noise afterwards because they set her hymns to ragtime.'
>
> 'What good does it do them?' said the V.A.D., '... and I have to put the roses in water!'
>
> I rode the highest horse of all: 'Her inquiries about their souls are an impertinence. Why should they be bothered?'
>
> These are the sort of the things they say in debating societies. But Life talks differently... Pinker said, 'Makes the po'r ole lady 'appy!' (111)

The control displayed by Martin-Nicholson is depicted in Bagnold's *Diary*, as are the petty complaints of upper-class VADs, and the disillusioned, atheistic proclamations of the intelligentsia. (The old lady and her 'inquiries' remind the reader of Owen's 'Disabled': 'Only a solemn man who brought him fruits/ *Thanked* him; and then inquired about his soul'.) The simple response of Pinker puts them all to shame, and Bagnold is thus 'explicitly disengaging herself from pacifists, jingoists or feminists'.[79]

In comparison to 'the boys', other characters from the hospital appear as insensitive, petty, dismissive. The ward Sisters are 'strangely unsexed' (35), formidable, like a 'fortress, unassailable, and whose sleeping guns may fire at any moment' (86). VADs act as schoolgirls who all just want to be liked, and 'there is a certain dreadful innocence about them too, as though each would protest, "In spite of our tasks, our often immodest tasks, our minds are as white as snow"' (34). Not surprisingly, Bagnold is scornful of such attitudes. She thinks they reflect the 'silliest, most mulish, incurious, unresponsive, condemning kind of an ideal' (35), and we sense that

[79] Tylee, *The Great War and Women's Consciousness*, 190.

it is not only the War that is the cause of this belief. The War has only highlighted the absurdity of such unrealistic expectations.

Visitors are even more satirized. They are depicted either as schoolchildren requiring control or as 'a race of gods' to be worshipped and fawned over. Like Pat Beauchamp, Bagnold is disdainful of these ladies who treat the nurses as servants and talk about life in wartime as if it were 'Cairo in the season'. One

> cried out with emotion when she saw the first officer limp into the Mess, 'And can some of them *walk*, then!' Perhaps she thought they came in to tea on stretchers with field bandages on. She quivered all over too, as she looked from one to the other, and I feel sure she went home and broke down, crying, 'What an experience . . . the actual wounds!' (17)

Bagnold wishes to disabuse them of their artificial impressions: '"Oh visitors. . . . if you could see what lies beneath the dressings!"' (102). *A Diary without Dates* is her attempt to show them this.

We also glimpse what lies beneath her own façade. She realizes that her work has changed her forever and it is the physical change, which the outside world sees and comments on:

> My ruined charms cry aloud for help.
>
> The caps wears away my front hair; my feet are widening from the everlasting boards; my hands won't take my rings.
>
> I was advised last night on the telephone to marry immediately before it was too late.
>
> A desperate remedy. I will try cold cream and hair tonics first. (47)

Though she will resort to beauty products, she does so in deliberate rebellion against what society deems she must do. The syntax of the final two sentences is a bold and humorous assertion of her independence. When others mark the change in her personality she is 'dumbfounded': 'Had I ever been "nice"?' (75), and on a particularly bad day she tells us: 'I am at anyone's mercy; I have lost 30 friends in one day. The 31st is in bed No. 11' (79). She longs to express her own personality. Instead of feeling a 'better' woman (as Dent proclaims), Bagnold is assailed by the 'vigorous and symmetrical vision of the ward' (86). She is in constant battle with outside expectations and with her own feelings of numbness: 'the struggle to feel pain, to repel the invading army of familiarity' (133). She worries that 'there are times when my heart fails me; when my eyes, my ears, my tongue, and my understanding fail me; when pain means nothing to me' (100), and believes that it is 'unsafe' to 'grow used to death': 'for if death becomes cheap it is the watcher, not the dying, who is poisoned' (90). She recognizes, but in the end, seems to find no solution for the 'deadlock', the paradox, that 'the pain of one creature cannot continue to have meaning for another. It is almost impossible to nurse a man well whose pain you do not imagine' (101). The questions she poses to herself are not unlike those of the other memoirists, but what distinguishes Bagnold are her resolutions—or lack thereof:

> I pause from laying my trays, and with a bunch of forks in my hand I stand still.
>
> They take the stretcher into a ward, and while I wait I know what they are doing behind the screens which stand around a bed against the wall. I hear the shuffle of feet as the men stand to attention, and the orderlies come out again, and the folds of the flag have ballooned up to receive and embrace a man's body.
>
> 'Where is he going?'
>
> 'To the mortuary.'
>
> 'Yes... but where else?' (28)

The other women would have had a more certain answer than this sceptical VAD. They would also have been more assured—or convinced themselves—that the dead will be remembered. For Bagnold, 'everything is written in water. We talk of tablets to the dead. There can be none but in the heart, and the heart fades' (104).

A Diary without Dates is consistently censorious and sardonic but also elegiac and lyrical:

> Those distant guns again tonight...
>
> Now a lull and now a bombardment; again a lull, and then batter, batter, and the windows tremble. Is the lull when *they* go over the top?
>
> I can only think of death to-night. I tried to think, just now, 'What is it, after all! Death comes anyway; this only hastens it.' But that won't do; no philosophy helps the pain of death. It is pity, pity, that I feel, and sometimes a sort of shame that I am here to write at all.
>
> Summer... Can it be summer through whose hot air the guns shake and tremble? The honeysuckle, whose little stalks twinkled and shone that January night, has broken at each woody end into its crumpled flower. (104)

Assailed by feelings of survivor's guilt, she sounds not unlike Kate Finzi, and she utilizes a similar repetition to enhance her meaning. 'Batter, batter' imitates the trembling of the windows and parallels the repetition of 'pity, pity'; the two words then correspond to each other: her heart is battered by pity. With no lengthy justifications, nature is used as a contrast to the mechanized war, which brings death, and ends the cycle of life. The guns intrude upon the summer's day—the honeysuckle, like the men she envisions going over the top, is crumpled and destroyed.

Though her mind wanders to the battlefield, she does not sensationalize or relish such a fixation. Indeed, she questions it:

> How strange that these people should still picture the minds of soldiers as filled with the glitter of bright bayonets and the glory of war! They think we need a vision of blood and ravage and death to turn us from our bright thoughts, to still the noise of the drum in our ears. The drums don't beat, the flags don't fly. . . .
>
> He should come down the left-hand side of the ward and hear what the dairyman says.
>
> 'I 'ates it nurse; I 'ates it. Them 'orses'll kill me; them drills . . . It's no life for a man, nurse.'
>
> The dairyman hasn't been to the Front; you needn't go to the Front to hate the war. (117)

In this way, Bagnold aligns herself more with post-war sentiment than with the beliefs of many of her nursing compatriots.

Her voice is one of sophisticated *ennui*, not schoolgirl enthusiasm. Acceptance based on patriotic ideals gives way to a weary resignation. She does not present a patriotic picture or a celebration of women's efforts in the War as do Dent or Thurstan. Instead, this memoir is a log of personal perceptions and endurance. In her epigraph, Bagnold says, 'I apologise to those whom I may hurt. Can I soothe them by pleading that one may only write what is true for oneself?'[80] She breaks the mould of conformity, which may be said to exist between the other memoirs. Absent also are 'official' sanctions as accorded to Finzi and Beauchamp. No military man's preface of praise introduces *A Diary without Dates*. Indeed, it resulted in her dismissal from the hospital where she nursed. She was said to have breached military discipline.[81] *The Bookman*'s review of the memoir is, therefore, a curious one: 'For all its unflinching realism and its traffic with sorrow, the book has

[80] Enid Bagnold, *A Diary without Dates* (London, 1918), frontispiece.

[81] Ouditt, *Fighting Forces, Writing Women*, 29; Tylee, *The Great War and Women's Consciousness*, 190; Anne Sebba, *Enid Bagnold: A Biography* (London, 1986), 62; Nigel Nicolson, 'Bagnold, Enid Algerine [*married name* Enid Algerine Jones, Lady Jones] (1889–1981)', *Oxford Dictionary of National Biography* (Oxford University Press, 2004).

charm—the charm of a genial and gracious personality' (*The Bookman*, March 1918).

The *Diary* comes the closest of all the memoirs considered here to demonstrating the enormous dislocation faced by women as a result of the Great War. Their roles in wartime, although for the most part traditionally feminine—encouraging men to fight, keeping the home fires burning, nursing the sick and wounded—were also profoundly indecorous in what active service exposed them to. The shock of their situations is reflected in the juxtaposition of the language they employed to tell their tales. In most cases, they relied on the florid prose of the nineteenth century, ornate passages loaded with adjectives, literary references, and obsolete expressions,[82] but the conflict necessitated the use of a new language, one specific to the War. This new language incorporated the graphic nomenclature of wounds, the terminology of trench warfare, and the slang of soldiers—words to which they had become accustomed and which formed their everyday wartime vocabulary. These inevitably sit uneasily with the archaic and sometimes precious prose that most memoirists employed, but together they created an amalgam of language. The jarring sensation this creates mimics the emotional or psychic dislocation between what these women had been taught to believe about 'glorious' conflict and what they had actually witnessed, between what they understood to be 'literary' language and the words now accessible to them to depict *their* war on paper.

The memoirs of individual women highlighted here show the ways in which this new technological and all-encompassing conflict intruded upon a literate, but largely conservative and traditional public consciousness. Enid Bagnold's memoir, in its 'quiet language'[83] and refusal to impose patriotic rhetoric on horror and sadness, bridges the divide between the literature of the War years and that of its aftermath.

Late twentieth-century historical works such as Lyn Macdonald's *The Roses of No Man's Land* perpetuate the elegiac memory of the active service woman:

> If the ghost that haunts the towns of Ypres and Arras and Albert is the statutory British Tommy, slogging with rifle and pack through its ruined streets to his well-documented destiny 'up the line', then the ghost of

[82] Sutherland, *On English Prose*, 101.

[83] Tylee, *The Great War and Women's Consciousness*, 190.

Boulogne and Étaples and Rouen ought to be a girl. She's called Elsie or Gladys or Dorothy, her ankles are swollen, her feet are aching, her hands reddened and rough. She has little money, no vote, and has almost forgotten what it feels like to be really warm. She sleeps in a tent. Unless she has told a diplomatic lie about her age, she is twenty-three. She is the daughter of a clergyman, a lawyer or a prosperous businessman, and has been privately educated and groomed to be a 'lady'. She wears the unbecoming outdoor uniform of a V.A.D. or an army nurse. She is on active service, and as much a part of the war as Tommy Atkins.[84]

Macdonald's syntax, rhythm, and vocabulary contribute to a romantic image that is not overshadowed by her attempt to depict a realistic, gritty representation of the girl on active service with her swollen ankles, aching feet, and rough hands. Indeed, these unpleasant side effects become part of the cherished memory. Veterans of the Great War could be equally elegiac in retrospect: 'I don't remember anybody or any section being less than their best, decent selves in that first war. . . . Everybody just went hell-for-leather.'[85] Julian Allan's recollection at 101 years of age accords with a consistent theme of the popular writing of 1914–18. Not every veteran would have agreed with her nor would every historian put the same gloss as Macdonald on women's active service. Peace activists, too, surely would find it difficult to tolerate the more jingoistic elements of both the memoirs and the romance novels that have been discussed here. Their literary counterparts who produced the language and narrative of protest in works of fiction and poetry (which other studies of the period have admirably documented and critiqued) were similarly disquieted, even outraged. However, this book has tried to demonstrate how another kind of literature of war was being fashioned, disseminated, and taken up by an eager readership. Perhaps when you wanted to forget, if only for a little while, the horrors and complex moral implications of war, you didn't turn to *Le Feu*.

The texts I have considered offer individual—and, in most cases, now-forgotten—women's responses to the Great War, and illustrate the multifarious ways in which this conflict was interpreted and

[84] Macdonald, *The Roses of No Man's Land*, 11.

[85] Julian Allan, personal interview, 26 May 1994, Rayner's Nursing Home, Chesham, Buckinghamshire. Julian Phelps Allan (1892–1996), sculptor, was a captain in the Women's Auxiliary Corps and in charge of a camp of 200 people near Dieppe during the Great War. Called up for service in the Second World War, she was promoted to the rank of colonel, and was the first President of the ATS War Office Selection Board.

represented. Although the rendering of each set of experiences is unique, certain common themes recur: the extolling of sacrifice, the acceptance of grief, the impulse to memorialize. The problem of representing the reality of war is never resolved,[86] for the writers return in most cases to the socialized notions of heroism and the nobility of death on the battlefield, in response to the more brutal aspects of mechanized warfare. Literary narrative can produce an ordering of discordant experience and throughout the novels and memoirs there is a need to idealize, to present exemplars of behaviour and right-thinking that will sustain both sexes in the face of overwhelming loss and dislocation. War art, as Stuart Sillars has argued, can be 'psychologically and ideologically supportive', as it provides 'some immediate guidance and reassurance in the first shock of tumultuous news' and is a 'cathartic release for the artist'.[87] As a means of coming to terms with grief, loss, and cultural upheaval, the practice of writing was as important to the professional novelists as it was to the memoirists.

As commercial products, it may not seem that such books of 'light entertainment' were written to assuage a sense of loss or 'survivor's guilt', but most romantic novelists would have experienced the loss of someone they loved in the course of those four years. Berta Ruck, for instance, dedicated *Khaki and Kisses* to the memory of her brother, Laurence Ruck, who was killed, aged 26, at Neuve Chapelle in March 1915. At the very least, they were aware of other people's losses for, as Elizabeth Marsland points out,

> the gap between combatant and civilian attitudes was narrower than many protest poems pretend, or than the after-the-event promoters of the 'two nations' concept maintain.... While one cannot doubt that the soldiers' experience at the Front was far beyond the comprehension of most people who had not seen action, civilians were by no means uninformed about the reality of the war.... News reports certainly veiled the facts, but casualty lists gave an indication of the massive scale of the destruction and the large numbers of the severely wounded and handicapped men returning from the Front bore witness to the devastating effects of modern weapons.[88]

[86] Critics continually grapple with this problem. Evelyn Cobley, in *Representing War: Form and Ideology in First World War Narratives* (1993), argues that writers produce rather than reproduce their war experience, and in the preface to *Facing Armageddon* (1996), Hugh Cecil and Peter Liddle question the extent to which war can ever really be described.

[87] Stuart Sillars, *Art and Survival in First World War Britain* (London, 1987), 5.

[88] Elizabeth A. Marsland, *The Nation's Cause: French, English, and German Poetry of the First World War* (London and New York, 1991), 159.

As Chapter 3 illustrated, novelists took great pains to cast war casualties in the most heroic light and even though many soldiers no doubt returned from the trenches decrying the 'glorious' gloss on horrific wounds as bunk, romance novels still sold, still responded to a public demand for the reassurance they offered. Sales of *Richard Chatterton, V.C.*, for instance, actually *increased* post-1916. The ideology propounded in the popular writing of the Great War, the seemingly throw-away sentiments used to play down suffering and that made such suffering part of a heroic endeavour that ignored the larger implications, are without doubt disturbing, even horrific. Berta Ruck's admonition that 'You' could be 'twice as much of man, now that you'll have to get on with one leg, as you were when you were dancing and fooling about on two!' has engendered much laughter when I have quoted it at conferences and seminars. Yet we might wonder whether such an admonition might *also* have raised an eyebrow or two of the readers of 1915. We must see as well that the intent behind that statement was to convince the maimed soldier, and certainly his wife or sweetheart, the loss was worth *something*, that it was not a worthless sacrifice. In time of war and with a lifetime of disability ahead, such a message cannot be dismissed out of hand.

The high-flown rhetoric of the memoirs must also be seen in this light. Santanu Das is right to argue that post-war memoirs are more able to delve into the psyche than those produced in wartime.[89] Women like Vera Brittain and Mary Borden were tapping into the cultural climate of disillusion about the War in that period of the second flowering of war literature in the late 1920s and early 1930s. Their own emotional distance from the intimate experience of nursing also contributed to the tone and message of their consciously literary texts. However, both wartime and post-war memoirs served the same *essential* function for their authors, that of ordering the experience of unimaginable suffering and of the feelings of helplessness to mitigate that suffering. Each had a political function as well. As this book has tried to demonstrate, many memoirs and novels of 1914–18, for all the chinks in the armour we might perceive, attested to the continuing righteousness of the cause and asserted patriotic values. It was left to their post-Armistice counterparts to record and render into literary form the

[89] Das, *The Sense of Touch*, 171.

disillusion experienced by so many veterans, male and female, in the interwar period.

To ignore or dismiss the less elite literature of the Great War is not only to obscure part of women's experience, but to lose continuity with the past. It is easy to condemn generals as 'Donkeys', to agree with and extol Owen and Sassoon, to laugh knowingly at the satire of *Blackadder Goes Forth*. It is more difficult, but no less important, to interrogate the ideology and language of writers who recorded the Great War in a different way and justified the sacrifices made in its name. Yet the words of Julian Allan ring true: 'the more you have read of the literature of that time, the more you will know of the Britain of World War I.'

Appendix 1

Items on a Boer War Theme in *The Girl's Own Paper*, *The Girl's Realm*, and *The Lady's Realm*, 1899–1902

The number of items on a Boer War theme, including fiction, non-fiction, and advertisements, appearing in *The Girl's Own Paper*, *The Girl's Realm*, and *The Lady's Realm* between 1899 and 1902 are as follows:

The Girl's Own Paper included one article per month on a Boer War theme from December 1899 to 1902 out of approximately sixteen to twenty regular items per monthly issue.

The Girl's Realm contained approximately twenty-five regular items per issue:

Month/Year	*No. of items on a Boer War theme*
December 1899	2
January 1900	4
February 1900	6
March 1900	6
April 1900	2
May 1900	4
June 1900	5
July 1900	5
August 1900	2
September 1900	1
Oct 1900–Sept 1901	missing from Bodleian
November 1901	—
December 1901	1

January 1902	—
February 1902	1
March 1902 and April 1902	—
May 1902	1
June 1902	1

The Lady's Realm featured approximately twenty-five regular items per issue:

Month/Year	*No. of items on a Boer War theme*
September 1899	1
January 1900	8
February 1900	8
March 1900	8
April 1900	6
May 1900	2
June 1900	6
July 1900	1
August 1900	2
September 1900	1
Oct 1900–Nov 1900	—
December 1900	1
January–April 1901	—
May 1901	1
June 1901	1
July 1901	1

Appendix 2

Schedule of Wellington House Literature

The following are publishers and the number of pamphlets or books they produced for the government agency, 1914–18:

Publisher	*No. of pamphlets/books*
Hodder & Stoughton	134
T. Fisher Unwin	80
Darling & Son	48
Sir Joseph Causton & Sons	22
Nelson	18
Macmillan	18
Eyre & Spottiswode	16
Burrap, Mathieson & Sprague	14
Jas. Truscott & Sons, Ltd.	14
George Allen & Unwin	13
Oxford University Press (including The Clarendon Press & Humphrey Milford)	13
Constable & Co.	12
Longmans, Green & Co.	10
Heinemann	9
W. Speaight & Sons	7
Cassell	6
Chapman & Hall	6
Chatto & Windus	6
Methuen	6
John Murray	6
Putnam	6
Cambridge University Press	2

J. M. Dent	2
John Lane	2
George Harrap	1
Hutchinson	1

Appendix 3

Biographies of Main Authors

Ruby Mildred Ayres (1881–1955) was the daughter of Charles Pryor Ayres (1850–1914), an architect, and his wife Alice Whitford, née Griggs (1855–1903). Ruby Ayres wrote fairy stories as a child, entertained her schoolmates with romantic tales, and won a short story competition sponsored by the *Boy's Own Paper.* At 25 she began writing other types of fiction, partly, she said, to pass the time while her husband Reginald William Pocock (1880–1948), an insurance broker, whom she had married in 1909, was at work. They had no children. By the time she published *Richard Chatterton, V.C.*, her first novel, in 1915, she had written stories for almost every newspaper and periodical in the country. She later did work for the film industries in London and America (C. M. P. Taylor, 'Ayres, Ruby Mildred (1881–1955)', *Oxford Dictionary of National Biography*, Oxford University Press, 2004; *Who Was Who*, vol. v). Her *Times* obituary noted that 'of her day and age, she became synonymous with romantic fiction' (*The Times*, 15 November 1955).

Enid Algerine Bagnold (1889–1981) was the elder child and only daughter of Arthur Henry Bagnold (1854–1943), a military engineer, and his wife Ethel, née Alger (1866–1931). She spent her childhood in Jamaica and after attending Prior's Field school, Godalming, Surrey, she took a flat in Chelsea, studied under Walter Sickert, and became friends with members of the bohemian artistic community, including Henri Gaudier-Brzeska. She worked for the magazine *Hearth and Home* before the Great War. Although *A Diary without Dates* resulted in her being sacked from the London hospital where she worked as a VAD, the public's reaction was enthusiastic. She married Sir (George) Roderick Jones (1877–1962) in 1920 and published her first novel, *The Happy Foreigner*, in the same year. Her best-known work, *National Velvet*, was published in 1935 and the subsequent 1941 film featured Elizabeth Taylor in her first starring role.

The Squire (1938) is considered by many to be her best novel, but she also published plays, including *Lottie Dundass* (1941) and *The Chalk Garden* (1955). She published her autobiography in 1969. Appointed CBE in 1976, she continued to write and publish into the 1980s (Nigel Nicolson, 'Bagnold, Enid Algerine [*married name* Enid Algerine Jones, Lady Jones] (1889–1981)', *Oxford Dictionary of National Biography*, Oxford University Press, 2004; Anne Sebba, *Enid Bagnold: A Biography* (1986)).

Florence Louisa Barclay (1862–1920) was perhaps most well known for her best-selling novel *The Rosary* (1909). Her other wartime novels are *In Hoc Vince* (1915) and *The White Ladies of Worcester* (1917). She was married to the Revd Charles W. Barclay and had two sons and six daughters. Barclay stressed that she wrote for those who asked 'merely to be pleased, rested, interested, amused, inspired to a more living faith in the beauty of human affection and the goodness of God' (Cadogan, *And Then Their Hearts Stood Still,* 57). She vowed 'never to write a line which could introduce the taint of sin or the shadow of shame into any home'.

Olive Annie Dent (1884/5–1930) was born at Kelloe, Co. Durham, the daughter of Abraham Dent, a joiner, and his wife Mary Annie, née Richardson. After the War she became a journalist in London. Her *Times* obituary characterized *A V.A.D. in France* as 'a naively enthusiastic and emotional record, which nevertheless presents a vivid picture of the day-to-day lives of the nurses' (*The Times*, 25 March 1930). She never married (birth certificate; probate record).

Kate John Finzi was born on 28 February 1890 at 77 St Helens Gardens, Kensington, the eldest child and only daughter of John Abraham Finzi, a ship broker and his wife Eliza ('Lizzie') Emma, née Leverson. Her younger brother was the composer Gerald Finzi. Kate Finzi began her voluntary service on 7 August 1914 with the 56/London (Marylebone) detachment of the Red Cross. Her personnel record states that she went to Ostend to assist Belgian refugees in 1914 and then worked with the YMCA in Boulogne in 1915. She also volunteered as a special military probationer for service in Malta. Two of her brothers died on active service. On 20 May 1917 at Richmond Registry Office she married Alexander Laidlaw Gilmour (b. 1895/96), a 2nd Lieutenant with the 7th Northamptonshire Fusiliers. Details of her later life are unknown (British Red Cross Museum and Archives; birth certificate; marriage certificate).

Janet Russell Laing (1870–1953), née Carstairs, was born at Balwearie, Perthshire. She was married to Henry William Laing, MD (1854–1931), who, having practised medicine in Kirkcaldy for twenty-seven years, joined the RAMC on the outbreak of war in 1914 and served as medical officer with the 2/7th Battalion of the Black Watch regiment. Janet Laing lived at The South Gate, Wardlaw Gardens, St Andrews from 1914 to *c.*1935. Her husband's obituary noted that she did 'much for musical culture' in the town (*St Andrews Citizen*, 28 November 1921). She published eight novels between 1903 and 1929, three with J. M. Dent and five with Hodder & Stoughton. In addition to *Before the Wind*, titles included *The Borderlanders* (1904), *The Man with the Lamp* (1919), and *The Villa Jane* (1929). She also published two one-act comedies, co-written with Paterson Whyte: *It's a Tryin' Time* (1932) and *Easy-Oasy* (1936). She died at Fortingall, Perthshire, and was buried with her husband in the Western Cemetery, St Andrews (J. M. Dent Archive, University of North Carolina, Chapel Hill Library; Manuscripts Department, University of St Andrews Library).

Marie Adelaide Elizabeth Renée Julia Belloc Lowndes (1868–1947) was the daughter of Louis Marie Belloc (1830–1872), a French barrister and his wife Elizabeth (Bessie) Rayner Parkes (1829–1925), the prominent British feminist. Marie Belloc's younger brother was the writer Hilaire Belloc. She grew up in Paris and in London, and her formal education was limited to two years at a convent school in Sussex, where she went to live with her mother after the death of her father in 1872. Belloc Lowdnes wrote from the age of 16 onwards and began her professional career with W. T. Stead, editor of the *Pall Mall Gazette*. She not only contributed to the family income but also subsidized her brother's education. She married Frederick Sawney Archibald Lowndes (1867–1940), a journalist for *The Times*, and they had one son and two daughters. Her early work was royal biography and historical romance, but her most famous novel is *The Lodger* (1913), based on the Jack the Ripper case. She wrote over 60 books including 40 novels, several plays, a volume of short stories, and series of autobiographical works. An active supporter of the women's suffrage movement, she also encouraged young writers, including Graham Greene and Hugh Walpole (David Doughan, 'Lowndes, Marie Adelaide Elizabeth Renée Julia Belloc (1868–1947)', *Oxford Dictionary of National Biography*, Oxford University Press, 2004; *Continuum*

Encyclopedia of British Literarture). Berta Ruck observed that 'Just as some people collect stamps, Marie Belloc Lowndes collected writers, and how she loved to entertain them!' (Berta Ruck, *A Smile for the Past* (1959), 100).

Bessie Marchant (1862–1941) was the writer 'who most successfully adapted the adventure tale to put contemporary girls in the central heroic role. [She was] often described as "the girls' Henty." Author of well over a hundred books published between 1894 and 1939, she almost always set her tales in the wilds of empire or in exciting foreign places where laws of modesty and decorum did not obtain—though even she generally managed some sort of refeminization at the story's end' (Sally Mitchell, *The New Girl: Girl's Culture in England, 1880–1915* (New York, 1995), 116). She was married to the Revd Jabez Ambrose Comfort in 1889 and had one daughter. *Molly Angel's Adventures: A Story of Belgium under German Occupation* (1915) was another of Marchant's wartime tales (*Who Was Who*, vol. iv).

Mary Eliza L. (known as Joan) Martin-Nicholson (b. 1876) sent her manuscript of *My Experiences on Three Fronts* to Stanley Unwin in April 1916, after he asked to read it sometime in late 1915/early 1916. Having been 'called up on account of the shortage of qualified nurses', she was at this time sister in charge 'of a simply huge surgical ward for the "Big Push" men straight from the front in the Kings Lancashire Military Hospital.' She wrote later to Unwin: 'I am driven to death up here but am having a splendid time'. She doubted whether her patients in Blackpool would be able to afford the 4/6 price of her memoir, 'however much they like the sister'. Generally pleased by the response of the press to her published memoir, Martin-Nicholson was nevertheless upset by a review in a Belfast paper that complained the memoir 'bangs the high melodramatic note'. The reviewer doubted whether 'her petty experiences' engendered much interest since the 'book itself . . . convey[s] to the reader so little'. Despite this, in a letter of 10 March 1917 she expresses pleasure at the decent sales ('428 to date') and the 'jolly good notices from the papers'. Little else is known of her life (Records of George Allen & Unwin, Ltd., MS3282, University of Reading Library).

Amy Roberta Ruck (1878–1978) was born in India, the daughter of Arthur Ashley Ruck, lieutenant, Isle of Man Regiment (8th Foot) and his wife Elizabeth Eleanor, née D'Arcy. From the age of two she was raised in Wales. She went to St Winifred's School in Bangor, and worked briefly as an *au pair* in Germany before studying at the Lambeth School of Art with the intention of becoming a book illustrator. She then studied art at the Slade and at Calorossi's in Paris before turning her hand to writing in about 1912, when her serial for *Home Chat,* 'His Official Fiancée', was admired by a publisher and turned into a book. This launched her career. In her long lifetime, she published over 150 books, turning out between one and three per year, including several volumes of autobiography. She regarded her work as 'the amusement business', without pretensions to literary greatness. *The Times* noted how she was 'a novelist of popular stamp... taking herself seriously enough as a novelist though without entertaining extravagant notions regarding the merit of her work as literature' (*The Times,* 12 August 1978). She was married to the author Oliver Onions (1873–1961), who took the name George Oliver, and had two sons. Joanne Shattock notes how 'Virginia Woolf probably inadvertently put her name (as Bert*h*a Ruck) on a tombstone in *Jacob's Room* (1922), causing an exchange of solicitors' letters and their eventual congenial meeting' (Joanne Shattock, *The Oxford Guide to British Women Writers* (Oxford and New York, 1993), 376). She died just 10 days after her 100th birthday at her home in Aberdovey, Wales (Brian Alderson, 'Ruck, Amy Roberta (1878–1978)', rev. Sayoni Basu, *Oxford Dictionary of National Biography*, Oxford University Press, 2004).

Violetta Thurstan (1879–1978) was born Anna Violet on 4 February 1879 in Hastings, Sussex, the only daughter of Edward Paget Thurstan. She was educated in France and Germany and at St Andrews University before joining the British Red Cross Society (No. 46, Westminster Detachment) in 1913. She was called up for service on 4 August 1914. Thurstan was awarded the Russian Order of St George Medal 'for courage and devotion', the Belgian Order of Queen Elizabeth, the Military Medal, the Bronze Star, and four Service Chevrons. She returned to Russia in 1915 to help organize hospital units for refugees. Once back in England, she returned to her pre-war post at the National Union of Trained Nurses. She soon became Matron at the Hôpital de l'Océan at La Panne Belgium, five miles from the Front until July 1917, when she was transferred to a British Dressing Station at Coxyde. On 27 August the Dressing Station was shelled by the Germans and she was wounded by falling timber when the hut in which she was working was hit. Nevertheless, 'she continued to work and assist in the evacuation of the helpless wounded, a most stimulating example to all' and for which she was awarded the Military Medal (*An Historical Roll*, 17; and Barbara McLaren, *Women of the War*, 88–9). After a brief sick-leave in England she went to Macedonia in charge of a field ambulance and served there until August 1918. She saw out the War serving with the Royal Air Force in England. Her two brothers served in the Royal Navy and the Royal Air Force. Thurstan published two other books during the War, *The People Who Run: The Tragedy of Refugees in Russia* (1916) and *A Text Book of War Nursing* (1917). She served in the WRNS during the Second World War and, a devout Catholic, was active in relief work in its aftermath. 'Violetta could be overbearing, and it is easy to understand how. Her range of experiences by 1947 made her formidable. Most colleagues considered her to be generous, firm but unsympathetic to those she felt "did not meet the mark"' (Muriel Somerfield and Ann Bellingham, *Violetta Thurston: A Celebration*, Jamieson Library (1993), 52). Violetta Thurstan became an expert in weaving and dyes for weaving. *The Use of Vegetable Dyes* has gone through numerous editions since its first publication in 1930, the most recent version appearing in 1988. She also wrote *A Short History of Decorative Textiles and Tapestries* (1934), *Weaving Patterns of Today and Yesterday* (1934), and *Weaving without Tears* (1956) and was President of the Cornwall Guild of Weavers, Spinners and Dyers. She published two novels, *Stormy Petrel* (1964) and *The Foolish Virgin* (1966). She returned to her Great War memories with *The Hounds of War Unleashed* (1978). Her military medals, nine in all, were buried with her at Penryn, Cornwall.

Catharine Marguerite Beauchamp [Pat] Washington, née Waddell (1892–1972), was born near Wetheral, Cumberland, the daughter of Cranston Waddell and Catherine Beatrice Beauchamp Thompson. She was awarded the *Croix de Guerre* with Silver Star and the Belgian *ordre de la reine Elizabeth*. When the units serving in France were disbanded and the Corps relocated to London, Beauchamp, 'quite undismayed by having a tin leg', became its Secretary in 1920. She was instrumental in the post-war FANY organization, including its annual camps. Her marriage to Capt. P. Washington in 1922 was noticed in *The Times*, which described her memoir as 'a cheery, vivid, enthusiastic account of her two and a half years' work in France'. In almost humorous understatement it recorded how during her war work with the FANY 'she had the misfortune to lose a leg as the result of a motor smash' (*The Times*, 28 July 1922). In the spring of 1940 Pat Beauchamp oversaw a mobile canteen to supply Polish troops based at Coëtquidan in Brittany. When France fell, she and her colleagues escaped to England, and when Polish troops were accommodated in tented camps on various estates in south-west Scotland, she and other members of the FANY continued their canteen work. She documented this service in her 1942 book *Eagles in Exile*. (Lynette Beardwood, 'Washington, Catharine Marguerite Beauchamp (1892–1972)', *Oxford Dictionary of National Biography*, Oxford University Press, 2004.) 'One of the Corps' most vigorous and vocal members, since before the First World War died at Christmas 1972' (Hugh Popham, *F.A.N.Y.: The Story of the Women's Transport Service 1907–1984* (London, 1984), 48, 75, 133). Popham's book also reproduces a photograph of Beauchamp with Polish soldiers at a Scottish camp. She is one of two women amongst a large group of men, wearing 'her cap at the Beatty angle'.

Bibliography

PRIMARY SOURCES

Periodicals

The Athenaeum
The Bookman
Boy's Own Paper, 1879–1967
The British Girl's Annual, compiled by editors of *The Girl's Realm*, 1910–28
The Daily Graphic Special War Cartoons, nos. 1, 3, 5 (1914)
The Empire Annual for Girls, 1909–30
The Englishwoman, vol. xxxv, no. 103, July 1917
The Gem Library, 1907–29
The Girls' Empire, 1902–4
The Girls' Friend, 1907–29
The Girls' Home, 1910–1915
The Girl's Own Paper, 1880–1950
The Girl's Realm, 1898–1915
The Girls' Reader, 1908–1915
Home Chat, 1895–1959
The Lady's Periodical, 1901–192
The Lady's Realm, 1896–1916
Nelson's Girls' Annual, 1914
The New Statesman
Our Girls, 1915–1919
Our Outlook, 1908–1920
The Outlook
The Times Literary Supplement
The War Illustrated: A Picture-Record of Events by Land, Sea and Air, 1914–1919
Women's Volunteer Reserve Magazine

Fiction

Anon., *Aunt Sara and the War: A Tale of Transformations* (London: Burns & Oates, 1915).

Askew, Claude and Alice, *Nurse* (London: Hodder & Stoughton, 1916).

Ayres, Ruby M., *Richard Chatterton, V.C.* (London: Hodder & Stoughton, 1915).
Barbusse, Henri, *Under* Fire (London: J. M. Dent & Sons, 1916).
Barclay, Florence L., *My Heart's Right There* (London and New York: G. P. Putnam & Sons, 1914).
Black, Dorothy, *Her Lonely Soldier* (London: Hodder & Stoughton, 1916).
Blundell, Mary Evans, *Penton's Captain* (London: Chapman & Hall, 1916).
Bottome, Phyllis, *A Servant of Reality* (London: Hodder & Stoughton, 1919).
Brazil, Angela, *The Fortunes of Philippa* (London: Blackie & Sons, 1907).
——, *The Nicest Girl in the School* (London: Blackie & Sons, 1910).
Brereton, Captain, *With French at the Front* (London, Glasgow, and Bombay: Blackie & Sons, 1915).
Chesney, George, *The Battle of Dorking: Reminiscences of a Volunteer* [1871] (Oxford and New York: Oxford University Press, 1997).
Childers, Erskine, *The Riddle of the Sands* (London: Nelson, 1910).
Clarke, Isabel, *The Potter's House* (London: Hutchinson, 1916).
Conyers, Dorothea, *The Scratch Pack* (London: Hutchinson, 1916).
'Dane, Clemence' (Winifred Ashton), *First the Blade* (London: Heinemann, 1918).
——, *Regiment of Women* (London: Heinemann, 1917).
Doyle, Arthur Conan, *Danger! and Other Stories* (London: John Murray, 1918).
Gilson, Capt. Charles, *A Motor Scout in Flanders* (London, Glasgow, and Bombay: Blackie & Sons, 1915).
Graves, Clothilde Ines Mary, *That Which Hath Wings* (London: Heinemann, 1918).
Harradan, Beatrice, *Where Your Treasure Is* (London: Hutchinson, 1918).
Heilgers, Louise, *Somewhere in France: Stories of the Great War* (London: Dryden, 1915).
Hocking, Joseph, *All for a Scrap of Paper: A Romance of the Present War* (London: Hodder & Stoughton, 1915).
——, *Dearer Than Life: A Romance of the Great War* (London: Hodder & Stoughton, 1915).
Keating, Joseph, *Tipperary Tommy: A Novel of the Great War* (London: Hodder & Stoughton, 1915).
Laing, Janet, *Before the Wind* (London and Toronto: J. M. Dent, 1918).
——, *The Man with the Lamp* (London and Toronto: J. M. Dent, 1919).
Leighton, Marie Connor, *The Baked Bread* (London: Hodder & Stoughton, 1917).
——, *Boy of My Heart* (London: Hodder & Stoughton, 1916).
Le Queux, William, *Annette of the Argonne: A Story of the French Front* (London: Hurst & Blackett, 1916).
——, *The Invasion of 1910: With a Full Account of the Siege of London* (London: Eveleigh Nash, 1906).

Lowndes, Marie Adelaide Belloc, '*Good Old Anna*' (London: Hutchinson, 1915).

——, *Out of the War?* (London: Chapman & Hall, 1918).

Macaulay, Rose, *Non-Combatants and Others* (London: Hodder & Stoughton, 1916).

——, *What Not* (London: Constable, 1919).

Marchant, Bessie, *A Girl Munition Worker* (London, Glasgow, and Bombay: Blackie & Son, 1917).

Newbolt, Henry, *Tales of the Great War* (London: Longmans Green & Co., 1917).

Orchard, Evelyn, *The Greater Glory* (London: Hodder & Stoughton, 1916).

Paradise, Dorothy Chester, *If There Must Be Battles* (London: George Allen & Unwin, 1916).

Petter, Evelyn Branscombe, *Miss Velanty's Disclosure* (London: Chapman & Hall, 1916).

Pettman, Grace, *Ordered to the Front* (London: John Bateman, 1915).

Radziwill, Princess Catherine, *Because It Was Written* (London: Cassell, 1916).

Ruck, Berta, *The Bridge of Kisses* (London: Hodder & Stoughton, 1917).

——, *The Girls at His Billet* (London: Hutchinson, 1916).

——, *Khaki & Kisses* (London: Hutchinson, 1915).

——, *The Lad with Wings* (London: Hutchinson, 1915).

Saki (Hector Munro), *When William Came* (1914; Oxford and New York: Oxford University Press, 1997).

Scott, Edith H., *Mistress Reality* (London: George Allen & Unwin, 1916).

Swan, Annie S., *The Woman's Part* (London: Hodder & Stoughton, 1916).

The Times Red Cross Story Book, by famous novelists serving in His Majesty's forces (London: Hodder & Stoughton, 1915).

Ward, Mrs Humphry, '*Missing*' (London, Glasgow, Melbourne, and Auckland: W. Collins Sons & Co. 1917).

Wells, H. G., *Ann Veronica* (London: J. M. Dent, 1909).

Memoirs

Aldrich, Mildred, *A Hilltop on the Marne* (New York: Grosset & Dunlap, 1915).

——, *On the Edge of the War Zone* (London: Constable, 1917).

An English Governess, *What I Found Out in the House of a German Prince* (London: Chapman & Hall, 1915).

Anon., *Diary of a Nursing Sister on the Western Front* (Edinburgh: Blackwood, 1915).

Anon. (Grace MacDougall), *Nursing Adventures: A F.A.N.Y. in France* (London: Heinemann, 1919).

Ashton, Harold, *First From the Front* (London: Arthur Pearson, 1914).

Bagnold, Enid, *A Diary without Dates* (London: Heinemann, 1918).

Beauchamp, Pat, *Fanny Goes to War* (London: John Murray, 1919).

Blunden, Edmund, *De Bello Germanico: A Fragment of Trench History* (Hawstead: G. A. Blunden, 1930).

——, *Undertones of War* (London: R. Cobden-Sanderson, 1928).

Bowser, Thekla, *The Story of British V.A.D. Work in the Great War* (London: Andrew Melrose, 1917).

Brittain, Vera, *Testament of Youth* (London: Victor Gollancz, 1933).

Buswell, Leslie, *Ambulance No. 10: Personal Letters from the Front* (London and Boston: Houghton Mifflin, 1917).

Cannan, May Wedderburn, *Grey Ghosts and Voices* (Kineton: Roundwood Press, 1976).

Carr, Kent, *Women Who Dared: Heroines of the Great War* (London: S. W. Partridge & Co., 1920).

C.E.L., *My Man: Letters from a Wife to a Husband 'Somewhere in France'* (New York: George H. Doran, 1916).

Cosens, Monica, *Lloyd George's Munition Girls* (London: Hutchinson, 1916).

Croft, Brig.-Gen. H. Page, *Twenty-Two Months Under Fire* (London: John Murray, 1917).

Dent, Olive, *A V.A.D. in France* (London: Grant Richards, 1917).

Dinning, Hector, *By-Ways on Active Service: Notes from an Australian Journal* (London: Constable, 1918).

Dolbey, Robert Valentine, *A Regimental Surgeon in War and Prison* (London: John Murray, 1917).

Doyle, Arthur Conan, *Memories and Adventures* (Boston: Little, Brown, & Co., 1924).

Finzi, Kate, *Eighteen Months in the War Zone* (London: Cassell & Co., 1916).

Fisher, Phil J., *Khaki Vignettes: Six Months Chaplain to the Troops in England and Fifteen Months in France* (London: Joseph Johnson, 1917).

Gardiner, A. G., *The War Lords* (London and Toronto: J. M. Dent & Sons, 1915).

Gervis, Henry, *Arms and the Doctor: Being the Military Experiences of a Middle-Aged Medical Man* (London: Daniel, 1920).

Gillam, John G., *Gallipoli Diary* (London: George Allen & Unwin, 1918).

Graves, Robert, *Goodbye to All That* (New York, Anchor Books/Doubleday, 1985).

Hall, Norman James, *Kitchener's Mob* (Boston and New York: Houghton Mifflin, 1916).

Houghton, Mary, *In the Enemy's Country: Being the Diary of a Little Tour in Germany and Elsewhere during the Early Days of the War* (London: Chatto & Windus, 1915).

Hurst, Gerald B., *With the Manchesters in the East* (Manchester: Manchester University Press, 1917).

Lauder, Harry, *A Minstrel in France* (London: Andrew Melrose, 1918).

Liveing, Edward, *Attack: An Infantry Subaltern's Impressions of July 1st 1916* (London: Heinemann, 1918).

Luard, K. E., *Unknown Warriors: Extracts from the Letters of K. E. Luard, R. R. C. Nursing Sister in France 1914–1918* (London: Chatto & Windus, 1930).

MacGill, Patrick, *The Great Push: An Episode of the Great War* (London: Herbert Jenkins, 1917).

MacNaughton, Sarah, *A Woman's Diary of the War* (London: Nelson, 1915).

Martin-Nicholson, Sister, *My Experiences on Three Fronts* (London: George Allen & Unwin, 1916).

Moore, F. Frankfort, *The Romance of a Red Cross Hospital* (London: Hutchinson, & Co., 1915).

Sandes, Flora, *An English Woman Sergeant in the Serbian Army* (London: Hodder & Stoughton, 1916).

Sassoon, Siegfried, *Memoirs of a Fox-Hunting Man* (London: Faber & Gwyer, 1928).

——, *Memoirs of an Infantry* Officer (London: Faber & Faber, 1930).

——, *Sherston's Progress* (London: Faber & Faber, 1936).

Sellers, Revd W. E., *With Our Fighting Men* (London: The Religious Tract Society,1915).

Sinclair, May, *Journal of Impressions in Belgium* (London: Hutchinson, 1915).

Stobart, Mrs St Clair, *The Flaming Sword in Serbia and Elsewhere* (London: Hodder & Stoughton, 1916).

Street, G. S., *At Home in the War* (London: Heinemann, 1918).

Thurstan, Violetta, *Field Hospital and Flying Column* (London: Putnam,1915).

Non-fiction

Angell, Norman, *The Great Illusion: A Study of the Relation of Military Power to National Advantage* (London: Heinemann, 1912).

Barker, Elsa, *War Letters from the Living Dead Man* (London: William Rider & Son, 1915).

Benett, W., *England's Mission* (Oxford: Oxford University Press, 1914).

von Bernhardi, General Friedrich, *Germany and the Next War* (London: Edward Arnold, 1914).

Billington, Mary Francis, *The Red Cross in War: Woman's Part in the Relief of Suffering* (London: Hodder & Stoughton, 1914).

Caine, Hall, *The Drama of 365 Days: Scenes in the Great War* (London: Heinemann, 1915).

Carter, Huntley (ed.), *Women's Suffrage and Militancy* (London: Frank Palmer, 1911).

Churchill, Lady Randolph, *Small Talks on Big Subjects* (London: Arthur Pearson, 1916).

Corelli, Marie, *'Woman or Suffragette?' A Question of National Choice* (London: Arthur Pearson, 1907).

Cosby, Dudley S. A., *Towards Universal Peace* (Bedford: Bedfordshire Times, 1915).

Doyle, Arthur Conan, *To Arms!* (London: Hodder & Stoughton, 1914).

Erichson, Erich, *Forced to Fight: The Tale of a Schleswig Dane* (London: Heinemann, 1917).

Green, the Revd James, C. M. G., *The Angel of Mons* (Sydney: Australian Christian World Printing and Publishing House, n. d.).

Hill, William Thompson, *The Martyrdom of Nurse Cavell: The Life Story of the Victim of Germany's Most Barbarous Crime* (London: Hutchinson, 1915).

Hobhouse, Emily, *The Brunt of War and Where It Fell* (London: Methuen & Co., 1902).

Hobhouse (Margaret Heywood), Mrs Henry, *'I Appeal Unto Caesar': The Case of the Conscientious Objector* (London: George Allen & Unwin, 1917).

Hollander, Bernard, *Woman: Her Brain, Mental Capacity and Character* (London: The Ethological Society, 1908).

Kellogg, Charlotte, *Women of Belgium: Turning Tragedy to Triumph* (New York and London: Funk & Wagnalls, 1917).

Kipling, Rudyard, *France at War* (London: Macmillan, 1915).

Maclaren, Barbara, *Women of the War* (London: Hodder & Stoughton, 1917).

M.E.S., *An Englishwoman's Home* (London: Sampson, Low, Marston & Co., 1909).

Mr Punch's History of the Great War (London: Cassell & Co., 1919).

Murray, Gilbert, *Can War Ever Be Right?* (Oxford: Oxford University Press, 1914).

——, *Thoughts on the War* (Oxford: Oxford University Press, 1914).

Ogden C.K. and Florence, Mary Sargant, *Militarism vs. Feminism* (London: George Allen & Unwin, 1915).

O'Neill, Elizabeth, *The War, 1914: A History and an Explanation for Boys and Girls* (London: T. C. & E. C. Jack, 1914).

O'Neill, Elizabeth, *The War, 1914–1915: A History and an Explanation for Boys and Girls* (London: T. C. & E. C. Jack, 1915).

Oxenham, John, *Everywoman and War: A Suggestion and its Application* (London: Headley Bros., 1915).

Pollard, Eliza F., *Florence Nightingale: The Wounded Soldier's Friend* (London: S. W. Partridge & Co., 1891).

Prothero, G. W., *Our Duty and Our Interest in the War* (London: John Murray, 1914).

Protheroe, Ernest, *A Noble Woman: The Life Story of Edith Cavell* (London: The Epworth Press/J. Alfred Sharp, 1916).

Reich, Emil, *Germany's Swelled Head* (London: Walsall Press, 1914).

Robinson, Arthur W., *The Response of Woman to Her Call To-Day* (London, New York, Bombay, and Calcutta: Longmans & Co. 1913).

Sanday, W., *The Meaning of the War for Germany and Great Britain: An Attempt at Synthesis* (Oxford: Clarendon Press, 1915).

Scharlieb, Mary, *Womanhood and Race-Regeneration* (London: Cassell & Co., 1912).

The Truth about German Atrocities: Founded on the Report of the Committee on Alleged German Outrages (London: Harrison & Sons, by authority of HM Stationery Office, 1915).

Vivian, E. Charles, and J. E. Hodder-Williams, *The Way of the Red Cross* (London, New York, and Toronto: Hodder & Stoughton for *The Times*, 1915).

Ward, Mrs Humphry, *England's Effort* (London: John Murray, 1916).

——, *Towards the Goal* (London: John Murray, 1917).

Pageants/Plays

Bell, Maud, *What of the Night? And Other Sketches* (London: Arthur Stockwell, 1917).

Creagh-Henry, May, *The Unknown Warrior* (London and New York: Macmillan, 1923).

Davidson, Gladys, *Britannia's Pageant of Peace* (1919).

——, *Britannia's Revue* (1914).

'Discipline', *Women's Volunteer Reserve Magazine*, 1/7 (July 1916), 135–8.

John, Gwen, *The Luck of War* (London and Glasgow: Gowens & Gray, 1922).

Holmes, Alec, 'The Munition Worker: A Play in One Scene', *The Englishwoman*, 33/99 (March 1917).

PAT, *The Hayes Munitionettes: Departmental or Popular Choruses* (Shepherd's Bush: C. A. Murray, 1916).

'A Patriot' (Guy du Maurier), *An Englishman's Home* (London: Edward Arnold, 1909).

Patry, Rose I., *Britain's Defenders or Peggy's Peep into Fairyland, a Fairy Play* (London and New York: Samuel French, 1919).

——, *The Vision of a New World: A Short Peace Pageant* (London and New York: Samuel French, 1919).
Sherriff, R. C., *Journey's End* (London: Victor Gollancz, 1929).

Poetry

Binyon, Laurence, *The Four Years* (London: Elkin Matthews, 1919).
Brittain, Vera, *Verses of a V.A.D.* (London: Erskine MacDonald, 1918).
Cannan, May Wedderburn, *The Splendid Days: Poems* (Oxford: B. H. Blackwell, 1919).
——, *In War Time: Poems* (Oxford: B. H. Blackwell, 1917).
Edwards, Mabel C., and Mary Booth, *The Fiery Cross: An Anthology* (London: Grant Richards, 1915).
Gurney, Ivor, *The Poems of Ivor Gurney*, ed. Leonard Clark (London: Chatto & Windus, 1973).
Owen, Wilfred, *The Poems of Wilfred Owen*, ed. Jon Stallworthy (London: Hogarth Press, 1985).
Paths of Glory: A Collection of Poems Written during the Great War, 1914–1919 (London: George Allen & Unwin, 1919).
Poems of To-Day: An Anthology (London: Sidgwick & Jackson, 1917).
Pope, Jesse, *Jesse Pope's War Poems* (London: Grant Richards, 1915).
Rosenberg, Isaac, *The Poems and Plays of Isaac Rosenberg: A Critical Edition*, ed. Vivien Noakes (Oxford: Oxford University Press, 2004).
Sassoon, Siegfried, *The Counter-Attack, and Other Poems* (London: Heinemann, 1918).

SECONDARY SOURCES

Adie, Kate, *Corsets to Camouflage: Women and War* (London: Hodder & Stoughton, 2003).
Atkins, John, *The British Spy Novel: Styles in Treachery* (London: John Calder, 1984).
Attenborough, John, *A Living Memory: Hodder & Stoughton Publishers 1868–1975* (London: Hodder, 1975).
Attridge, Steve, *Nationalism, Imperialism and Identity in Late Victorian Culture: Civil and Military Worlds* (Basingstoke: Palgrave, 2003).
Auchmuty, Rosemary, *A World of Girls* (London: Woman's Press, 1992).
Baden-Powell, Miss, and Sir Robert Baden-Powell, *How Girls Can Help to Build the Empire: The Handbook for Girl Guides* (London: T. Nelson & Sons, 1912; facsimile edition: London: Girl Guides Association, 1993).
Barfield, Owen, *Poetic Diction* (London: Faber & Gwyer, 1928).

Bell, Susan Groag, and Marilyn Yalom (eds.), *Revealing Lives: Autobiography and Gender* (Albany: State University of New York Press, 1990).

Beauman, Nicola, *A Very Great Profession: The Woman's Novel 1914–39* (London: Virago, 1983).

Beetham, Margaret, *A Magazine of Her Own?: Domesticity and Desire in the Women's Magazine, 1800–1914* (London and New York: Routledge, 1996).

Bergonzi, Bernard, *Heroes' Twilight* (Manchester: Carcanet, 1996 (3rd ed.)).

Bloom, Clive, *Literature and Culture in Modern Britain, 1900–1929* (London: Longmans, 1993).

Blunden, Edmund, Cyril Falls, H. M. Tomlinson, R. Wright (eds.), *A Booklist on the War, 1914–1918* (London: The Reader, 1930).

Bodkin, Maud, *Archetypal Patterns in Poetry* (Oxford: Oxford University Press, 1963).

Booth, Wayne C., *The Rhetoric of Fiction* (Chicago: University of Chicago Press, 1961).

Bourke, Joanna, *Dismembering the Male: Men's Bodies, Britain and the Great War* (London: Reaktion Books, 1996).

Bowra, C. M., *Poetry and Politics 1900–1960* (Cambridge: Cambridge University Press, 1966).

Bracco, Rosa Maria, *Merchants of Hope: British Middlebrow Writers and the First World War, 1919–1939* (Providence R. I., and Oxford: Berghahn, 1993).

Braybon, Gail, *Women Workers in the First World War* (London: Croom Helm, 1981).

Brodzki, Bela, and Celeste Schenck, *Life Lines: Theorizing Women's Autobiography* (Ithaca, N.Y.: Cornell University Press, 1988).

Brooks, Cleanth, and Robert Penn Warren, *Understanding Poetry* (New York: Henry Holt, 1938).

Brown, Heloise, *'The Truest Form of Patriotism': Pacifist Feminism in Britain, 1870–1902* (Manchester: Manchester University Press, 2003).

Buitenhuis, Peter, *The Great War of Words: Literature as Propaganda 1914–18 and After* (London: B. T. Batsford, 1989).

Burdett, Carolyn, *Olive Schreiner and the Progress of Feminism: Evolution, Gender and Empire* (Basingstoke: Palgrave, 2001).

Bush, Julia, *Edwardian Ladies and Imperial Power* (London: Leicester University Press, 2000).

Cadogan, Mary, *And Then Their Hearts Stood Still: An Exuberant Look at Romantic Fiction Past and Present* (London: Macmillan, 1994).

——, *You're a Brick, Angela! A New Look at Girls' Fiction, 1839–1975* (London: Victor Gollancz, 1976).

——, and Patricia Craig, *Women and Children First: The Fiction of Two World Wars* (London: Victor Gollancz, 1978).

Caesar, Adrian, *Taking It Like a Man: Suffering, Sexuality and the War Poets* (Manchester and New York: Manchester University Press, 1993).

Cardinal, Agnès, Dorothy Goldman, and Judith Hathaway (eds.), *Women's Writing on the First World War* (Oxford: Oxford University Press, 1999).

Carey, John, *The Intellectual and the Masses: Pride and Prejudice among the Literary Intelligensia* (London: Faber, 1992).

Carline, Richard, *Pictures in the Post: The Story of the Picture Postcard and Its Place in the History of Popular Art* (Bedford: G. Fraser, 1959).

Carpenter, Humphrey, and Mari Pritchard, *Oxford Companion to Children's Literature* (Oxford: Oxford University Press, 1984).

Cawelti, John G., *Adventure, Mystery, and Romance: Formula Stories as Art and Popular Culture* (Chicago and London: University of Chicago Press, 1976).

Cecil, Hugh, and Peter H. Liddle (eds.), *Facing Armageddon 1914–18: The War Experienced* (London: Leo Cooper, 1996).

Chamberlain, J. Edward, and Sander L. Gilman (eds.), *Degeneration: The Dark Side of Progress* (New York: Columbia University Press, 1985).

Chapple, J. A. V., *Documentary and Imaginative Literature: 1880–1920* (London: Blandford Press, 1970).

Clark, Alan, *The Donkeys* (London: Hutchinson, 1961).

Clarke, I. F., *The Great War with Germany: Fictions and Fantasies of the War-to-Come* (Liverpool: Liverpool University Press, 1997).

——, *The Tale of the Future: From the Beginning to the Present Day, a Check-List* (London: Library Association, 1961).

——, *The Tale of the Great War, 1871–1914: Fictions of Future Warfare and of Battles Still-to-Come* (Liverpool: Liverpool University Press, 1995).

——, *Voices Prophesying War* (London and New York: Oxford University Press, 1966).

Cobley, Evelyn, *Representing War: Form and Ideology in First World War Narratives* (Toronto, Buffalo, and London: University of Toronto Press, 1993).

Coetzee, Frans, and Marilyn Sherin-Coetzee (eds.), *Authority, Identity and the Social History of the Great War* (Providence, R.I., and Oxford: Berghahn Books, 1995).

Cohn, Jan, *Romance and the Erotics of Property: Mass-Market Fiction for Women* (Durham and London: Duke University Press, 1988).

Collins, L. J., *Theatre at War, 1914–18* (London: Macmillan,1998).

Constantine, Stephen, Maurice W. Kirby, and Mary B. Rose (eds.), *The First World War in British History* (London, New York, Sydney, and Auckland: Edward Arnold, 1995).

Cooke, Miriam, and Angela Woollacott, *Gendering War Talk* (Princeton: Princeton University Press, 1993).

Cooper, Helen M., Adrienne Auslander Munich, and Susan Merrill Squier (eds.), *Arms and the Woman: War, Gender, and Literary Representation* (Chapel Hill and London: University of North Carolina Press, 1989).

Das, Santanu, *The Sense of Touch in First World War Literature*, Ph.D. dissertation, University of Cambridge (Cambridge, 2002).

Davin, Anna, 'Imperialism and Motherhood', *History Workshop: A Journal of Social Historians* 5 (Spring, 1978), 9–65.

Dent, J. M., *The Memoirs of J. M. Dent: 1849–1926* (London: J. M. Dent & Sons, 1928).

Dodds, E. R., *Missing Persons: An Autobiography* (Oxford: Clarendon Press, 1977).

Dolden, A. Stuart, *Cannon Fodder: An Infantryman's Life on the Western Front, 1914–18* (Poole: Blandford Press, 1980).

Doyle, Arthur Conan, *The Great Boer* War (London: John Murray, 1900).

Egan, Susanna, *Patterns of Experience in Autobiography* (Chapel Hill and London: University of North Carolina Press, 1984).

Falls, Cyril, *War Books: An Annotated Bibliography of Books about the Great War* (London: P. Davies, 1989).

Feather, John, *A History of British Publishing* (London and New York: Routledge, 1988).

Fleishman, Avron, *Figures of Autobiography: The Language of Self-Writing in Victorian and Modern England* (Los Angeles: University of California Press, 1983).

Flint, Kate, *The Woman Reader* (Oxford: Clarendon Press, 1993).

Fowler, Bridget, *The Alienated Reader: Woman and Popular Romantic Literature in the Twentieth Century* (New York and London: Harvester Wheatsheaf, 1991).

Fox, John, *Forgotten Divisions: The First World War from Both Sides of No Man's Land* (Cheshire: Sigma Press, 1994).

Fraisse, Geneviève, and Michelle Perrot (eds.), *A History of Women in the West, vol. IV: Emerging Feminism from Revolution to World War* (Cambridge, Mass., and London: Harvard University Press, 1993).

Freud, Sigmund, 'Creative Writers and Daydreaming', *Art & Literature*, Freud Pelican Library, xxiv (Harmondsworth: Penguin Books, 1985).

——, 'Thoughts for the Times on War and Death', *Civilization, Society and Religion*, Freud Pelican Library, xxii (Harmondsworth: Penguin Books, 1985).

Friedl, Bettina (ed.), *On to Victory: Propaganda Plays of the Woman Suffrage Movement* (Boston: Northeastern University Press, 1987).

Fry, Pauline, 'The Domestic Front: Women and the Great War', *Focus on Robert Graves and His Contemporaries*, 2/1, (Spring 1993) pp. 33–6.

Fussell, Paul, *The Great War and Modern Memory* (Oxford: Oxford University Press, 1975).

Girouard, Mark, *The Return to Camelot: Chivalry and the English Gentleman* (New Haven, Conn.: Yale University Press, 1981).

Goldman, Dorothy (ed.), *Women and World War I: The Written Response* (Basingstoke: Macmillan, 1993).

Grayzel, Susan R., *Women's Identities at War: Gender, Motherhood, and Politics in Britain and France during the First World War* (Chapel Hill: University of North Carolina Press, 1999).

Green, Martin, *Dreams of Adventure, Deeds of Empire: A Wide-Ranging and Provocative Examination of the Great Tradition of the Literature of Adventure* (London: Routledge, 1980).

Greenslade, William, *Degeneration, Culture and the Novel, 1880–1940* (Cambridge: Cambridge University Press, 1994).

Griffiths, Gareth, *Women's Factory Work in World War I* (Stroud, Gloucestershire: Alan Sutton, 1991).

Haggard, H. Rider, *The Private Diaries of Sir H. Rider Haggard: 1914–1925* (London: Cassell, 1980).

Harrison, Brian, 'For Church, Queen and Family: The Girls' Friendly Society 1874–1920', *Past and Present*, 61 (November 1973).

Heilbrun, Caroline, and Margaret Higonnet, *The Representation of Women in Fiction* (Baltimore, Md., and London: Johns Hopkins University Press, 1983).

Heilmann, Barbara, and Margaret Beetham (eds.), *New Woman Hybridities: Femininity, Feminism and International Consumer Culture, 1880–1930* (London and New York: Routledge, 2004).

Hibberd, Dominic, *Owen the Poet* (London: Macmillan, 1986).

Higonnet, Margaret Randolph, Sonya Michel, Jane Jenson, and Margaret Collins Weitz (eds.), *Behind the Lines: Gender and the Two World Wars* (New Haven, Conn., and London: Yale University Press, 1987).

Hodge, Julie, *Innocent Flowers: Women in the Edwardian Theatre* (London: Virago, 1981).

Hynes, Samuel, *The Soldiers' Tale: Bearing Witness to Modern War* (London: Pimlico, 1998).

——, *A War Imagined: The First World War and English Culture* (New York: Collier Books/Macmillan, 1990).

James, Lawrence, *The Rise and Fall of the British Empire* (London: Little, Brown, 1994).

Keating, Peter, *The Haunted Study: A Social History of the English Novel 1875–1914* (London: Secker & Warburg, 1989).

Kelly, Andrew, *Cinema and the Great War* (London and New York: Routledge, 1997).

Khan, Nosheen, *Women's Poetry of the First World War* (New York, London, Toronto, Sydney, and Tokyo: Harvester Wheatsheaf, 1988).

Kipling, Rudyard, *Rudyard Kipling's Verse: The Definitive Edition* (London: Hodder & Stoughton, 1940).

Laffin, John, *World War I in Postcards* (Gloucester: Alan Sutton, 1988).

Lambert, Angela, *Unquiet Souls: A Social History of the Illustrious, Irreverent, Intimate Group of British Aristocrats Known as 'the Souls'* (New York, Cambridge, Philadelphia, San Francisco, and London: Harper & Row, 1984).

Landow, George P., *Victorian Thinkers* (Oxford: Oxford University Press, 1993).

Lasswell, Harold D., *Propaganda Technique in the World War* (Cambridge, Mass., and London: M.I.T. Press, 1927).

Ledger, Sally, and Roger Luckhurst (eds.), *The Fin de Siècle: A Reader in Cultural History c.1880–1900* (Oxford: Oxford University Press, 2000).

Leed, Eric J., *No Man's Land: Contrast and Identity in World War I* (Cambridge: Cambridge University Press, 1974).

McAleer, Joseph, *Popular Reading and Publishing in Britain, 1914–1950* (Oxford: Clarendon Press, 1992).

Macdonald, Lyn, *The Roses of No Man's Land* (London: Joseph, 1980).

Macdonald, Sharon, Pat Holden, and Shirley Ardener (eds.), *Images of Women in Peace and War: Cross-Cultural and Historical Perspectives* (London: Macmillan, 1987).

MacKenzie, John (ed.), *Imperialism and Popular Culture* (Manchester: Manchester University Press, 1986).

Mansfield, Katherine, *The Collected Stories of Katherine Mansfield* (London: Constable, 1945).

Marlow, Joyce (ed.), *Virago Book of Women and the Great War, 1914–1918* (London: Virago, 1998).

Marsland, Elizabeth A., *The Nation's Cause: French, English, and German Poetry of the First World War* (London and New York: Routledge, 1991).

Marwick, Arthur, *The Deluge: British Society and the First World War* (London: Bodley Head, 1965).

Meaney, Gerardine, *(Un)Like Subjects: Women, Theory, Fiction* (London and New York: Routledge, 1993).

Messinger, Gary S., *British Propaganda and the State in the First World War* (Manchester: Manchester University Press, 1992).

Milloy, Jean, and Rebecca O'Rourke, *The Woman Reader: Learning and Teaching Women's Writing* (London and New York: Routledge, 1991).

Mitchell, Sally, *The New Girl: Girls' Culture in England, 1880–1915* (New York: Columbia University Press, 1995).

Montefiore, Jan, *Feminism and Poetry* (London: Pandora, 1994).

Moore, T. Sturge, *Some Soldier Poets* (New York: Harcourt, Brace & Howe, 1920).

Morgan, Charles, *The House of Macmillan (1843–1943)* (London: Macmillan, 1944).

Mumby, F. A., *Publishing and Bookselling* (London: Jonathan Cape, 1930).

Murdoch, Brian, *Fighting Songs and Warring Words: Popular Lyrics of Two World Wars* (London and New York: Routledge, 1990).

Nash, Walter, *The Language of Popular Fiction* (London and New York: Routledge, 1990).

Nelson, Claudia, *Boys Will Be Girls: The Feminine Ethic and British Children's Fiction, 1857–1917* (New Brunswick, N.J., and London: Rutgers University Press, 1991).

Nowell-Smith, Simon, *The House of Cassell: 1848–1958* (London: Cassell & Co., 1958).

Orwell, George, 'Boys' Weeklies', *Inside the Whale and Other Essays* (London: Gollancz, 1940).

Ouditt, Sharon, *Fighting Forces, Writing Women: Identity and Ideology in the First World War* (London and New York: Routledge, 1994).

Owen, Wilfred, *Selected Letters*, ed. John Bell (Oxford: Oxford University Press, 1985).

Oxford Dictionary of National Biography (Oxford: Oxford University Press, 2004).

Pakenham, Thomas, *The Boer War* (London: Weidenfeld & Nicolson, 1993).

Paret, Peter, Beth Irwin Lewis, and Paul Paret, *Persuasive Images: Posters of War and Revolution* (Princeton: Princeton University Press, 1992).

Peel, Mrs C. S., *How We Lived Then, 1914–18: A Sketch of Social and Domestic Life in England during the War* (London: John Lane, The Bodley Head, 1929).

Person, Ethel S., *The Force of Fantasy: Its Roles, Its Benefits and What it Reveals about Our Lives* (London: HarperCollins, 1997).

Pick, Daniel, *Faces of Degeneration: A European Disorder, c.1848–c.1918* (Cambridge: Cambridge University Press, 1989).

Pinsky, Robert, *Poetry and the World* (New York: Ecco Press, 1988).

Plain, Gill, *Women's Fiction of the Second World War: Gender, Power and Resistance* (Edinburgh: Edinburgh University Press, 1996).

Posonby, Arthur, *Falsehoods in War-Time* (London: George Allen & Unwin, 1928).

Potter, Jane, 'Interview with Rayner Unwin', *Publishing History* 41 (1997).

——, '"A Great Purifier": The Great War in Women's Romances and Memoirs, 1914–1918', in Suzanne Raitt and Trudi Tate (eds.), *Women's Fiction and the Great War* (Oxford: Clarendon Press, 1997).

Press, John, *A Map of Modern English Verse* (Oxford: Oxford University Press, 1969).

Proctor, Tammy, *Female Intelligence: Women and Espionage in the First World War* (New York and London: New York University Press, 2003).

Propp, Vladimir, 'Fairy-Tale Transformations', *Readings in Russian Poetics: Formalist and Structuralist View,* trans. Ladislav Matejka & Krystyna Pomorska (Cambridge, Mass.: Massachussetts Institute of Technology, 1971).

——, *Theory and History of Folklore,* trans. Adriana Y. Martin and Richard P. Martin (Minneapolis: University of Minneapolis Press, 1984).

Radford, Jean (ed.), *The Progress of Romance* (London and New York: Routledge & Kegan Paul, 1986).

Radway, Janice, *Reading the Romance* (London: Verso, 1987).

Raitt, Suzanne, and Trudi Tate (eds.), *Women's Fiction and the Great War* (Oxford: Clarendon Press, 1997).

Ramazani, Jahan, *Poetry of Mourning: The Modern Elegy from Hardy to Heaney* (Chicago and London: University of Chicago Press, 1994).

Read, Herbert, *Collected Essays in Literary Criticism* (London: Faber & Faber, 1969).

——, *English Prose Style* (London: G. Bell & Sons, 1952).

Reed, David, *The Popular Magazine in Britain and the United States 1880–1960* (London: British Library, 1997).

Reilly, Catherine, *Scars Upon My Heart: Women's Poetry and Verse of the First World War* (London: Virago, 1981).

Richards, Thomas, *The Commodity Culture of Victorian England: Advertising and Spectacle, 1851–1914* (Stanford: Stanford University Press, 1990).

Robb, George, *British Culture and the First World War* (Basingstoke: Palgrave, 2002).

Robson, W. W., *The Definition of Literature and Other Essays* (Cambridge: Cambridge University Press, 1982).

Russell, Bertrand, *Autobiography, vol ii.* (London: George Allen & Unwin, 1969).

Saunders, M. L., and Philip M. Taylor, *British Propaganda during the First World War, 1914–18* (London: Macmillan, 1982).

Sceats, Sarah, and Gail Cunningham, *Image and Power: Women in Fiction in the Twentieth Century* (London New York: Longman, 1996).

Sebba, Anne, *Enid Bagnold: The Authorized Biography* (London: Weidenfield and Nicolson, 1986).

Second Report on the Work Conducted for the Government at Wellington House, with introductory remarks by C. F. G. Masterman, 1 February 1916.

Showalter, Elaine, *A Literature of Their Own: British Women Novelists from Brontës to Lessing* (London: Virago, 1978).

Sillars, Stuart, *Art and Survival in First World War Britain* (London: Macmillan,1987).

Smith, Angela K., *The Second Battlefield: Women, Modernism and the First World* War (Manchester: Manchester University Press, 2000).

——, *Women's Writing of the First World War: An Anthology* (Manchester: Manchester University Press, 2000).

Smith, Sidonie, *A Poetics of Women's Autobiography: Marginality and the Fictions of Self-Representation* (Bloomington: Indiana University Press, 1987).

Somerfield, Muriel, and Ann Bellingham, *Violetta Thurstan: A Celebration* (Newmill, Penzance, Cornwall: Jamieson Library, 1993).

Spacks, Patricia Meyer, *The Female Imagination* (London: George Allen & Unwin, 1976).

Stallworthy, Jon, 'Survivors' Songs in Welsh Poetry', Annual Gwyn Jones Lecture, University College (Cardiff, 1981).

—— (ed.), *Oxford Book of War Poetry* (Oxford: Oxford University Press, 1984).

——, *Wilfred Owen* (Oxford: Oxford University Press, 1974).

Stanley, Peter, *What did YOU do in the War, Daddy?* (Melbourne: Oxford University Press, 1983).

Stearn, Roger T.,'The Mysterious Mr LeQueux', *Soldiers of the Queen* 70 (Spring 1992).

——, 'Victorian and Edwardian Fiction of Future War', *Soldiers of the Queen* 69 (June 1992).

Steiner, George, *The Death of Tragedy* (London: Faber, 1961).

Storr, Anthony, *Freud* (Oxford: Oxford University Press, 1989).

Suleiman, Susan Rubin, 'War Memories: On Autobiographical Reading', *New Literary History: A Journal of Theory and Interpretation*, 24:3 (Summer 1993), 363–75.

Tate, Trudi, *Modernism, History and the First World War* (Manchester: Manchester University Press, 1998).

Taylor, A. J. P., *The First World War: An Illustrated History* (Harmondsworth, Middlesex: Penguin, 1966).

Thompson, Michael, '"Outdaring with a Kiss All-Powerful Wrath": Images of War, Images of Death', *Focus on Robert Graves and His Contemporaries*, 1/7 (June 1988), 3–7.

Thompson, Tierl (ed.), *Dear Girl: The Diaries and Letters of Two Working Women, 1987–1917* (London: Women's Press, 1987).

Todd, Janet (ed.), *Dictionary of British Women Writers* (London and New York: Routledge, 1989).

Trotter, David, *The English Novel in History, 1895–1920* (London: Routledge, 1993).

Trout, Steven, 'Women in Richard Aldington's Fiction', *Focus on Robert Graves and his Contemporaries*, 2/1, (Spring 1993) 22–32.

Tuchman, Barbara, *August 1914* (London: Constable, 1962).

Tylee, Claire M., *The Great War and Women's Consciousness: Images of Militarism and Womanhood in Women's Writings, 1914–1964* (Iowa City: University of Iowa Press, 1990).

——, '"Munitions of the Mind": Travel Writing, Imperial Discourse and Great War Propaganda by Mrs Humphry Ward', *English Literature in Transition 1880–1920* v. 38:2 (1996), 171–92.

Unwin, Sir Stanley, *Publishing in Peace and War* (London: George Allen & Unwin, 1944).

——, *The Truth about Publishing* (London: George Allen & Unwin, 1926).

——, *The Truth about a Publisher* (London: George Allen & Unwin, 1960).

van Wyk-Smith, Malvern, *Drummer Hodge: The Poetry of the Anglo-Boer War, 1899–1902* (Oxford: Clarendon Press, 1978).

Vaughn, Edwin Campion, *Some Desperate Glory* (London: Macmillan, 1981).

Vicinus, Martha, *Independent Women: Work and Community for Single Women, 1850–1920* (London: Virago, 1985)

Ward, Irene, *F.A.N.Y. Invicta* (London: Hutchinson, 1955).

Waugh, Arthur, *A Hundred Years of Publishing: Being the Story of Chapman & Hall, Ltd.* (London: Chapman & Hall, 1930).

Webb, Barry, *Edmund Blunden* (New Haven, Conn., and London: Yale University Press, 1990).

Weimann, Robert, *Structure and Society in Literary History: Studies in the History of Historical Criticism* (London: Lawrence & Wishart, 1977).

Whaley, Joachim (ed.), *Mirrors of Mortality: Studies in the Social History of Death* (London: Europa Publications, 1981).

Wheelwright, Julie, *Amazons and Military Maids: Women who Dressed as Men in Pursuit of Life, Liberty and Happiness* (London: Pandora, 1989).

Wilson, Trevor, *The Myriad Faces of War: Britain and the Great War, 1914–1918* (Cambridge: Cambridge University Press, 1986).

Winship, Janice, *Inside Women's Magazines* (London: Pandora, 1987).

Winter, J. M., *The Great War and the British People* (London: Macmillan, 1985).

Woolf, Virginia, *Three Guineas* (London: Hogarth Press, 1938).

Woollacott, Angela, *On Her Their Lives Depend: Munitions Workers in the Great War* (Berkeley: University of California Press, 1994).

Zinsser, William (ed.), *Inventing the Truth: The Art and Craft of Memoir* (Boston: Houghton Mifflin, 1987).

Index